mediterranean FRESH

also by joyce goldstein

ANTIPASTI: Fabulous Appetizers and Small Plates

ITALIAN SLOW AND SAVORY

SOLO SUPPERS: Simple Delicious Meals to Cook for Yourself

SAFFRON SHORES: Jewish Cooking of the Southern Mediterranean

ENOTECA: Simple, Delicious Recipes in the Italian Wine Bar Tradition

SEPHARDIC FLAVORS: Jewish Cooking of the Mediterranean

SAVORING SPAIN AND PORTUGAL: Recipes and Reflections on Iberian Cooking

CUCINA EBRAICA: Flavors of the Italian Jewish Kitchen

MEDITERRANEAN COOKING

KITCHEN CONVERSATIONS: Robust Recipes and Lessons in Flavor from One of America's Most Innovative Chefs

TAVERNA: The Best of Casual Mediterranean Cooking

MEDITERRANEAN THE BEAUTIFUL: Authentic Recipes from the Mediterranean Lands

FESTIVE OCCASIONS

CASUAL OCCASIONS

BEEF, FISH

SOUP FOR SUPPER

FOOD AND WINE PAIRING

BACK TO SQUARE ONE: Old-World Food in a New-World Kitchen

THE MEDITERRANEAN KITCHEN

FEEDBACK: Cooking as Communication

mediterranean FRESH

A COMPENDIUM OF ONE-PLATE SALAD MEALS AND MIX-AND-MATCH DRESSINGS

joyce goldstein

PHOTOGRAPHY BY
andre baranowski

FOOD STYLING BY
melissa hamilton

FOREWORD BY
dan barber

WINE ESSAY BY
evan goldstein

W. W. NORTON & COMPANY
NEW YORK   LONDON

For information about permission to reproduce selections from this book, write to
Permissions, W. W. Norton & Company, Inc., 500 Fifth Avenue, New York, NY 10110

For information about special discounts for bulk purchases, please contacct W. W.
Norton Special Sales at specialsales@wwnorton.com or 800-233-4830

Manufacturing by RR Donnelley, Crawfordsville
Book design by Kathleen McMillan
Production managers: Andrew Marasia and Sue Carlson

Library of Congress Cataloging-in-Publication Data

Goldstein, Joyce Esersky.
    Mediterranean fresh : a compendium of one-plate salad meals and
mix-and-match dressings / Joyce Goldstein ; photographs by Andre Baranowski ;
food styling by Melissa Hamilton ; foreword by Dan Barber ; wine essay by
Evan Goldstein.—1st ed.
    p. cm.
    Includes index.
    ISBN 978-0-393-06500-8 (hardcover)
1. Salads. 2. Salad dressing. 3. Cookery, Mediterranean. I. Title.
    TX740.G547 2008
    641.8'3—dc22

                                        2008006087

W. W. Norton & Company, Inc., 500 Fifth Avenue, New York, N.Y. 10110
www.wwnorton.com

W. W. Norton & Company Ltd., Castle House, 75/76 Wells Street, London W1T 3QT

1 2 3 4 5 6 7 8 9 0

to all those cooks who
are crazy about salads—
may your oils never go
rancid and your greens
never go limp

contents

foreword

BY DAN BARBER

FIFTEEN YEARS AGO I went west in search of great food. Back then, if you were an aspiring chef and serious about food, you went to France. I went to California.

I had just graduated from college, full of idealism and chutzpah. I thought I'd try my hand at cooking (how hard could that be?), and despite that it might have infuriated my father, or perhaps because it might, I went straight to San Francisco. I'd read about Joyce Goldstein, the woman who was redefining California cuisine at her Square One restaurant, and I figured she was in need of a cocky wise guy who had worked the cooking line in a few nice burger joints.

Expert foodie friends of my father's introduced us. (I suppose my father thought if I was going to throw away my elite New England university degree I ought to do it with the best of them. That Joyce was Jewish, indisputably the Nana by the Bay, well, that didn't hurt either.)

I walked in the night of my introduction and, like a blast of cool air off the bay, got a whiff of what everyone in the world was talking about: California cuisine. I looked around at the greatest collection of happy, fit, and good-postured people I'd ever seen. They weren't just liking the food, they were smitten, infatuated, and collectively so approving of what was on their plates—everyone seemed to nod in agreement with each bite—I

thought the energy of the place would just about levitate the tables. And there, in the middle of it all, was Joyce. Indeed she seemed, at only five feet tall, to gently float above it all, greeting the admirers, admiring the regulars, and then, back in the kitchen, cupping one hand over a hot soup to waft in a few of the intense aromas, while with the other sprinkling salt onto a salad just leaving the kitchen. She was a joy to behold because she was joyous, so tickled to be in her chef whites she seemed to wriggle with the sheer excitement of it.

A black bean soup that night was incredible. Each bite was loaded with texture and aroma and a deep, rich taste I didn't know a bean was capable of delivering. The rest of the meal is a blur. I spent the evening studying the cooking line, which wasn't difficult as Square One had an open kitchen. Back then, in a world without Food Networks, it was like sitting in front of the space shuttle: you'd seen pictures, but up close you could only gaze in wonderment, bright kitchen lights illuminating these cooks as movie stars.

As luck would have it, there was a guy three-in on the cooking line that was roughly my age, at about the same height. I watched him intently and replaced his hands with mine, because if you were an expert at making your own reality like I was, you could imagine yourself cooking the food as you stared at the brightly lit kitchen stage. My hands kept replacing his as we moved food over the stove, onto the cutting board, and finally onto the gleaming white plates. By the time I had finished the bean soup, I had mastered his job. *Not that hard*. Square One, I decided, was where I was going to work.

We were on desserts when the kinetic Chef Goldstein came to say hello. I looked up at her, my family friends in the midst of introducing me, the aspiring chef, and I must have had it written all over my face: I WILL WORK HERE.

"We don't have any openings," she said, interrupting my stare. "No openings and no one leaving anytime soon, but let me know if I can help you get into a kitchen."

I must have turned red because she pulled up a chair and sat with us as I swallowed the outline of the cooking dream I had just convinced myself was real.

It would be nice to write that by the end of our talk she saw my potential and on the spot reconsidered, offered me a job, and the rest is history. I love happy endings. Alas (or maybe not), she didn't see the urgency of the hire.

As she was getting up to go back to the kitchen, I stood up to shake her hand and asked, "Any advice on becoming a chef?" It was one of those moments that I look back on and cringe—an overwrought question a collar-raised teenager might ask—but she neither cringed nor hesitated.

"Ask questions" she said. "Ask a hundred questions a day. Ask a thousand if you can get away with it. When you start working in kitchens, assume nothing. Nada. You know nothing. Don't pretend. Don't pretend you know how to roast a chicken or braise a carrot or make a salad, because you don't know how to dress it, or how to season it, or how to balance it. Nothing. So ask. And then ask again."

She spoke in such a straightforward, honest tone—what a fellow-chef friend refers to as "Joycespeak"—that I've never forgotten the words.

I'm reminded of the tone yet again with this book. A robust portrait of salad and its many forms, *Mediterranean Fresh* is enviable in its clarity and encyclopedic in its variety.

It's pure Joycespeak, and the recipes are too: refreshingly simple, dazzlingly creative, and eternally humble in the face of great ingredients. Here is a book for any inquisitive cook who knows he doesn't know it all—a book by Joyce, the consummate teacher and perpetual student.

acknowledgments

A GIANT THANK YOU TO GREG Drescher. This book was really his inspiration. He invited me to participate at a restaurant retreat at the Culinary Institute of America at Greystone, in the Napa Valley. My assignment was to show restaurateurs that salads could be much more than the salad-bar concept. For my demonstration I made twelve Mediterranean salad dressings for a tasting and then worked with the CIA staff to prepare twenty-four salads that used the dressings. Because of the success of this presentation, Greg invited me to repeat this seminar a few more times for various groups at the CIA.

I want to thank my editor, Maria Guarnaschelli, who attended one of my Mediterranean salad dressing demos at the CIA and said, "I love those tastes and I want this book." Thank you for giving me the opportunity to go salad crazy. Thanks also to Maria's assistants, Sarah Rothbard and Margaret Maloney, and to Andrew Marasia, Nancy Palmquist, Susan Sanfrey, and the entire Norton team.

Thanks to my friend Mark Furstenberg, who paired some of his wonderful breads and sandwiches with my salad dressings and mayonnaises. It was delicious fun for all who ate them.

Thanks to CIA chefs Toni Sakaguchi and David Thater for helping me prepare for those extensive demos where we fed the masses.

Thank you to fabulously gifted photographer Andre Baranowski for his impeccable eye and to stylist Melissa Hamilton for making the food look so seductively beautiful. Thank you to Liz Duvall for patient and careful copyediting and to Kathleen McMillan for the bright and colorful design layout.

Thank you to Alice Waters, who changed the way lettuces are sold in markets and farmers' markets across the country. Who knew about mesclun until she started using it at Chez Panisse? We are all eating better because of her.

Thanks to Andy Powning of Greenleaf and Andy Griffin of Mariquita Farm, for great produce and excellent educational information via witty and erudite newsletters.

Thanks to my son, Evan, for his wise wine words.

Thanks to my fellow "tart mouths": Paul Buscemi, Gary Woo, Gerald Gass, Kathleen Blake, Barbara Haimes, Ari Weinzweig, and the late, greatly missed Barbara Tropp and Catherine Brandel. We tasted olive oils and vinegars and talked vinaigrettes until we were satisfied.

tO THE AVERAGE AMERICAN DINER, THE

word *salad* conjures up an image of a bowl of leafy greens tossed with a dressing, served as a precursor to the meal. But in the regions that surround the Mediterranean Sea—southern Europe, North Africa, and parts of the Middle East—*salad* may first call to mind a dish entirely devoid of greens. In many of these countries, the term connotes a grain salad like tabbouleh, or a vegetable salad of grilled eggplant, or a seafood salad of calamari in a lemony dressing. Rather than defining the word *salad*, leafy greens are merely one category in a selection of incredibly diverse dishes that dazzle the palate with variety, complexity, and bright flavor.

IN THE MEDITERRANEAN, A SALAD may be assembled with the freshest uncooked seasonal ingredients and allowed to marinate briefly: cucumber salads, tomato, avocado, and fruit salads, even chopped vegetable salads and plates of raw fish receive this treatment. Other kinds of salads are prepared with cooked ingredients and given time to absorb the dressings and develop complex flavors. Many of these prepared salads fall into the popular category known as small plates—antipasti, hors d'oeuvres, tapas, and meze—and are served at room temperature. Still others are composed salads, or an assortment of cooked or cooked and raw ingredients arranged on a plate and then drizzled with salad dressing.

There are as many options for when to serve a salad as there are for what exactly a salad contains. A salad is often the first bite a hungry diner eats after being seated at the table; it can set the tone of the meal to come. In Italy or France, however, a light and cleanly dressed salad might be served as a palate refresher after the meal. And in some instances, salad can be a meal in itself. A large salad can be a satisfying supper. A selection of small plates can be an entire meal. An assortment of prepared salads is a creative way to entertain guests and sate their appetites.

what's in a name?

SO IF A SALAD ISN'T DEFINED BY its components or by when it's served, what exactly is it? The word *salad* is derived from *sale*, the Latin word for salt, and *insalata*, or salad, translates as "salted." Salt heightens and reveals flavors. The key ingredients for flavor balance in a salad are salt and acidity in the form of vinegar, citrus juice, or a combination of the two. A fat such as oil, yogurt, cream, or tahini might be the major component in a salad dressing, but it is the combination of salt and acidity that makes or breaks the dressing and in turn defines a dish as a salad.

The key to successful salads and small plates lies in the balance the dressing provides. Yet the ingredients in a perfectly balanced dressing must complement the salad itself in addition to one another. If the dressing is too tame, assertive components will take over and the dish will be out of balance. If it is too sharp, delicately flavored ingredients will be overpowered and lost. If the dressing is too heavy or viscous, tender leaves will be buried. It is truly a balancing act. And my aim with this book is to make you into an expert in this game of balance and harmony.

dress to impress

YOU WILL NOTICE AS YOU READ the recipes that the amount of salad dressing I recommend is an approximation. I am not being intentionally vague here—there are good reasons for this. Salad making is not an exact science, like baking. The ingredients cannot be precisely measured. A little more or less here or there is not going to make or break the recipe.

For example, if I call for two medium tomatoes or one large eggplant for a dish, is the tomato you use what I would call medium, or is it large? What about the eggplant? Will the eggplant be the same size every time you make the salad? What yield did you get from the chopped bell pepper—half a cup this time, or more? How big is your handful of salad greens as opposed to mine? These are constant variables that affect the amount of dressing that you add to the bowl.

There is also the absorption factor. Bean, grain, and potato salads drink dressing, especially if they are warm when you add the dressing to the bowl. After 15 or 20 minutes, those salads may be dry and the flavor of the dressing may have dissipated. You will probably want to add a bit more dressing so the ingredients have some moistness and movement on the fork and the flavor of the dressing is again perceptible.

Personal preferences are also a factor. Some of us like our salads rather dry, with just a bare gloss of dressing. Others like a little more. I am one of the latter. I don't want a soggy salad, but if the dressing is good, I want to taste it. I don't want just a hint of its flavor. And if there is a tiny bit too much, I can leave it on the plate or mop it up with a piece of bread.

So here is my advice: add the dressing gradually, in increments. After you add some, toss the salad, and then taste a leaf or bean. If the salad is dry, add more dressing. Your mouth is ultimately the judge.

Any leftover dressing will keep and can be used again on a salad or possibly as a marinade. You may even be inspired to use it in your cooking or create a new dish.

salad boot camp

BEFORE YOU CAN MATCH A SALAD and a dressing or decide whether to add an extra pinch of salt to a vinaigrette, you need to learn how to taste. Only by trial and error, by constant tasting, can you develop a seasoned palate and learn how to create the appropriate dressing for a salad of bitter greens or mild greens, or a salad with fruits or nuts or beans or seafood. With cooked and composed salads, the ante is raised even higher.

In my work as a restaurant consultant, I run a workshop for professional cooks called Salad Boot Camp. Because it requires extreme concentration, each session runs about 1 1/2 hours. But before we even begin discussing salt and acidity or the different types of salads the cooks have on their menus, we taste. I have the cooks taste all of the varied lettuces and greens, all of the oils and vinegars in the kitchen. Then we taste all of the salad dressings offered as options on the menu. Next I ask the cooks to dip each kind of lettuce into every dressing to see if they work well together. Then I have them dip pieces of cheese or fruit in all of the dressings, again to see which work well together. It can be a revelation to find that some of the dressings don't go with anything on the salad menu.

During a second session we taste ingredients that are often added to salads (nuts, cheese, beans, poultry, seafood) when they are cold, at room temperature, and warm. We taste nuts straight from the fridge and toasted nuts. We taste cold cheeses and cheeses brought to room temperature. We taste a shrimp and bean salad cold, at room temperature, and warmed, then compare the textures and tastes. We discuss and taste tossed salads and composed salads and see different ways to integrate protein such as fish or chicken. The cooks come away with a totally new understanding of what constitutes a salad, what makes a good salad, and what can make a good salad great.

With all kinds of salads, simple and composed, less is usually more: a few carefully selected ingredients dressed perfectly with an appropriate, well-chosen dressing are best. Making fine salads requires finesse. It entails a series of correct decisions and attention to fine details. Not only is salad preparation filled with culinary and creative pleasures, it is important for the development of the palate and learning how to taste. The cook gets a chance to work with sour, salty, bitter, and sweet flavors in so many astounding and subtle ways. Learning to play with these elements in a salad dressing or vinaigrette and then experimenting to see which dressing will complement the greens and other salad components to bring out their flavors without overpowering them is a critical balancing act. It takes time and experience to become attuned to the nuances of flavor, proportion, and acid balance. When you master the art of making salads, you will have a more finely tuned palate. You may not be able to sit in on my Salad Boot Camp, but

after reading this book you will be able to improve your salad skills and taste awareness too.

I know that many people today say they don't have time to cook. If eating well is important to you, you will find the time. It takes a bit of practice to build up speed and confidence and improve your knife skills, but the bottom line is that salads and salad dressings are fast and easy to prepare and give immediate satisfaction. Developing a fine palate takes time and practice, but it sure is fun along the way. If you want your salads to taste as if a master chef with years of experience created them, this book will lead the way. After forty years of teaching cooking and sixteen years of running restaurants specializing in foods of the Mediterranean, I have learned what kinds of salads and dressings the dining public loves. Rather than try to cover every salad, every small plate, and every dressing from all over the Mediterranean—an impossible task at best—I've made some careful choices and have winnowed the recipes to 46 versatile and easy-to-prepare dressings and 146 delicious salads and small plates as well as a few hot dishes to show the versatility of Mediterranean dressings as marinades and finishing sauces. These recipes should keep you well satisfied and your friends and family well fed.

WINE AND SALAD? A combination that is not top of mind for most folks. Indeed, at a sommelier competition that I attended several years ago, the room erupted in applause when, during a wine and food pairing query, the sommelier being examined replied that wine and salad did not go together and he'd recommend a flat mineral water such as Evian. Well, times have changed. And so have salads!

This cutting-edge book, *Mediterranean Fresh*, written so well by my mom, celebrates the new way of thinking about salads. And concurrent with the evolution of salads has come a new role at table for wine.

Traditionally, a salad was defined simply as assorted greens, tossed with a vinaigrette and served with minimal fanfare and without much, if any, thought to wine. The "no wine with salad" rule was birthed from this classic position, as these one-size-fits-all green salads were served primarily as palate cleansers post the entrée and pre-dessert in Western European countries. At that point in the meal the wine remaining on the table was inevitably a medium- to full-bodied, low-acid red wine. Such a partnering was a disaster, prompting the pundits to forever assert wine's relationship with salads to be a nonstarter.

Today, people are embracing salads of all kinds. They love the diversity and array of flavors, the variety of Mother Nature's bounty of produce, and the panoply of interpretations, ingredients, textures, and dressings. They love the sheer flexibility of salads that can take on the character of appetizer or main course, palate cleanser or, in the case of fruit salad, dessert. So, it isn't surprising that people look for the same diversity and flexibility when it comes to pairing wine with salad. As with all wine and food pairings that I explore, wine with salad has minimal rules, but several guidelines that are worth keeping in mind. What follows is my thinking and approach toward finding happiness for wine lovers at the global salad bar.

the golden rule

AS MOST DRESSINGS HAVE AN acidic base, it's critical that the acidity (tartness factor) of the wine served is equal to or slightly greater than the acidity of the dressing and/or salad, or the wine will come off as a shrill shadow of itself. Since white wines generally come from cooler climates and as such have higher acidity levels, they are almost always the best choice. Select a wine that is sharp, refreshing, and redolent of bright, tart fruit character to mirror the same in a dressing. Wines such as Sauvignon Blanc (from New Zealand, South Africa, France, Chile, and, of course, California),

Pinot Grigio (from Italy and California, and more austere examples from France and Oregon), Albariño (from Spain), and Grüner Veltliner (from Austria) would typify this genre.

This point made, you will have more flexibility in pairing a wider range of wines if you take the pressure off the dressing. This can be done in one of the following ways:

PARE BACK THE VINEGAR. By doing so you'll drop the acid in the vinaigrette, making it easier to match with a wine. You can also employ softer, wine-friendly vinegars such as balsamic in lieu of the standard red or white wine vinegars so commonly employed.

USE SOFTER ACIDITY FOR YOUR DRESSING. Citric acid, in the form of citrus (lemon, lime, or grapefruit juices) is far softer on wine than vinegar and mirrors many of wine's inherent core flavors. The use of *verjus*, a sour liquid made from unripe, unfermented grapes, is also by definition more wine friendly. Finally, incorporating a splash of the wine you are serving (or a similar wine) into the dressing itself as the acid base will all but guarantee a successful equalizing of acidity levels between the wine and the salad.

TAKE THE EMPHASIS OFF THE DRESSING. Adding more ingredients to an otherwise classic salad, or making a composed or serving an entrée salad,

means that the wine will be matched less to a "sauce" and more to an array of ingredients. When smoked trout or chicken, toasted almonds, oranges, and sweet red onions are layered over a bed of dressed greens, the wine will gravitate toward the totality of the salad's ingredients and away from the dressed lettuces.

when it's not a classic dressing

AS THIS BOOK EXPLORES, THERE are many types of dressings and so, no silver bullet rules for pairings.

CREAM DRESSINGS. The softness and silky texture of a yogurt, tahini, or cream-based dressing will enable you to choose a wine that also is creamy and velvety. Smooth, rich Chardonnays (from all over), unctuous Marsannes and Roussannes (from France, Australia, and California), and wines made from Sémillon (France, Washington State, and Australia) are perfect pairings with these types of dressed salads.

MAYONNAISE DRESSINGS. As they are essentially void of any defining acidic character, dressings such as aioli, remoulade, or simply a mayo base "spiked" with mustard, saffron, or a little cayenne make for very wine-friendly matches. You will need a wine with some body, to stand up to the richness of the mayonnaise, and flavors that accentuate or are brought out by the dressing. For example, the earthiness of an aioli's garlic demands similarly earthy wines from France, Spain, Italy, or Portugal, while an herbal-scented tarragon mayonnaise calls for an equally herbal Sauvignon Blanc (see above).

UNIQUE DRESSINGS. Pesto (based on fresh basil) is almost always best with clean, green, and citrusy white wines. I especially love Sauvignon Blanc, Pinot Grigio, and local "Italianate" whites (Tocai Friulano, Vernaccia, and Vermentino, to name three). With olivey tapenade, seek out wines that have a similar profile and adequate acidity—for black olives this can range from peppery red grapes like Carignan, Mourvèdre, and Tempranillo, while green olives cry out for wines more akin to those that "love pesto."

PLAIN OILS. Whether it be with the finest virgin olive oil, or a drizzling of hazelnut or walnut oil, or a slight trickle of sesame, the wine pairing will likely be based on the ingredients, *not* the oil. A fish or shellfish crudo or beef carpaccio has more to do with the fish and meat and less with the oil. That said, nut oils do pair well with wines that are by definition "nuttier" (through oak aging or simply bottle aging over time).

speaking of ingredients . . .

FROM THE WINE'S STANDPOINT, there are many salads that are indeed ingredient driven. Slices of meat or a cold roasted chicken can, in context, be a salad. Here you are best off selecting wines to go with . . . meat and poultry. Pasta salads, grain-based salads (couscous, for example), and bean salads have richer texture, where the starch provides a canvas for fuller-bodied wines. Make sure to select a wine that has some flesh to pair with these types of salads. Slower-cooked vegetables, such as roasted peppers and eggplant, also require richer wines.

variety is king

DO NOT OVERLOOK THE RANGE of wines available to you. While it's true as a guiding principle that you'll have a higher level of satisfaction with the profile that white wines provide against salads, dry rosé wines, light reds, Champagne and other sparkling wines, and lightly fortified wines, such as fino sherry, can add range and diversity to your pairings at table.

So, armed with information and, I hope, newfound wine and salad curiosity, read on, and play with your wines . . . and salads!

MEDITERRANEAN SALADS AND SMALL PLATES

1

MEDITERRANEAN SALADS AND SMALL PLATES

I HAVE SORTED THE MEDITERRANEAN SALADS into seven categories. leafy greens, vegetable salads, fruit-based salads, grain salads, and bean salads are the basic five. These salads can be enriched with proteins such as pieces of cooked chicken, strips of prosciutto or Serrano ham, hard-boiled eggs, slivers of an omelet, canned or fresh cooked tuna, poached salmon, cooked shrimp and other shellfish, cheese in slices or shavings or crumbled, and toasted nuts. Sometimes, however, the proteins become the star of the plate, so the two other categories are seafood salads and poultry and meat salads.

ALL OF THESE SALADS SHARE certain signature flavors and ingredients that distinguish their cuisines and reflect their culinary heritage. To reveal maximum flavor, most of them are served at room temperature. To my mind, American salads are often served way too cold, placed on chilled plates, even accompanied by chilled forks. My teeth ache just thinking about it. And yet if you stop to consider it, you'll realize that many salad ingredients do not taste best when cold. Yes, leafy greens, cucumbers, and radishes should be chilled to retain their crisp texture, but cheeses, olives, tomatoes, and toasted nuts taste best when served at room temperature, as do vinaigrettes, because chilled olive oil congeals in a most unappealing way. Most Mediterranean salads are served at room temperature for maximum flavor intensity.

In the contemporary kitchen, there is a trend to serve some of the salad components warm and add them at the last minute. This contrast in temperature— a warm dressing against cool greens, or some quickly sautéed shrimp piled atop a mound of marinated beans—adds a bit of drama to the salad and highlights the flavors and textures of the diverse ingredients. The sensual juxtaposition of warm and cold makes salads more interesting and adds to the overall balance and harmony of the dishes.

Before you embark on preparing these salads, please read the chapters on salad dressings so you will be familiar with the styles of dressing and their flavor attributes. Often I give a few choices of dressing for each dish, so by reading about the dressings, you will know which one you want to select this time around. Or try two and see which you prefer. They are not that hard or time-consuming to prepare, so you can play with both and discover what pleases your personal palate.

it's easy being green: leafy salads

THE ROMANS INTRODUCED leafy salads to Europe, but it was the Arabs who created the tradition of starting a meal with a salad. In Spain, following the Arab tradition, salads are served on big platters placed at the center of the table, dressed to order, and eaten communally. You will find individually plated green salads in Italy and France. Some are judiciously embellished with a few sliced oranges, slivers of apple or pear, croutons, cooked eggs, strips of ham, crumbled cheese, canned tuna, chickpeas, olives, and pimientos or nuts. Not all at the same time, mind you.

This chapter includes salads in which the major ingredient is a leafy green or a combination of greens, such as mesclun, head lettuces like romaine or butter lettuce, spinach, Belgian endive, arugula, radicchio, even a few hand-gathered or "spontaneous" greens such as fennel greens, baby mustard, and purslane. There are also two salads of cooked leafy greens, *horta* from Greece and cooked greens with preserved lemon from Morocco.

The most widely used term for assorted young or "baby" salad greens is *mesclun*. (The word comes from the Latin for "miscellaneous.") Mesclun or "spring mix" is now available in most supermarkets, sold in bulk bins or prewashed in bags. Many are labeled organic, but alas, most are no longer local. These baby salad green assortments have made salad preparation easier for the home cook, since you don't have to break down and clean head lettuces. I usually buy my greens at the farmers' market or scoop them out of large bins in the supermarket. I never buy prebagged greens. I like to pick what I want, and I often combine different greens from the various bins.

If you are working with individual heads of lettuce instead of mesclun, separate the leaves from the central core. Some cooks like to keep the leaves whole for a dramatic presentation at the table. Such salads require a knife as well as a fork to eat. If you don't want the diner to have to do any extra work, tear the leaves into pieces that can be picked up easily with a fork.

Before preparing a leafy salad, wash the greens well, even if the package says they are organic and prewashed. Spin them dry, in batches, in a salad spinner. Then pat them gently with dish towels. The leaves must be impeccably dry so they do not dilute the dressing. Once your greens are prepped, you may wrap them in a dish towel or layer them in paper towels in a plastic bag and store them in the fridge until you are ready to assemble the salad. They will keep for three or four days quite nicely.

The best dressings for simple leafy salads are vinaigrettes, citrus dressings, and a few cream-based dressings. When it comes to dressing delicate salad leaves, you do not want anything too weighty or viscous. It's wise to check on the balance of your chosen dressing *before* you toss the greens. Dip a leaf in it to see if the dressing has enough salt and acid. The time to correct the balance is now, before you give the salad the final toss.

the art of the toss

IDEALLY A LEAFY SALAD IS tossed in a very large bowl. Glass, stainless steel, or ceramic is best. Wooden salad bowls, because they are porous, can develop off flavors. Clean hands are probably your best tools for tossing and dressing salads, because metal salad implements can bruise delicate ingredients. I know this sounds messy, but if you watch restaurant cooks at a salad station, you will undoubtedly see the flash of gloved hands at work. However, if you do not want to use your hands or latex gloves, wooden tongs or tongs with plastic tips will aid you in this task.

I always sprinkle the greens lightly with sea salt first and then add the dressing. Adding more salt to the dressing does not compensate for salting the greens. I find that the greens themselves need a bit of salt to reveal their flavors. The salt granules partially dissolve on the leaves and then the gloss of dressing coats the leaves and adds the final salt balance.

After sprinkling the salt, add the dressing in a circular fashion, drizzling it around the edge of the bowl, and then toss the greens. This "necklace" of dressing, as my late friend Barbara Tropp called it, will drip down the sides of the bowl to coat it and will help dress the greens faster and more evenly.

When dining out, you might be presented with a plate of greens and cruets of oil and vinegar. No tossing utensils. I know you are advised to drizzle everything with oil and then add vinegar and salt and mix it with your fork. In a way, this cruet business implies that dressing the salad is child's play and anyone can throw a salad together, even the diner. But to a nut like me, someone who is sensitive to the nuances of salad dressing, this raises the issue of balance. Unless you have a way to combine a balanced mixture of oil and vinegar and toss it with the greens, the results can be really hit-or-miss. You'll get pools of oil, tart jolts of vinegar. When I was living in Italy, many a waiter watched in amazement and amusement as I gamely tried to "mix" a balanced salad dressing of oil and vinegar in my soupspoon with my fork! It was a challenge.

basic ingredients

LET'S LOOK AT THE LETTUCES and greens that you may find at your market or farmers' market which can be included in your salad or mesclun.

AMARANTH is a wild beet but does not have the bulb at the root. Its slightly rounded leaves may be tinged with red and are mildly sweet. It can be eaten raw or cooked. It is often included in mesclun or spring mix. Red wine vinaigrettes are the best foil.

ARUGULA is also called rocket or rucola. This popular salad green goes back to the days of the early Romans. When young, the dark green leaves are small and tender, but as they mature they become large and a bit tough. Arugula is a member of the mustard family but less bitter than mustard greens. Its taste is more peppery, like watercress, and rather nutty. It can be paired and tempered with milder lettuces such as Bibb or butter lettuce or matched for flavor with bitter Belgian endive or radicchio. It adds contrast to fruit-based salads. Because it is bitter, the best dressings for arugula are citrus-based or those enhanced with sweeter vinegars like balsamic. *Arugula sylvetta* and *rocolla* are the wild arugulas; their leaves are smaller than domestic arugula and notched, spearlike and delicate in appearance. They may be sharper

mesclun

in flavor than the regular arugula, but as they are so small, they are less powerful than the full-size leaves.

BASIL now comes in many varieties, from oval to round silky-leaved Genovese to purple or opal basil, lemon basil, and Thai basil, all with small pointy leaves. Basil has a sweet minty taste and lovely perfume. Use whole leaves in salads, cut them in slivers and add to dressings, or turn them into pesto for pesto dressing. Avoid basil with tough, leathery leaves; this means it has been in the sun too long.

BELGIAN ENDIVE is in the chicory family. It grows in compact torpedo-shaped heads about 5 inches long, with white leaves tipped with pale yellow-green (although there is now a red variety, with white leaves tipped with red). The leaves have a mild crunch and are bitter in taste. You can cut them crosswise or lengthwise or leave them whole for salads. To use, cut off the end and separate the leaves. You will have to do this a few times as you get closer to the center of each head. Endive requires a dressing that coats and tempers the bitterness. It does well with creamy dressings; with mustard-based dressings, which echo the bitterness in the leaves and require mild and neutral additions such as mushrooms or toasted nuts; or with sweeter citrus dressings paired with toasted nuts and sweet fruit or salty cheese.

BUTTER LETTUCES, including **BIBB** or **LIMESTONE LETTUCE,** are soft, small heads of cup-shaped tender leaves, very mild and sweet in flavor.

mustard greens

boston bibb lettuce

These require mild salad dressings that will not overpower their delicate sweetness. They can take a dressing with some coating quality, like those with a cream or mayonnaise base. Little Gem is a cross between butter

arugula

microgreens

mâche

mizuna

Belgian endive and radicchio. It has been cultivated by the same company that grows most of the commercial radicchio in the United States, California Vegetable Specialties. It shares a taste profile with endive and radicchio: bitter. The leaves are variegated white and red. It loves an assertive dressing or one with a hint of sweetness.

ESCAROLE is also in the chicory family. It has broad flat dark-green leaves in compact heads and a bit of crunch. It can be eaten raw or cooked. It also needs a full-flavored dressing.

FENNEL FRONDS are the feathery tops of fennel bulbs. They taste like anise and are lovely in salads, especially those with seafood and citrus.

ICEBERG is a round, compact, pale-green head of rather bland-tasting lettuce. It's best for crunchy texture because it's short on taste. It is often served in wedges here but is not used in the Mediterranean.

LEAF LETTUCES include the loose heads of red leaf and oak leaf lettuce. The leaves are soft, tender, and mild in flavor. The dressings should not overpower these delicately flavored greens. Stay mild or creamy.

MÂCHE is also known as lamb's lettuce. It is mildly sweet, with little round dark-green leaves. Like leaf lettuces, it needs a mild dressing.

MICROGREENS are tiny versions of grownup leaves, harvested when quite young, about a week old. They are small but intense in flavor. And they are costly. Some of the more popular are radish leaves, arugula, beet, mustard, mizuna, pepper cress, and red kale. They are used by chefs and will be at our markets soon.

MINT's sweetly fragrant, serrated pointy leaves can be added whole to salads or cut into fine strips and used in dressings. Peppermint leaves are smaller than those of other mints and have slightly more bite. Mint pairs well with fruit and citrus dressings; it accents milder greens and provides sweetness to bitter ones.

MIZUNA is a mustard green of Japanese origin, also cultivated in

romaine

upland
cress

China. It has feathery, deeply serrated dark-green leaves on white juicy stalks, with a mild mustard taste and a lovely delicate texture. It is often added to mixes of baby salad greens.

MUSTARD GREENS are pungent and bitter, with a bite. Baby mustard leaves are often part of a salad mix. The large leaves are good for cooking. Cut them into thin strips and sauté or steam.

NASTURTIUM LEAVES AND BLOSSOMS add notes of brilliant orange and gold to a salad. They are a bit peppery. They are sometimes included in mesclun or spring mix.

PARSLEY has small flat dark-green leaves that are only mildly piquant and are wonderful in salads. I prefer flat-leaf parsley to curly parsley because it has a sweeter, cleaner taste.

PURSLANE has thick round leaves that resemble those of a jade plant or succulent. They are tangy and juicy and add crunch to a salad. They

are used in Middle Eastern salads and can handle a creamy dressing or one with citrus.

RADICCHIO is a member of the chicory family and a native of the Veneto in Italy. The three styles are named after towns in the region. Treviso has elongated red-and-white leaves (the green version is Pan di Zucchero). Rosso di Verona or Palla rossa is a round, compact head of red leaves veined with white, and Castelfranco comes in rosette-like heads but the leaves are white and pale gold, with small veins of red and pale green. Radicchio is bitter and nutty in flavor and can be served raw or cooked. Crunchy when raw, it needs dressings that are sweet or nutty. Radicchio grills well too.

ROMAINE or **COS LETTUCES** are heads of long pale-green leaves, crisp in texture. Their tender centers are prized, as the large outer leaves with their heavy central veins can be tough. Leaves can be used whole if small or cut crosswise. Romaine pairs well with other crunchy salad accompaniments, like radishes, cucumbers, and onions, as well as with slivers of fruit and nuts. It shows best with creamy dressings or dressings that have some richness.

SORREL has long oval leaves with a sour lemony taste. It is tender in texture but intense in flavor, so you may want to cut the leaves up a bit. When cooked, it tends to turn brown and become very soft and slippery.

SWISS CHARD leaves, tiny in size, are found in salad mixes when they are tender and sweet. The large leaves are good for steaming, sautéing, and braising.

SPINACH was introduced by the Moors to Spain in the sixteenth century and is now grown all over the Mediterranean. It comes in large bunched leaves with stems and needs to be washed many times, as it tends to be quite sandy. Baby spinach comes in bulk and is tender and mild in taste. The leaves are bright green. (Old

fennel

spinach turns yellow and is to be avoided.) Spinach takes to a variety of dressings and accompaniments, as it is neutral and mild.

TATSOI leaves are round, paddle-shaped, and dark green with pale greenish stalks. A bit crunchy, they are often part of a salad mix.

WATERCRESS has small round dark-green leaves on crunchy stems. It comes in bunches, some with roots attached. It is very peppery and nutty, offers a good contrast in fruit-based salads, and pairs well with bitter endive. It does best with citrus dressings.

measuring greens

IN THE FOLLOWING RECIPES, I measure greens by the handful, by the pound, or by cups. One pound of greens equals about 12 large handfuls—quite a lot, and more than you will usually need. Half this amount, 6 large handfuls, equals about 1/2 pound or 12 loosely packed cups—enough to make 6 large individual salads, 8 smaller salads, or a bed for other ingredients on a platter. Similarly, 4 large handfuls (1/3 pound, or 8 cups) is enough to make 4 individual salads. As with dressings, the amount you need depends to some degree on the nature of the ingredients on the day you make your salad, so remember that these quantities are approximate.

Measuring greens that come by the bunch or head is different from measuring loose lettuce and mesclun salad mix. Bunches of escarole, frisee, Swiss chard, and broccoli rabe are of varying sizes and weights. So the weights and measurements for *horta* are approximate.

2 to 2 1/2 pounds bulk gives you about 8 cups trimmed greens (by trimming I mean removing all thick or tough stems), which cooks down to about 2 1/2 cups. 1 1/2 to 2 pounds untrimmed greens (by head or bunch) gives you 6 to 7 cups trimmed and cut up greens, which cooks down to about 2 cups.

green salad with croutons and gruyère cheese

THIS IS THE BOTTOM LINE, a basic green salad with a sprinkling of herbs, a few croutons, and a bit of cheese. Master this and the rest will come to you easily.

There are two ways to make croutons. You can brush slices of bread with oil and bake them, as directed below, or you can fry them in oil—very tasty but much richer. If you want to fry them, cut a rustic loaf into 3/4-inch-thick slices, remove the crusts, and then cut the slices into 3/4-inch cubes. Warm some oil in a sauté pan and fry the cubes, turning and stirring, until they are golden. Drain on paper towels.

> **1/2 small baguette**
> **Olive oil**
> **1 garlic clove (optional)**
> **1/2 pound assorted lettuces, well washed and dried (about 12 loosely packed cups)**
> **2 tablespoons chopped fresh tarragon, chervil, or chives, or to taste**
> **1/3 pound Gruyère or Emmenthaler cheese, sliced 1/8-inch thick and cut into strips about 1 1/2 inches long, at room temperature**
> **About 1/2 cup basic vinaigrette (page 268)**

Heat the oven to 350 degrees F.

Slice the baguette into 1/4-inch-thick rounds and place on a baking sheet. Brush the rounds with olive oil and bake until crisp and golden, 10 to 15 minutes. Check on them midway to see how they are browning; you don't want them to be too dark. While warm, rub each crouton with the garlic clove if you want a hint of garlic in the salad. (You can omit this step and use a garlic vinaigrette or omit garlic altogether.) Or cut the bread into cubes, toss with oil, and bake until golden, stirring from time to time for even browning.

Toss the lettuces, herbs, cheese strips, and croutons in a bowl with the vinaigrette. Serve at once.

ALTERNATE DRESSINGS:
garlic vinaigrette (page 269),
sherry vinaigrette (page 270).

insalata capricciosa

CAPRICCIOSA IS ITALIAN FOR "ON A WHIM" or "as the spirit moves you." The base of the salad can be torn leaves of romaine, butter lettuce, or mesclun. Then, capriciously, but judiciously and with taste, add whatever you like. You might select diced cucumbers, strips or slivers of carrots, cooked chickpeas, or a few olives. Mix them well with a garlicky vinaigrette and add a few croutons (see page 37) if desired. I like to grate the carrots on the large holes of a box grater—they are wider than those done with the small holes, which tend to break easily.

> 1 1/2 to 2 cups cooked chickpeas (see pages 189–90), or canned chickpeas
> About 3/4 cup garlic vinaigrette (page 269)
> 12 cups torn romaine lettuce (about 1/2 pound after trimming, or
>   6 large handfuls)
> 2 cups seeded diced cucumbers
> 1 cup grated carrots (use the large holes of a box grater)
> Toasted croutons (optional)

If using canned beans, rinse well. In a bowl, toss the chickpeas with 1/4 cup vinaigrette and marinate for about 30 minutes.

Combine all of the salad ingredients in a large bowl and toss with enough of the remaining vinaigrette to coat.

ALTERNATE DRESSINGS:
sherry vinaigrette (page 270),
red wine vinaigrette (page 268).

NOTE: *Most regular supermarket cucumbers are waxed and must be peeled and seeded. English cucumbers do not require peeling but must also be seeded. Japanese and Persian cucumbers do not need to be peeled and the seeds are negligible.*

green salad with sautéed mushrooms and warm shallot vinaigrette

CONTRASTING TEMPERATURES CREATES an interesting and sensual dish. The French love leafy salads dressed with warm vinaigrette. The cool leaves wilt just a bit and become coated with the dressing in a very unctuous way. Sautéed mushrooms are also wonderful additions to a green salad. Again, add them while they are warm to the cool crisp greens for maximum effect.

> 1/2 pound flavorful fresh mushrooms, such as chanterelles, matsutakes, or creminis
> 4 large handfuls of young, tender salad greens (about 8 cups or 1/3 pound), chilled
> 2 to 3 tablespoons extra-virgin olive oil
> 2 teaspoons minced garlic
> Sea salt and freshly ground black pepper
> About 1/2 cup mustard shallot vinaigrette (page 271)

Trim the stems of the mushrooms and then wipe the mushrooms clean with paper towels. If using chanterelles or creminis, slice 1/4-inch thick. You may want to cut matsutakes a bit thinner.

Place the chilled salad greens in a large bowl.

In a large sauté pan, heat 2 tablespoons olive oil over medium heat. Add the mushrooms and garlic and sauté, adding a bit more oil if the mushrooms begin to stick or scorch. Cook until the mushrooms are tender, about 5 minutes. Season with salt and pepper to taste and slide them onto a plate.

Quickly deglaze the pan with vinaigrette and then pour the warm dressing and warm mushrooms over the salad greens. Mix well. Distribute among 4 salad plates and serve at once.

VARIATION:
You may add cooked green beans to this salad.

ALTERNATE DRESSINGS:
balsamic vinaigrette (page 276),
sherry vinaigrette (page 270).
You may add hazelnuts to the salad and use
hazelnut vinaigrette (page 273).

green salad with lardons, mushrooms, and chopped egg SALADE AUX LARDONS

IN THE OLD DAYS OF CLASSIC CUISINE, before creativity and chaos set in, recipe terms were familiar to the dining public. People knew that lardons were strips of bacon or salt pork. Finely chopped hard-boiled egg yolk was called "mimosa" because it was supposed to resemble the golden blossoms of the mimosa tree. But today I don't think many people have ever seen a mimosa or know what it is in culinary lingo. Besides, I hate to discard egg whites, so for the garnish on this salad I often use whole eggs, finely chopped. A poached egg (see photo) is the classic garnish for this bistro salad, but for those who are nervous about poaching, I offer the foolproof chopped-egg option.

I like tender leaves for this salad—young chicory (frisée), baby spinach, or even butter lettuce. I want the mushrooms firm, so I don't cook them. A zesty vinaigrette is needed to cut through the meatiness of the lardons, which can be made with bacon or pancetta. And for extra punch I warm the dressing in the pan before mixing it with the salad.

> 2 cups white or brown mushrooms, sliced 1/8-inch thick
>
> About 1/2 cup red wine vinaigrette (page 268)
>
> 8 cups well-washed chicory, baby spinach, or butter lettuce (about 1/3 pound)
>
> 1/2 cup thinly sliced green onions (white and green parts)
>
> Sea salt and freshly ground black pepper
>
> 1 to 2 tablespoons olive oil
>
> 4 ounces pancetta or bacon, sliced 1/4-inch thick and cut crosswise into strips about 1/4-inch wide (lardons)
>
> 2 hard-boiled eggs, finely chopped, or 4 poached eggs

In a bowl, toss the mushrooms with a few tablespoons of the vinaigrette and marinate for 10 minutes.

Place the salad greens and green onions in a salad bowl. Sprinkle lightly with salt and pepper.

Add the oil to a small sauté pan over medium heat and cook the strips of pancetta until they are somewhat crunchy, about 5 minutes. Remove from the pan and set aside.

Add the remaining vinaigrette to the pan and mix well to warm the dressing.

Add the mushrooms to the salad bowl, add the warm dressing, and toss well to coat. Distribute among 4 salad plates and top with pancetta and egg. Serve at once.

ALTERNATE DRESSINGS:
sherry vinaigrette (page 270),
balsamic vinaigrette (page 276).

facing page: green salad with lardons, mushrooms, and a poached egg

green salad with cucumbers, walnuts, and mustard shallot vinaigrette

HERE THE TANGY MUSTARD VINAIGRETTE coats the lettuce leaves and adds a little zip to the crunchy but bland cucumbers. You can make the vinaigrette early in the day and toast the walnuts a few hours ahead. Try to keep the walnuts in large pieces, easy to pick up with a fork. Let them macerate in some of the dressing. Then it's just toss and serve.

> 1 1/4 cups walnuts, toasted and coarsely chopped
> About 3/4 cup mustard shallot vinaigrette (page 271)
> 6 large handfuls of butter or romaine lettuce (about 1/2 pound)
> 2 cucumbers, peeled, seeded, and diced (about 4 cups)
> 3 tablespoons chopped fresh dill (optional)
> Sea salt and freshly ground black pepper

In a small bowl, toss the walnuts with 1/4 cup vinaigrette and let them absorb the dressing for about 15 minutes.

Combine the lettuces, cucumbers, walnuts, and dill, if using, in a large salad bowl. Toss with enough of the remaining vinaigrette to coat and add salt and pepper to taste. Serve at once.

ALTERNATE DRESSINGS:
walnut vinaigrette (page 273).
walnut cream dressing (page 312)
can be lovely here if you use soft lettuces like butter,
oak leaf, and red leaf.

andalusian green salad with eggs, ham, and tomato vinaigrette

AS FAR BACK AS A.D. 500, lettuces, carrots, asparagus, leeks, garlic, and wild herbs and greens were used in salads all over the Mediterranean. Dressings were made from fermented grapes and figs. In the caliphate of Al Andaluz, in Spain, spring onions and citrus juices were eventually added to the dressings. After the discovery of the New World, tomatoes and peppers became salad standbys. In this delightful Andalusian salad, those New World tomatoes are incorporated into the vinaigrette.

2 heads romaine or butter lettuce, trimmed and well washed and dried
1/2 cup tomato vinaigrette, or as needed (page 282)
2 hard-boiled eggs, sliced
2 or 3 green onions, thinly sliced (white and green parts)
1/4 pound Serrano ham, cut in thin strips
1/4 cup assorted black or green olives

Tear the lettuce into bite-sized pieces and put them in a salad bowl. Toss with some of the dressing to coat. Arrange on a platter and top with eggs, green onions, ham, and olives. Spoon the rest of the dressing on top.

ALTERNATE DRESSINGS:
sherry vinaigrette (page 270),
lemon mayonnaise dressing (page 316).

romaine, gorgonzola, and walnut salad

DID YOU EVER WONDER why some salads become classics? It might be the perfect balance of contrasting textures—creamy, crisp, and crunchy—or of contrasting flavors—bitter and sweet, like apples or figs and endive or sweet beets and salty cheese. This classic salad is good to have in your repertoire, as it is a definite crowd-pleaser. It has the creamy (cheese), crisp (romaine), and crunchy (walnuts) formula.

Gorgonzola dolce is the sweet version of this fabulously rich blue-veined cheese. If you cannot find it at your market, substitute Roquefort or a similar blue cheese. If you want to add a sweet component to contrast with the saltiness of the cheese and the bitterness of the nuts, figs or grapes make a nice addition. In the winter you may add slices of persimmon, as in the photo, or slices of ripe pear.

It is important to toast the nuts to maximize their nutty taste. Do not refrigerate after toasting. The cheese will also taste best if it is served at room temperature.

> **1 cup walnuts, preferably halves**
> **3/4 cup to 1 cup walnut vinaigrette (page 273)**
> **3 medium heads romaine lettuce**
> **1/2 pound Gorgonzola dolce**

Heat the oven to 350 degrees F.

Toast the walnuts on a baking sheet for 8 to 10 minutes, stirring occasionally. Chop coarsely, or break them up with your fingers. Do not make them too small to pick up on a fork. Place the toasted walnuts in a small bowl and macerate in 3 to 4 tablespoons vinaigrette for about 15 minutes.

Remove all broken and discolored leaves from the romaine. Wash the lettuce leaves and dry well. Break the leaves into 1 1/2-inch-long pieces, easy to pick up with a fork. (If you opt for the more dramatic presentation of whole leaves, be sure to serve a knife with the salad.) Place in a large salad bowl.

With your fingers, break the Gorgonzola into bite-sized morsels.

Add the walnuts and enough of the remaining vinaigrette to coat the lettuce, and toss. Divide among 6 salad plates, top with crumbled cheese, and serve.

(continued on next page)

facing page: romaine, gorgonzola, and walnut salad with persimmons and hazelnut vinaigrette

VARIATION:
If you would like to add fruit, use 6 ripe figs, cut into quarters,
or 1 cup red or black seedless grapes, cut in half, or 2 small ripe pears,
halved, cored, and cut into thin wedges, or 2 ripe Fuyu persimmons,
cut in thin wedges or sliced.

ALTERNATE DRESSINGS:
Use hazelnuts instead of walnuts with
hazelnut vinaigrette (page 273);
lemon cream dressing (page 308);
gorgonzola cream dressing (page 313),
cutting back on the crumbled cheese if you like.

NOTE: *It is always best to buy walnut halves rather than walnut pieces.
The latter are often too small to pick up with a fork. When you buy
halves, you have the control. Toast them, then break or chop them into
pieces that will fit on a fork, about 1/2 inch.*

crunchy garden salad with yogurt dressing

COOL AND REFRESHING, the tangy, creamy yogurt dressing offers a fine counterpoint to the mild, crisp romaine and cucumbers while tempering the bitter zip of the radishes and green onions.

2 smallish English cucumbers, seeded and cut in 1/2-inch dice, or
    4 Persian or Japanese cucumbers, cut in 1/4-inch slices
1 bunch radishes, sliced paper-thin
Sea salt
6 small hearts of romaine, cut in 2-inch lengths
6 green onions, finely chopped (white and green parts)
About 1 cup yogurt dressing (page 306)
1/4 cup chopped fresh dill
Freshly ground black pepper

If you have time, sprinkle the cucumbers and radishes with salt and let them sit for 5 to 10 minutes, then rinse and dry. They will release less water into the dressing.

Combine the lettuce, cucumbers, radishes, and green onions in a salad bowl. Toss with enough dressing to coat. Garnish the salad with chopped dill and black pepper to taste and serve immediately.

ALTERNATE DRESSINGS:
tahini dressing (page 303),
lemon cream dressing (page 308).

spinach salad
à la grecque

I LIKE TO TAKE a classic spinach salad and give it a Greek flavor profile. Spinach is the ideal green for this salad, especially if you can find small, tender leaves, as it is only mildly bitter. But you can use assorted lettuces. Adding beets and beans makes this more substantial. I often add cooked shrimp to make this a meal in a bowl.

In a salad of this complexity, with leafy greens, starchy beans, sweet and earthy beets, tangy onions, fleshy, bitter olives, and salty, crumbly cheese—so many diverse elements of texture and taste—the vinaigrette is the key that ties all the components together. Lemon juice alone is not deep enough in flavor to stand up to the onions. Vinegar alone is too strong and can overpower the sweetness of the beets and make the cheese taste too sour. The combination of lemon and vinegar provides the right balance of acidity.

You could add diced or sliced cucumber to this salad in place of the more filling white beans. They are mildly bitter and add an element of cool crispness.

> 1 small red onion, thinly sliced
> About 1 1/2 cups mint vinaigrette
> 2 cups cooked white beans (optional)
> 6 large or 12 small beets, cooked
> 1 pound cooked shrimp (optional)
> 6 to 8 large handfuls of baby spinach or assorted lettuces, well washed
>   and dried (about 1/2 pound)
> 1/2 pound feta cheese, coarsely crumbled, for garnish
> 1 cup Kalamata olives, for garnish

Marinate the onions in 2 to 3 tablespoons of the mint vinaigrette for about 15 minutes to soften them and lessen their bite.

If using beans, toss them in 1/4 cup vinaigrette to marinate for about 30 minutes.

Cut large beets in half and then into 1/4-inch slices. If the beets are small, cut them into quarters or eighths. Toss with a few tablespoons vinaigrette.

If using shrimp, toss them with a bit of dressing as well.

In a large salad bowl, combine the marinated onions and beets (and beans or shrimp if using) with the spinach and toss with enough of the remaining vinaigrette to coat. Distribute among individual salad plates and sprinkle with feta and olives. Serve immediately.

ALTERNATE DRESSING:
oregano garlic vinaigrette (page 284).

spinach salad with potatoes, oranges, and catalan vinaigrette

ORANGES AND POTATOES MIGHT SEEM like an odd couple, but they are not an unusual salad combo in the Mediterranean. In her wonderful book, *The Glorious Foods of Greece*, Diane Kochilas talks of a Greek salad of potatoes and oranges with a bit of red onion and olives, tossed in a simple oil and vinegar dressing. My version is from Spain and combines potatoes, oranges, celery, tomatoes, and baby spinach with Catalan vinaigrette. I am particularly fond of this salad and have prepared it at numerous events sponsored by the U.S. Potato Board. It is always a hit. People are pleasantly surprised by the combination of earthy potatoes and tart oranges and tomatoes, accented with the crunch of celery. I am sure the dressing, with nuts and citrus juice, has a great deal to do with its popularity.

> 4 large handfuls of spinach leaves, well washed (about 1/3 pound)
> About 1 cup Catalan vinaigrette (page 278)
> 3 oranges
> 8 small new potatoes (about 1 pound), boiled and sliced,
>   or quartered if small
> 1 cup diced celery, cut 1/4-inch thick
> 1/2 cup finely diced red onion
> 2 ripe tomatoes, peeled, seeded, and diced

Toss the spinach leaves with some of the vinaigrette and divide them among 4 salad plates.

Working with 1 orange at a time, cut a thin slice off the top and bottom to reveal the flesh. Stand the orange upright and remove the peel in wide strips, cutting downward and following the contour of the fruit. Holding the orange over a bowl, cut along both sides of each segment, releasing the segments from the membrane and letting them drop into the bowl. Use the knife tip to pry any seeds from the segments. Squeeze the membrane over the bowl to collect extra juice, which you can add to the dressing at serving time if you like.

Place the remaining ingredients in a large bowl with the remaining vinaigrette and toss. Top each serving of spinach with some vegetables and orange segments and serve.

ALTERNATE DRESSINGS:
mint vinaigrette (page 280),
or add 1/2 cup toasted almonds, omit the tomatoes,
and use **tomato vinaigrette** (page 282).

spinach and chicory salad with cauliflower, artichokes, and tapenade vinaigrette

THIS IS CALLED *caponata di verdure* in Italy and is commonly dressed with anchovy garlic vinaigrette. I like to use tapenade dressing because it is richer in texture and stands up well to the strongly flavored cauliflower and artichokes. The toasted bread crumbs add another layer of texture to this rather substantial dish.

> 1 medium head cauliflower, cut into florets (about 2 cups)
> 4 artichokes
> 1/3 cup olive oil
> 1/3 cup water, plus more if needed
> 2 tablespoons fresh lemon juice
> Sea salt and freshly ground black pepper
> 4 cups spinach leaves (a scant 1/3 pound)
> 4 cups torn chicory (about 2 handfuls)
> About 1 cup tapenade vinaigrette (page 322)
> 1 cup diced celery, cut 1/4-inch thick
> 1 cup diced cucumbers, preferably Japanese (seeded and peeled if not), cut
>   1/2-inch thick
> 1 1/3 cups toasted bread crumbs (recipe follows)

Cook the cauliflower in boiling salted water over medium-high heat until it is a little past al dente, 5 to 8 minutes. Refresh in cold water and pat dry.

Remove all of the artichokes' leaves, scoop out the fuzzy chokes, and cut the artichokes into thick slices or wedges. In a sauté pan, cook over medium-high heat in the olive oil and water, stirring often, until the artichokes are tender and the water has been absorbed 15 to 20 minutes. Remove the artichokes to a large bowl, drizzle with the lemon juice, and season with salt and pepper to taste.

Toss the spinach and chicory with enough dressing to coat the leaves and arrange on individual salad plates. Toss the cauliflower, artichokes, celery, and cucumbers with the remaining dressing and strew these over the greens. Sprinkle generously with the toasted bread crumbs and serve.

ALTERNATE DRESSINGS:
anchovy garlic vinaigrette (page 286),
oregano garlic vinaigrette (page 284).

toasted bread crumbs

HEAT THE OVEN to 375 degrees F. Place 2 cups cubed fresh Italian or French bread, crusts removed, in a food processor. Process the bread with pulses to form coarse crumbs. Transfer to a bowl and toss the crumbs with 1 teaspoon salt, 1/2 teaspoon freshly ground black pepper, and 1/4 cup olive oil. Spread the crumbs on a baking sheet. Bake, stirring occasionally for even browning, until golden, about 15 minutes. Yield: about 1 1/3 cups.

COMPOSED SALADS

Composed salads are an assortment of cooked or cooked and raw ingredients arranged on a plate and then drizzled with salad dressing. *Salade Niçoise* (page 227) is a perfect example. For the cook, composed salads can be an arena of great creativity, both in the choice of ingredients and in the selection of appropriate dressings to accompany these ingredients. Composed salads appear in different sections throughout this book. They are not just random collections of leftovers but are often the result of careful thought and selection.

spinach salad with mushrooms, walnuts, and lemon mustard cream dressing

MANY MEDITERRANEAN RECIPES PAIR mushrooms and nuts. In Italy, hazelnuts are the complement for assorted local mushrooms. In Spain, almonds are often part of the duet. In this Greek-inspired salad, walnuts are combined with mushrooms and spinach. I've chosen lemon mustard cream dressing because I like the way it coats and unifies the salad.

> 1 1/2 cups thinly sliced white or cremini mushrooms
> About 1 cup lemon mustard cream dressing (page 308)
> 1 cup walnuts, toasted and very coarsely chopped
> 6 large handfuls of small spinach leaves, well washed and dried
>   (about 1/2 pound)

In a medium bowl, toss the mushrooms with 1/4 cup of the dressing. In a small bowl, toss the walnuts with a few tablespoons of the dressing. Marinate both for 10 minutes.

In a salad bowl, toss the spinach with enough of the remaining dressing to coat. Add the mushrooms and nuts, toss again, and serve.

VARIATION:

Omit the mushrooms, add 2 to 3 cooked beets, sliced, and use **walnut vinaigrette** (page 273) or **gorgonzola cream dressing** (page 313).

ALTERNATE DRESSINGS:

Use hazelnuts and **hazelnut cream dressing** (page 311) or **hazelnut vinaigrette** (page 273). You can also use **walnut cream dressing** (page 312), **mustard mayonnaise dressing** (page 316), or **tarragon mayonnaise dressing** (page 316).

serves 4

belgian endive, fennel, mushroom, and walnut salad

IN THIS FRENCH-INSPIRED SALAD, lemon mustard cream facilitates the delicate balancing act between bitter endive, bitter but toasty walnuts, crunchy, anise-scented sweet fennel, and earthy mushrooms. If you can't get fennel, try celery, which is milder and less sweet. With celery, you might want to play up the lemon by adding a bit more juice and maybe some grated lemon zest, to hold the bitter walnuts and endive in check, or switch to hazelnuts, which are sweeter than walnuts.

4 small heads Belgian endive
2 small bulbs fennel
1/4 pound white or cremini mushrooms, sliced 1/8-inch thick (about 2 cups)
About 1 cup lemon mustard cream dressing (page 308)
1 cup walnuts, toasted and coarsely chopped

Remove the root ends from the endive and separate the leaves.

Cut the fennel in half, remove the tough outer leaves, cut out the cores, and slice the fennel thin.

Combine the endive leaves, fennel slices, and mushrooms in a large salad bowl. Toss with enough dressing to coat and top with the chopped walnuts. Serve immediately.

VARIATION:
Omit the mushrooms and nuts and fold 2 to 3 tablespoons salmon roe caviar into the dressing.

ALTERNATE DRESSINGS:
gorgonzola cream or roquefort cream dressing (page 313), walnut vinaigrette (page 273) or walnut cream dressing (page 312), or use hazelnuts and hazelnut cream dressing (page 311).

fennel

arugula, mushroom, gruyère, and prosciutto salad with lemon mustard cream dressing

serves 6

HERE STRIPS OF prosciutto and cheese replace the nuts used in the previous two recipes. They add a salty element that is kept in balance by the cream in the dressing. Do not use paper-thin slices of prosciutto—the meat should hold together without shredding. Have both the cheese and the prosciutto at room temperature for maximum flavor.

> 6 large handfuls of arugula (about 1/2 pound)
> 3 heads Belgian endive, leaves separated
> About 1 1/2 cups lemon mustard cream dressing (page 308)
> 12 large white mushrooms, stems trimmed, sliced 1/8-inch thick
> 6 thin slices Gruyère or Emmenthaler cheese, cut into 2 1/2-inch-by-
>   1/8-inch strips
> 6 thin slices prosciutto, cut into 2 1/2-inch-by-1/8-inch strips

Toss the greens with half the dressing and divide them among 6 salad plates. Toss the mushrooms with enough dressing to coat and arrange on the greens. Lay the strips of cheese and prosciutto on top and drizzle lightly with the remaining dressing. Serve immediately.

ALTERNATE DRESSINGS:
balsamic vinaigrette (page 276),
sherry vinaigrette (page 270).

arugula and fennel salad with baked goat cheese and sun-dried tomato vinaigrette

THE RICH SWEETNESS OF SUN-DRIED TOMATOES works well to echo the sweetness of the fennel and is strong enough to work with the bitter greens. I like to throw a few basil and mint leaves into the mix for the surprise factor, and they add a subtle note of sweetness. The cheese is placed on top of the salad and is not dressed, so the vinegar does not make it taste bitter. What the warm goat cheese brings to the party is salt and a creamy texture, as well as a contrast in temperature, making the salad more than the sum of its parts.

1/2 cup dried bread crumbs
2 tablespoons chopped fresh mint
4 rounds fresh goat cheese, each about 1 inch thick
Extra-virgin olive oil

2 bulbs fennel, cut in half, cored, and thinly sliced
4 handfuls of small-leaf arugula (about 1/3 pound)
1/2 cup fresh basil leaves
1/2 cup fresh mint leaves
6 tablespoons oil-packed sun-dried tomatoes, cut in thin strips
About 3/4 cup sun-dried tomato vinaigrette (page 283)

Heat the oven to 350 degrees F.

Combine the bread crumbs and chopped mint in a shallow bowl. Brush each round of cheese with olive oil and then dip in the herbed bread crumbs. Place on a baking sheet. Bake until warm and creamy, 8 to 10 minutes.

While the cheese bakes, put the fennel, arugula, herbs, and sun-dried tomato strips in a bowl and toss with the vinaigrette. Distribute among 4 salad plates. Top each serving with a round of baked goat cheese and serve warm.

VARIATION:
If you don't want goat cheese rounds, you can top this salad with shavings of pecorino cheese.

ALTERNATE DRESSING:
mint vinaigrette (page 280).

belgian endive with apples and hazelnuts

THIS CLASSIC SALAD inspired by the French palate is always welcome at my table. Be sure the apples are tart and crisp for maximum contrast with the bitter greens and toasty nuts. For visual contrast, you might add radicchio in place of some of the endive, or use endigia, a colorful cross between endive and radicchio. Adding a few shavings of Parmesan or thin strips of nutty Gruyère makes the salad richer and adds a mild salt component. Or you can top it with a slice of baked goat cheese.

> 1/2 cup hazelnuts, toasted, skinned, and coarsely chopped
> 3/4 to 1 cup hazelnut vinaigrette (page 273)
> 4 medium heads Belgian endive, leaves separated
> 2 Pippin or Granny Smith apples, cored, halved, and thinly sliced
> Shavings of Parmesan or strips of Gruyère cheese, for garnish (optional)

Occasionally you can buy blanched hazelnuts with the skins already removed. If not, to remove the skins, heat the oven to 375 degrees F. Place the nuts on a baking sheet with sides or in a small baking pan. Toast until the peels are cracked and the nuts are fragrant, 10 to 12 minutes. Turn the nuts out onto a dish towel. Briskly and with some force, roll them around in the towel, scrunching them with your fingers to loosen the skins. You may not be able to get all the skins off, but that's all right.

Because hazelnuts are round, it's tricky to chop them. Do not use a food processor—it reduces some of the nuts to useless dust. To chop the nuts, lay out a small handful at a time and hit them with the flat side of a cleaver or a small frying pan. After you hit them, you may chop them with a knife, but don't chop them too small. You want pieces you can pick up with a fork. I find that the initial crushing is sufficient most of the time.

Toss the nuts with just enough vinaigrette to coat.

Either leave the endive leaves whole or cut them crosswise into 1-inch-wide pieces, easy to pick up with a fork. (If you leave the leaves whole, remember to serve a knife with the salad.) In a salad bowl, toss the endive with most of the remaining vinaigrette. Divide the leaves among 4 salad plates.

Top with the apple slices and drizzle with a little vinaigrette. Sprinkle with the nuts and garnish the cheese if you like. Serve immediately.

VARIATION:

If you want to top this salad with baked goat cheese, brush 1-inch-thick rounds of mild fresh cheese with extra-virgin olive oil, dip in dried bread crumbs, place on a baking sheet, and bake in a 350-degree F oven for 8 to 10 minutes. Serve the cheese warm.

facing page: belgian endive and radicchio with apples, hazelnuts, shavings of parmesan, and hazelnut vinaigrette

ALTERNATE DRESSING:

Use walnuts and **walnut vinaigrette** made with balsamic vinegar (page 273).

belgian endive, pear, fennel, and walnuts with roquefort cream dressing

BITTER BELGIAN ENDIVE WELCOMES a dressing with creaminess, mild sweetness, or notable acidity. When it is paired with fruit, a citrus-based dressing is ideal, but when you add a cheese component, the taste profile changes. If the cheese is a garnish, stay with citrus or a mild, sweet balsamic dressing. But if you want the cheese to have greater presence, then a cheese-based cream dressing is the answer. When combining sweet fruit and sweet fennel and salty cheese, the walnuts are a crucial bitter element to keep the salt in check.

> 1 cup walnuts, toasted and coarsely chopped
> 3/4 to 1 cup Roquefort cream dressing (page 313)
> 4 medium heads Belgian endive
> 2 small bulbs fennel
> 1 large or 2 small ripe Bartlett or Comice pears, halved, cored, and
>   thinly sliced (with peel)

Toss the nuts in a small bowl with a few tablespoons of the dressing and let sit to macerate for 10 to 15 minutes.

Remove the root ends from the endive and separate the leaves.

Cut the fennel bulbs in half, remove the tough outer leaves, cut out the cores, and slice the bulbs thin.

Combine the endive leaves and fennel in a large salad bowl. Toss with half the remaining dressing. Arrange on 4 salad plates.

Arrange the pears over the endive and fennel. Drizzle with the remaining dressing and top with the walnuts. Serve immediately.

VARIATION:
Substitute apples or figs for the pears.

ALTERNATE DRESSING:
walnut vinaigrette made with
balsamic vinegar (page 273).

belgian endive, radicchio, and orange salad with mint vinaigrette

I'LL NEVER FORGET THE FIRST TIME I ordered fresh orange juice in Rome and was served a glass of a shockingly red liquid. It was blood-orange juice, tart, floral, and perfumed, and I've been hooked on it ever since. Fortunately, blood oranges are now available at many markets. I love to use them in salads because of their jewel-like appearance. Of course you can use regular oranges here, or the pink-tinged Cara Caras, but they won't be quite as dramatic on the plate.

3 small heads Belgian endive, red or white

2 medium or 3 small heads radicchio

1/2 cup fresh mint leaves

About 3/4 cup mint vinaigrette (page 280)

3 blood or navel oranges, peeled, pith and seeds removed, cut into 1/4-inch-thick slices

1/4 cup thinly slivered mint leaves, for garnish (optional)

Remove the root ends from the endive and separate the leaves. Cut the radicchio heads in half and pull apart the leaves. Wash and dry thoroughly. Toss the endive, radicchio, and the mint leaves with the vinaigrette. Distribute among 6 salad plates. Top with the orange slices. Sprinkle with a little slivered mint if desired. Serve immediately.

ALTERNATE DRESSINGS:
catalan vinaigrette (page 278),
orange balsamic vinaigrette (page 277).

grilled radicchio salad with beets, oranges, and balsamic vinaigrette

A RECENT RESTAURANT TREND trickling into the home kitchen is to grill lettuces like romaine or radicchio for salads. Grilling adds a smoky undertone to the greens while wilting them a bit. This dish is really pretty, all tones of red, pink, and orange. We are playing with many kinds of sweetness: sweet beets and raisins and the tart sweetness of oranges. You might wonder why I don't dress this salad with a citrus dressing. Orange juice is just too sweet and mild to brighten the salad by itself. You need the tang of vinegar for depth to keep the dish from becoming too cloying or wimpy, and to stand up to the bitterness of the radicchio.

2 large or 4 small heads Treviso radicchio
Extra-virgin olive oil
4 small beets, cooked and cut in eighths or thinner
2 blood oranges, sliced, or 2 navel oranges, segmented
About 3/4 cup balsamic vinaigrette (page 276)
1/4 cup golden raisins plumped in water, orange juice, or marsala
1/4 cup pine nuts, toasted

Make a fire in a charcoal grill or preheat a broiler, gas grill, or ridged stovetop grill pan.

If the radicchio is large, cut it into quarters lengthwise. If not, cut in half. Pull apart the leaves. If they seem gritty, wash quickly and dry really well. Brush the wedges of radicchio lightly with the olive oil and cook on a grill, under the broiler, or in a ridged grill pan until they are charred on the outside but still tender within, turning occasionally, 5 to 8 minutes. Transfer to a platter or 4 salad plates. Top with the beets and orange segments.

Pour the vinaigrette into a small sauté pan and add the raisins and pine nuts. Warm the dressing for a few minutes, then pour it over the radicchio, beets, and oranges. Serve warm.

ALTERNATE DRESSINGS:
orange balsamic vinaigrette made with nut oil (page 277),
sherry vinaigrette (page 270),
or use almonds rather than pine nuts with
catalan vinaigrette (page 278).

italian parsley salad with walnuts and pecorino

I REMEMBER THAT THE FIRST TIME we served this at my restaurant, Square One, a guest asked the waiter, "The parsley salad—it's not made with parsley, is it?" At the time this concept was a bit unusual for the average American diner. So why did we try it? Because on a visit to Istanbul I ate a truly delicious salad that seduced me into using parsley as a salad green. One time the salad was served as part of a meze assortment; another time it was an accompaniment to a very rich lamb sausage. I love the clean taste of parsley dressed simply with lemon juice and olive oil, but I knew this salad might be a hard sell as is ("It's not parsley, is it?"), so I added those old crowd-pleasers, crunch and salt. The salad successfully migrated from Turkey to Italy, and may be accompanied by crostini with chopped roasted eggplant or a puree of roasted peppers seasoned with garlic.

> 1/2 cup basic citrus dressing using lemon and olive oil (page 290)
> 6 small handfuls of fresh flat-leaf parsley leaves, torn into bite-sized
>   pieces or very coarsely chopped (about 4 bunches)
> 1/2 cup walnuts, toasted and coarsely chopped
> 1/2 cup grated pecorino cheese

Whisk the dressing directly in the salad bowl.

Add the parsley, walnuts, and pecorino and toss to coat.

Distribute the salad among 4 salad plates. Serve immediately.

greek parsley salad with tahini dressing
TAHINI SALATA

WHILE CALLED A SALAD, this is really a meze spread to be served with pita bread. I sometimes add toasted pine nuts to the parsley and tahini mixture, as I think they add texture and sweetness. If you don't have green onions on hand, you can use 4 tablespoons chopped chives instead.

1/2 cup tahini dressing (page 303), plus more if needed
Water
Sea salt, if needed
1 1/2 to 2 cups chopped fresh flat-leaf parsley
3 green onions, finely chopped (white and green parts)
2 tablespoons toasted pine nuts, coarsely chopped (optional)
Pita bread, cut into triangles and warmed

Put the tahini dressing in a blender or a small food processor and beat in a bit of water to make it thin enough to coat the leaves. Salt is crucial for the balance of flavor, so dip a leaf of parsley into the dressing and add salt if needed.

In a salad bowl, toss the parsley, green onions, and toasted pine nuts with the dressing. Serve with the pita bread for scooping.

facing page: greek parsley salad
with tahini dressing

puntarelle e peperoni

IN ROME IN SPRINGTIME, as you walk through the open markets you can watch people trimming Catalogna chicory, known locally as *puntarelle*. It is cut lengthwise and then chilled in ice water so it forms curls resembling the letter C. It used to be impossible to get *puntarelle* at American markets, so when I had a craving for this salad, I used chicory and dandelion greens. But now my market has the real deal.

Puntarelle salad is served with a vinaigrette loaded with anchovies. Their saltiness blends perfectly with the bitter greens. To play sweet against bitter, I add strips of roasted peppers, but I don't cut down on the anchovies. Their saltiness is needed for perfect balance.

> **4 small heads chicory or *puntarelle***
> **2 red peppers, roasted, stemmed, and seeded**
> **1 cup anchovy garlic vinaigrette (page 286)**

Trim the stem ends from the chicory and separate it into leaves. Wash well and then dry. If you have *puntarelle,* strip the soft green parts from the central stems and place the stems in a bowl of ice water until they curl. If the stems are wide cut them lengthwise. Dry well.

Cut the peppers into strips 1/3-inch wide.

Put the chicory and peppers into a salad bowl, toss with the vinaigrette, and serve.

puntarelle

belgian
endive

radicchio

collard green salad with yogurt dressing

THIS DISH IS A SPECIALTY of the Black Sea region of Turkey. Collard greens are cooked with onion, rice, tomatoes, and peppers; the mixture is then chilled and topped with yogurt dressing. You can also use purslane, dandelion greens, or beet greens for this dish.

    1/4 cup olive oil
    1 small onion or 4 green onions, chopped (about 1/2 cup)
    3 garlic cloves, minced (if you don't have garlic in the dressing)
    1/2 cup long-grain rice, such as basmati
    1 cup peeled, seeded, and diced tomatoes
    1/2 cup diced long green peppers, such as Anaheims
    2 pounds collard greens, coarsely chopped
    1 1/2 to 2 cups water
    1 cup yogurt dressing (page 306)
    Paprika or Aleppo pepper, for garnish

Warm the oil in a large sauté pan over medium heat. Add the onion and cook for about 5 minutes, until softened. Add the garlic, if using, and the rice, tomatoes, peppers, and greens and stir to combine. Add the water and reduce the heat to low. Cover the pan and cook until the greens are tender and all of the water has been absorbed, 15 to 20 minutes.

Transfer the mixture to a serving dish and chill. When cold, top with the yogurt dressing. Sprinkle with paprika or Aleppo pepper and serve cold.

cabbage slaw à la politika

POLITIKA REFERS TO THAT GIANT "POLIS" Constantinople, now cosmopolitan Istanbul. In other words, this salad has its origins in Turkey. The Greek version is usually prepared with cabbage and strips of bell peppers and onions. I find the peppers a bit too bitterly assertive for the already assertive cabbage and onions—the burp factor looms large—so I use sweeter, milder carrots and some strips of apple instead. The lemon mayonnaise dressing is a genial mediator for these diverse ingredients. For a more Greek flavor profile, try yogurt dressing.

> 1 small green cabbage, cut in half, cored, and shredded
> 2 to 3 medium carrots, grated
> 1 tart apple, peeled and cut into thin julienne strips
> 1 cup lemon mayonnaise dressing (page 316)

Place all of the ingredients in a salad bowl and toss with the dressing. Let the salad rest for a few hours before serving.

ALTERNATE DRESSINGS:
yogurt dressing (page 306),
lemon mustard cream dressing (page 308).

cooked wild greens
HORTA

serves 4

THE GREEKS ARE MAD FOR GREENS. They add them to soups and stews, tuck them into phyllo pies, and combine them with legumes. Instead of simply serving a salad of fresh wild greens, Greeks cook the greens and dress them with the classic *ladolemono*, an olive oil and lemon juice dressing. The traditional mixture of cooked greens is called *horta*, which translates as "weed," and is similar to *verdure spontanée* (see page 69). In Crete alone more than 300 indigenous herbs and greens are sometimes used for this dish.

As greens cook down quite a bit, be sure to have at least 1/2 pound per person. Some people believe that drinking the cooking juices contributes to long life and good health!

1 1/2 to 2 pounds assorted young, tender wild greens, such as arugula, sorrel, black mustard, dandelion greens, beet greens, escarole, kale, collard greens, and chicory (gives you 6 to 7 cups after trimming—cooks down to about 2 cups)
3/4 cup basic citrus dressing (page 290)
2 hard-boiled eggs, sliced, for garnish (optional)
1 cup black olives, for garnish (optional)

Trim the greens, discarding any tough stems.

Fill a sink with cold water and throw in the greens. Swish them around in the water and let any dirt settle to the bottom. Remove the greens with a slotted skimmer and place in a colander to drain.

Bring a large pot of lightly salted water to a boil over high heat, add the greens, and cook, uncovered, at a rolling boil until the greens are tender, about 10 minutes. Drain well. (Reserve the cooking juices if you'd like to try the broth. You might want to add a little salt and lemon juice.)

Serve the greens warm or cold. Dress with *ladolemono* at serving time. Garnish with hard-boiled eggs or olives if you like.

ALTERNATE DRESSING:
tahini dressing (page 303).

(continued on next page)

salad of cooked wild greens and preserved lemon dressing

THIS NORTH AFRICAN VERSION of *horta* can be served as a salad or as a bed for fish kebabs. You can also add slivers of fennel or slices of cooked artichokes if you like.

serves 4

1 pound (after trimming) assorted bitter greens, such as arugula, purslane, chard, mustard, and dandelion greens

3 tablespoons olive oil

3 cloves garlic, mashed with salt to a paste

1 bunch fresh flat-leaf parsley, stems removed, chopped

1 bunch fresh cilantro, stems removed, chopped

About 1/3 cup preserved lemon dressing (page 299)

Handful of oil-cured black olives, for garnish

Thinly slivered preserved lemon peel, for garnish (optional)

Wash the greens well and chop them coarsely. Boil or steam in a large pot until tender, about 10 minutes. Drain well.

Warm the oil in a medium sauté pan. Add the garlic paste, cooked greens, parsley, and cilantro and cook for a few minutes over medium heat to blend the flavors. Turn off the heat and dress the greens with the dressing.

Spoon the greens onto a serving platter and garnish with olives and with strips of lemon peel if you like. Serve warm.

ALTERNATE DRESSING:
basic citrus dressing (page 290).

GATHERED GREENS

All over the Mediterranean, people create salads and cooked dishes with what are called *verdure di campagna* or *verdure spontanée*, or "spontaneous greens." These are greens that grow wild in the countryside, including wild fennel, dandelion, purslane, hedge mustard, miner's lettuce, vitalba, luppolo, tarassaco, silene, and other weeds. (Franco Muzzio publishes a book by Jacopo Marinoni called *Cucina e salute, Kitchen and Health*, about the spontaneous greens from the Tre Venezie.) Of course, not all of these can be found growing here, but many wild greens are available in farmers' markets as well as in gardens and fields.

A long time ago, when I traveled to Sicily for the first time, my companion and I drove inland to Piazza Armerina to see the Roman mosaics. We had not called ahead, and the one major hotel was fully occupied by a film crew. Luckily, we found a room in a small local inn. We wandered into the tiny dining room in search of a simple dinner. I ordered *verdure spontanée*, having no idea what it was. I wondered why it was taking so long to come to the table. Then I looked out the window and saw two little old ladies out in the fields. They gathered some wild greens, washed them, and put them in a bowl. It was a memorable salad.

raw and cooked vegetable salads

BY FAR THE MOST EXTENSIVE category of Mediterranean salads and small plates is that based on vegetables. This chapter includes both raw and cooked vegetables seasoned with all manner of vinaigrettes and dressings.

Consider the following vegetables which appear on the Mediterranean table. The big three are eggplant, peppers, and tomatoes, solo or in combination.

EGGPLANT can be grilled, roasted, fried, stuffed, rolled, or mashed into a spread or dip. It can be anointed with creamy tahini or yogurt dressing, vinaigrettes, and citrus dressings. It is often paired with tomatoes and peppers, as in the Spanish *escalivada*. There are numerous Turkish, Greek, Italian, and Israeli eggplant dishes, as well as North African versions with preserved lemon, harissa, and charmoula.

PEPPERS can be roasted, grilled, sautéed, and stuffed. In Tunisia they are dressed with fiery harissa. They can be combined with roasted tomatoes, as in the classic North African *michwiya*, or paired with potatoes, as in some Spanish salads. They can be stuffed with rice, bread or cracked wheat, meat, or seafood.

TOMATOES are added to many a dish for a note of color and tart-sweet flavor, but they are stars on their own.

Served raw, they can be sliced, diced, stuffed, or used to flavor vinaigrettes. They are combined with mozzarella, feta, or goat cheese and dressed with pesto vinaigrette, oregano and anchovy or garlic vinaigrette, or tapenade dressing. They can also be roasted, sautéed, and braised.

SQUASHES: Zucchini can be fried, grilled, stuffed, marinated in mint vinaigrette *a scapece,* or drizzled with a rich yogurt dressing. The heartier winter or pumpkin squashes are sautéed or roasted, then marinated with vinaigrette or a citrus dressing. In North African salads they are roasted and mashed, then dressed with harissa.

CUCUMBERS are added to leafy salads for crunchy texture and cool relief. They can be added to chopped salads, or they can be served solo, tossed in a creamy dressing, as in Greek *tzatziki,* Turkish *cacik,* or Arabic *tarator.*

CELERY and **FENNEL** add crunch to leafy or chopped salads and provide a cool, clean contrast to seafood. Fennel is often paired with citrus for a sweet contrast to tart fruit.

CARROTS can be grated or shredded and served raw or added to leafy greens for color contrast. More often they are parboiled briefly and dressed while warm so they absorb the flavors of the dressing. Like winter squashes, they can also be mashed.

BEETS are boiled or roasted and served with citrus, mint, nuts, and cheese. In Greece, a common pairing is with feta and walnuts. Beets take to tahini or yogurt dressings as well as vinaigrettes and citrus dressings.

POTATOES are boiled or roasted. They are served as part of chopped salads or composed plates such as the Italian salad of potatoes, green beans, seafood, and pesto vinaigrette; or with cauliflower and a spicy Tunisian harissa vinaigrette.

ARTICHOKES can be paired with fruit or even cooked in citrus juice. They can be stuffed, pickled, or preserved and are most often served in Greece, Turkey, Morocco, and Italy.

CAULIFLOWER is parboiled and used in Italian, Spanish, and Tunisian salads. Its relative, broccoli, appears mostly in Italian salads. Because they are both rather assertive, they need strong dressings and vinaigrettes.

GREEN BEANS, ASPARAGUS, and **LEEKS** are blanched and dressed with citrus or other vinaigrettes or creamy dressings. They may star or be partnered with nuts, cheese, or eggs. They are used in composed salads as part of an ensemble sharing a common dressing.

Green beans, asparagus, and broccoli cannot be dressed ahead of time or they fade and turn gray-green.

CHOPPED SALADS

While some salads are loose in format, with leaves and other ingredients combined in a bowl, others use the same ingredients cut into small pieces. These are what we call chopped salads. They are not an American invention but a classic salad format in Turkey, Syria, Lebanon, Morocco, Spain, and Israel, where vegetables are chopped and dressed with vinaigrette. Classic chopped salads include the Spanish *pipirrana*, from Jaen (page 75), which combines tomatoes, onions, peppers, hard-boiled eggs, and ham; the Turkish *çoban* (page 73), or shepherd's salad, which combines diced tomatoes, cucumbers, onions, peppers, olives, and sometimes anchovy; and the Moroccan *merk hzina* (page 74), which is a mix of tomatoes, celery, onions, pepper, preserved lemon, and capers. Chopped salads are often extended with beans, grain, and bread; tabbouleh and farro salads are really chopped salads, as are bread salads like fattoush and panzanella.

turkish chopped salad
ÇOBAN SALATASI

IN MANY MEDITERRANEAN COUNTRIES, chopped salads are quite popular. This one from Turkey bears a close resemblance to the Spanish chopped salad called *pipirrana* (see page 75). Garlic is not traditional, but I find that it adds liveliness. I also like to add mint along with the parsley to brighten the taste even more. The Aleppo pepper provides a mild buzz, and sumac, if you use it, will increase the tartness of the salad.

If you want to assemble this a few hours ahead of time, be aware that the tomatoes will continue to give off water. Either add them at the last minute or drain excess liquid from the assembled salad and reseason it with dressing, salt, and pepper.

3 large ripe tomatoes, peeled, seeded, and chopped
2 small cucumbers, peeled, seeded, and chopped, or 1 English cucumber, seeded and chopped
1 medium red onion, finely minced
1 small bell pepper (green, red, or yellow) chopped (about 1/2 cup)
2 cloves garlic, minced (optional)
1/4 cup chopped fresh flat-leaf parsley
1/4 cup thinly slivered fresh mint
1/2 cup red wine vinaigrette (page 268)
Sea salt and freshly ground black pepper
2 teaspoons Aleppo pepper
2 teaspoons ground sumac (optional)
A few oil-cured black olives, for garnish

Drain the tomatoes in a colander for 20 minutes.

Combine all of the vegetables, garlic if using, and herbs in a salad bowl. Toss with the vinaigrette. Season to taste with salt pepper and add the Aleppo pepper. Add the sumac, if you like. Garnish with the olives and serve at room temperature.

VARIATION:
This salad may be extended with chopped greens such as arugula or purslane.

ALTERNATE DRESSINGS:
hot pepper vinaigrette (page 272),
mint vinaigrette (page 280).

facing page: turkish chopped salad with red wine vinaigrette, ready to be mixed. in the foreground, from left to right: sumac and aleppo pepper.

moroccan chopped salad
MERK HZINA

CHOPPED SALADS APPEAR WITH REGULARITY in North Africa.
Those made with just one vegetable are called *zahlouk* or *ajlouk*. This more
complex Moroccan chopped salad, *merk hzina*, is best dressed ahead of time
so the flavors have time to develop. But keep in mind that tomatoes give off
liquid as the salad sits, so you may need to readjust the seasoning at serving
time. If you want this to be a bit zingy, add the hot pepper.

6 large ripe tomatoes, peeled, seeded, and diced
1 medium red onion, minced
3 stalks celery, diced
1 bell pepper, diced
2 tablespoons salt-packed capers, rinsed
1 small hot chili pepper, chopped (optional)
1/2 teaspoon sea salt
1/2 teaspoon freshly ground pepper
About 1/2 cup preserved lemon dressing (page 299)
3 tablespoons chopped fresh flat-leaf parsley or cilantro, for garnish

Drain the tomatoes in a colander for 20 minutes.

Combine all of the ingredients in a salad bowl. Let sit at room temperature
for 2 hours before serving so the flavors mingle. Sprinkle with the parsley
or cilantro just before serving.

ALTERNATE DRESSINGS:
harissa dressing (page 329),
charmoula vinaigrette (page 326).

chopped summer salad from jaen
PIPIRRANA JIENENSE

serves 6

ATTEMPT THIS SALAD ONLY WHEN the tomatoes are perfectly ripe and flavorful. In Valencia, a salad with the same name uses salt cod instead of ham, contains a dash of hot pepper and chopped romaine, and has lemon juice in place of vinegar. In Murcia, a similar chopped salad garnished with tuna or sardines is called *mojete,* or "soak," because it is so delicious you want to soak bread in the juices. *Pipirrana* is not to be confused with *piperada,* a Basque omelet with fried peppers, tomatoes, and ham.

6 medium ripe tomatoes (2 pounds), peeled, seeded, and chopped
2 or 3 small green bell peppers, chopped
1 small onion, chopped
2 cloves garlic, minced
1 teaspoon sea salt
3 tablespoons chopped fresh flat-leaf parsley
2 hard-boiled eggs
About 1/2 cup sherry vinaigrette (page 270)
6 tablespoons diced ham, for garnish

Drain the tomatoes in a colander for 20 minutes.

Combine the tomatoes, peppers, and onion in a bowl. Add the garlic, salt, and parsley and mix.

Cut the eggs in half and place the yolks in a small bowl. Coarsely chop the whites and add them to the salad bowl. Mash the egg yolks and then beat them into the vinaigrette.

Toss the salad with the vinaigrette. Garnish with chopped ham and serve immediately.

ALTERNATE DRESSING:
red wine vinaigrette (page 268).

catalan chopped salad

MAYONNAISE-BASED DRESSINGS ARE IDEAL for chopped salads, because they add creaminess and help the ingredients cling together. The strong flavors here—bitter endive and onion, salty ham and anchovies—cry out for a mild, creamy dressing.

2 heads Belgian endive, cut crosswise into 1/2-inch-wide pieces, leaves separated

4 stalks celery, chopped

4 small spring onions, green parts only, chopped

4 ounces Serrano ham, diced

Half a 3-ounce jar of oil-packed anchovies (about 12), drained and minced

1 large clove garlic, minced

About 1/2 cup lemon mayonnaise dressing (page 316)

2 hard-boiled eggs, sliced, for garnish

Combine all the ingredients except the eggs in a salad bowl. Place the salad on a platter and garnish with the eggs. Serve immediately.

ALTERNATE DRESSINGS:
Omit the ham and use **tuna mayonnaise dressing** (page 316), or omit the anchovies and use **anchovy mayonnaise dressing** (page 316).

greek country salad

HORIATKI SALATA

serves 4

WHAT MAKES THE CLASSIC GREEK SALAD that appears on every taverna menu so special is the quality of the ingredients: intensely flavorful, organically grown tomatoes and cucumbers and tangy brined feta cheese and Kalamata olives. In many instances the salad is dressed only with extra-virgin olive oil. Although the vegetables are usually sliced in Greece, or cut in large chunks, I like to treat this as a chopped salad. My favorite way to dress it is with oregano garlic vinaigrette, as I think that brings all the ingredients together in a most harmonious way.

1/2 cup oregano garlic vinaigrette (page 284)
4 ripe but firm tomatoes, diced
1 cucumber, peeled and sliced 1/4-inch thick, or two Persian or
    Japanese cucumbers, diced
2 small green bell peppers, seeded and diced
1 red onion, finely chopped
3 cups torn or coarsely chopped salad greens, such as romaine or
    escarole (about 1/4 pound)
20 Kalamata olives, pitted
1/2 pound feta cheese, coarsely crumbled

At least 1 hour before serving, make the vinaigrette.

Drain the tomatoes in a colander for 20 minutes. Combine the salad ingredients in a large salad bowl and toss with the vinaigrette.

NOTE: *If you find raw onion a little strong, marinate it in a bit of the vinaigrette for 15 minutes to soften it and temper its bite.*

ALTERNATE DRESSING:
basic citrus dressing (page 290).

russian salad
INSALATA RUSSA

MANY YEARS AGO, I LIVED IN PERUGIA with a Jewish family named Coen. The cook in the household was a tiny lady in her eighties, Albertina. She was sweet and chatty but not a very good cook. This salad was her favorite, and when she presented it at table, she would say, "*Ecco il capolavoro*"— "Here's the masterpiece." The vegetables were always soggy, and the dressing was made with inferior olive oil. It took me years to think about serving this salad, but with a creamy, well-seasoned homemade mayonnaise dressing and perfectly cooked vegetables, I have come to enjoy it.

Essentially this is a chopped salad combined with a mayonnaise thinned with oil and vinegar. A similar salad is served in Greece, where it is called *rossiki,* which of course is Russian salad. In Piedmont, cooks sometimes puree canned oil-packed tuna into the mayonnaise dressing, like the tuna mayonnaise (page 000) served with vitello tonnato. It makes it richer and perhaps a bit more interesting. And if you love cooked tongue, chop some and fold it into the salad.

1 pound new potatoes, cooked, peeled, and diced

1/2 pound carrots, cooked and diced

1/2 pound green beans, cooked and cut in 1/2-inch pieces

1 cup peas, cooked

1 cup basic mayonnaise dressing (page 315), thinned with 1 to 2 tablespoons vinegar

1 cup chopped cooked tongue (optional)

1/2 cup chopped cornichons (optional)

1/2 cup pimiento-stuffed olives, cut in quarters (optional)

3 tablespoons salt-packed capers, rinsed (optional)

2 heads Belgian endive or 1 head romaine, leaves separated

Toss all of the ingredients except the endive together in a bowl. On a platter, make a bed of endive leaves, then spoon the salad on top and serve.

ALTERNATE DRESSING:
tuna mayonnaise dressing (page 316); do not use tongue.

chicken and potato salad
OLIVIEH

SALADE RUSSE CAME to Tehran with White Russian émigrés and has evolved into a very popular chicken salad called *olivieh*.

1/2 pound chicken, cooked and chopped
4 small new potatoes, cooked and chopped
4 hard-boiled eggs, chopped
1/4 pound gherkins, finely chopped
1 cup basic mayonnaise dressing (page 315)

In a bowl, combine the chicken, the potatoes, the hard-boiled eggs, the gherkins, and the mayonnaise dressing. Serve on a bed of endive leaves, as for the insalata russa.

grilled eggplant with pomegranate dressing

THIS PERSIAN SALAD OFFERS an unusual combination of bitter and tart flavors, offset by the sweetness of pine nuts and mint.

> 2 to 3 long slender eggplants (about 2 pounds)
> Extra-virgin olive oil
> Sea salt and freshly ground black pepper
> About 1/2 cup pomegranate citrus dressing (page 297)
> 3 tablespoons pomegranate seeds
> 3 tablespoons toasted pine nuts
> 2 tablespoons thinly slivered fresh mint

Make a fire in a charcoal grill or heat a gas grill.

You may peel the eggplants or not. Cut them into 1/2-inch-thick slices. Brush the slices liberally with olive oil and sprinkle them with salt and pepper to taste. Grill until tender and slightly browned, about 3 minutes per side.

Arrange the eggplant on a platter in overlapping slices. Drizzle with the dressing, top with the pomegranate seeds, pine nuts, and mint, and serve.

VARIATION:

You may serve roasted pepper strips instead of the eggplant, or alternate slices of eggplant with slices of roasted pepper.

ALTERNATE DRESSING:
mint vinaigrette (page 280).

NOTE: *If you don't want to heat up the grill, you may bake the eggplant. Heat the oven to 450 degrees F. Brush the eggplant slices liberally with olive oil and arrange them on baking sheets. Bake for about 20 minutes, turning once. The slices should be tender, translucent, and lightly browned.*

slow-roasted eggplant with pesto vinaigrette

THIS DISH IS BEST PREPARED with small globe eggplants. You also might try Japanese eggplants, as they have virtually no seeds and look lovely side by side on the plate.

> **3 large or 6 small globe eggplants or 12 small Japanese eggplants**
> **About 1/2 cup pesto vinaigrette (page 320)**
> **Sea salt and freshly ground black pepper**
> **3 ripe tomatoes, peeled, seeded, and chopped (optional)**

Heat the oven to 400 degrees F.

Prick the eggplants with a knife in a few places and put them on a baking sheet. Roast them, turning occasionally, until tender, 45 to 60 minutes for globe eggplants, 20 to 30 minutes for Japanese eggplants. (You can also broil or grill the eggplants, but be careful not to overcook them so they become too soft.)

Remove the eggplants from the oven, and when they are cool enough to handle, carefully cut away the stems and peel off the skins. Drain the peeled eggplants in a colander for about 30 minutes to rid them of excess moisture. Leave Japanese eggplants whole. Cut large globe eggplants in half and discard any large seed pockets, which are bitter and gritty on the tongue. If the halves are ragged-looking, chop the flesh coarsely.

Arrange the eggplants on a platter or divide among 6 salad plates. Dress with pesto vinaigrette and season to taste with salt and pepper. If you are using tomatoes, sprinkle them over the eggplants. Serve warm or at room temperature.

ALTERNATE DRESSINGS:
charmoula vinaigrette (page 326),
oregano garlic vinaigrette (page 284),
yogurt dressing (page 306),
tahini dressing (page 303).

serves
8 as
part of a
meze
assortment

turkish eggplant puree with yogurt dressing and walnuts

THE COMBINATION OF EGGPLANT AND YOGURT DRESSING is
not just reserved for the Persian kitchen. Turkish cooks also love to blend the
two. The natural bitterness of the eggplant and walnuts is tempered by the
tart, creamy yogurt. Even the chilies add a bitter edge. Sometimes the bitterness is too intense, so you might have to add more lemon juice for balance.
Serve this eggplant puree with wedges of warm pita bread.

4 large eggplants (3 to 4 pounds)
Juice of 2 lemons, plus more to taste
4 cloves garlic, green sprouts removed, minced
1 tablespoon extra-virgin olive oil, if needed
About 1 cup yogurt dressing (page 306)
4 tablespoons finely chopped fresh dill, mint, or cilantro
2 jalapeño peppers, very finely minced
2 teaspoons ground cumin, toasted (optional)
Sea salt and freshly ground black pepper
1/3 cup walnuts, toasted and chopped, for garnish
3 tablespoons chopped fresh flat-leaf parsley, for garnish
Crumbled feta cheese (optional)

For a smoky taste, grill the eggplants under the broiler, turning often,
or cook them slowly on a stovetop cast-iron griddle over medium heat,
turning them from time to time, until they are uniformly tender, about 20
minutes. You also may prick them with a fork in a few places, place them
on a baking sheet, and bake them in a 400-degree F oven until they are
soft throughout, about 1 hour. No matter which technique you choose,
remember to turn the eggplants occasionally until they are very soft.

Using tongs, put the eggplants in a colander or a perforated drainer tray.
Let stand until cool enough to handle.

Carefully remove the skins and put the eggplant pulp in a strainer to drain
for 10 minutes. Discard any large seed pockets; they are bitter and add
an unpleasant texture to the creamy eggplant puree. To keep the eggplant
white—a point of pride in Turkey—soak it briefly in water to which you've
added the lemon juice, or squeeze the juice directly over the eggplant.
After a few minutes, drain the pulp and squeeze it dry.

In a large bowl, coarsely puree or mash the eggplant with a potato masher
or a wooden spoon.

facing page: turkish eggplant puree
with yogurt dressing, feta, walnuts,
and warm pita

(continued on next page)

If the garlic is strong, or "hot," warm the oil over low heat in a small sauté pan, add the garlic, and cook for a minute or two to remove the bite. Add to the eggplant pulp.

Stir in the yogurt dressing, herb, jalapenos, and cumin, if using. Season with salt and pepper to taste. Place in a serving bowl or on a platter and sprinkle with chopped walnuts and parsley and with crumbled feta if you like. Serve with warm pita bread.

ALTERNATE DRESSINGS:
tahini dressing (page 303),
tarator dressing (page 305).

eggplants

chopped eggplant with preserved lemon
ZAHLOUK

ZAHLOUK, A CLASSIC MOROCCAN chopped eggplant salad, appears
on many a meze table. When tomatoes are in season, you may add some,
along with a few tablespoons of grated onion. The use of preserved lemon in
this dish is a signature of the town of Fez, but if you do not have any in your
pantry, use fresh lemon juice instead, or even a peeled, chopped fresh lemon.

2 1/2 to 3 pounds (3 medium) globe eggplants
1/2 cup olive oil, plus more if needed
2 grilled or roasted red peppers, peeled, deribbed, seeded, and chopped
3 cloves garlic, minced
3 ripe tomatoes, peeled, seeded, and diced (optional)
1/2 medium onion, grated (optional)
About 1/2 cup preserved lemon dressing (page 299)
1 teaspoon sea salt
4 tablespoons chopped fresh flat-leaf parsley

Peel alternating strips of the eggplants to make stripes. Cut them
into 1/2-inch-thick slices. Heat the olive oil in a large sauté pan over
medium-high heat and fry the eggplant in batches until golden, about 3
minutes per side. Drain on paper towels. When cool enough to handle, cut
the eggplants into 1-inch pieces.

In a large salad bowl, combine the eggplant with the remaining
ingredients. Mix well and serve at room temperature or cold.

NOTE: *If you want to reduce the amount of oil in this recipe, bake the
eggplants or cook them on a stovetop griddle instead of frying them. Heat
the oven to 450 degrees F. Prick each eggplant in a few places with a
fork. Roast on a baking sheet until tender but not mushy, turning a few
times for even cooking, about 45 minutes. Let stand until cool enough to
handle, then peel and cut into 1 1/2-inch cubes. Place in a colander to
drain and then transfer to a salad bowl. You will need to mix some olive
oil into the salad for flavor and texture.*

ALTERNATE DRESSINGS:
charmoula vinaigrette (page 326),
charmoula citrus dressing (page 326),
oregano garlic vinaigrette (page 284),
red wine vinaigrette (page 268).

roasted eggplant with tahini dressing

BABA GHANOUJ

THIS EGGPLANT SPREAD IS POPULAR in Syria, Lebanon, and Israel.
Warm wedges of pita bread or crunchy vegetables such as carrots, radishes,
green onions, and cucumbers are the best accompaniments.

3 to 4 large globe eggplants
About 3/4 cup tahini dressing (page 303)
Sea salt and freshly ground black pepper

GARNISHES
3 tablespoons toasted pine nuts
3 tablespoons chopped fresh flat-leaf parsley
1 teaspoon ground cumin (optional)
2 tablespoons pomegranate seeds (optional)

For a smoky taste, grill the eggplants under the broiler, turning often,
or cook them slowly on a stovetop cast-iron griddle over medium heat,
turning them for even cooking, until they are uniformly tender, about 20
minutes. You also may prick them with a fork in a few places, place them
on a baking sheet, and bake them in a 400-degree F oven until they are
soft throughout, about 1 hour. No matter which technique you choose,
remember to turn the eggplants occasionally until they are very soft.

Using tongs, put the eggplants in a colander or a perforated drainer tray.
Let stand until cool enough to handle.

Carefully remove the skins and put the eggplant pulp in a strainer to drain
for 10 minutes. Discard any large seed pockets; they are bitter and add an
unpleasant texture to the creamy eggplant puree.

Mash the eggplant in a bowl or transfer to the container of a food
processor and pulse to create a coarse puree. Add the tahini dressing
and salt and pepper to taste.

Transfer the puree to a plate or a shallow bowl. Sprinkle with pine nuts
and parsley, and with cumin and pomegranate seeds if you like. Serve at
room temperature.

HOW TO
COOK EGGPLANT

While eggplant is a beloved vegetable in the Mediterranean kitchen, it has never captivated the American palate to the same degree that it does in Turkey, Greece, Italy, Spain, North Africa, and the Middle East. I have a theory about this, and it has to do with how eggplant is cooked and served. When sliced and grilled or baked, eggplant is often served undercooked and is therefore bitter. When fried, because it can absorb lots of oil, people fear that it will be too oily, and so they undercook it: bitter again.

Here is a helpful visual clue to judge eggplant doneness. When you are cooking the vegetable, notice that it starts out white and opaque. When it is fully cooked, it is translucent and very pale green. The translucence comes from the absorption of just enough oil, proper heat, and sufficient cooking time. White areas indicate undercooking. So aim for total translucency and your eggplant will be mild and sweet.

cheese-stuffed eggplant rolls
with tapenade vinaigrette

THESE ROLLS are an ideal vehicle for tapenade vinaigrette. Grill the eggplant slices for a slightly smoky flavor, or simply fry them. (Zucchini can be prepared the same way; cut it lengthwise into slices 1/3-inch thick and grill or sauté.) Do not cut the eggplants too thin—they shrink when grilled. You want them to have enough body to hold the filling and be flexible enough to roll. If they are too thin, they will be flimsy and will tear when you try to roll them.

> 2 globe eggplants, peeled and sliced lengthwise 1/3- to 1/2-inch thick
>   (about 18 slices)
> 1/2 cup extra-virgin olive oil, plus more if needed
> Sea salt and freshly ground black pepper
> 1 cup soft fresh goat cheese, or strips of fresh mozzarella or fontina cheese
> 1/4 cup chopped fresh flat-leaf parsley, or 1/8 cup parsley and 1/8 cup
>   chopped fresh basil
> About 1 cup tapenade vinaigrette (page 322)

To grill the eggplant slices, prepare a hot fire in a charcoal grill. When the fire is ready, brush the eggplant slices on both sides with the olive oil and sprinkle with salt and pepper. Place the eggplant directly over the fire and grill, turning once, until tender and translucent but not too soft and not too dark, about 5 minutes total. Remove from the grill.

To fry the eggplant slices, layer them in a colander, lightly salting the layers, and let stand for 30 minutes to drain. Pat the eggplant slices completely dry with paper towels. In a large sauté pan, heat the olive oil over medium heat. Working in batches, add the eggplant slices and fry, turning once, until translucent and tender but not too soft, 6 to 8 minutes total. Transfer to paper towels to drain. Repeat with the remaining slices.

To make the filling, combine the cheese and parsley. Season to taste with pepper. Place a little cheese on each eggplant slice and roll up.

Set the rolls seam side down on a platter and spoon on the tapenade vinaigrette. Serve at room temperature.

You may also serve the eggplant rolls warm. Heat the oven to 350 degrees F. Lightly oil a baking dish large enough to accommodate the eggplant rolls in a single layer. Arrange the rolls seam side down in the dish. Warm them for 15 minutes and then drizzle with the dressing.

VARIATION:
Use the stuffing for the red pepper rolls (page 98)
instead of the cheese and parsley.

ALTERNATE DRESSINGS:
pesto vinaigrette (page 320),
oregano garlic vinaigrette (page 284).

facing page: cheese-stuffed eggplant
rolls with tapenade vinaigrette

spanish salad of grilled eggplant, onions, and peppers ESCALIVADA

IN CATALAN, *ESCALIVAR* MEANS "TO GRILL." Grilling produces the characteristic smoky taste that is essential to *escalivada*. If you don't want to light a fire every time you crave this Catalan dish, broil the vegetables or cook them directly on the burner or on a heavy stovetop griddle, or you can oven-roast them.

Escalivada is most versatile. Serve it as an accompaniment to grilled meat, tuck it into ham or chicken sandwiches, or present it at room temperature as part of a tapas assortment.

> 2 medium onions
> Olive oil
> 3 globe eggplants
> 2 red bell peppers
> 3 medium tomatoes
> About 1 cup oregano garlic vinaigrette (page 284)
> Sea salt and freshly ground black pepper
> Chopped fresh flat-leaf parsley, for garnish

If roasting, heat the oven to 400 degrees F.

Put the unpeeled onions in a baking pan and rub them with a little olive oil. Roast until tender, at least 1 hour. Let stand until cool enough to handle, then peel and slice 1/2-inch thick.

Prick the eggplants in several places with a fork and place them in a baking pan. Roast until soft but not mushy, about 45 minutes. Turn them occasionally for even cooking. When they are uniformly tender, remove from the oven and let stand. After they cool, peel them and tear the flesh into large strips (discard any large seed pockets). Place in a colander to drain.

If you prefer a smoky flavor, grill or broil the eggplants or soften them on a stovetop cast-iron griddle, turning often for consistent cooking. You do not need to prick them with a fork if they are not going in the oven.

Roast the peppers on a rack in a broiler or over a direct flame, turning often with tongs, until charred on all sides. Place them in a plastic container or a paper or plastic bag and close. Allow the peppers to steam inside the container for about 20 minutes. When they are cool enough to handle, peel off the skins with your fingers and scrape off any stubborn pieces of peel with a knife blade. A few flakes of peel are acceptable. If possible, do not wash the peppers. Cut them in half, remove the seeds and ribs, and cut the peppers into strips about 1/2-inch wide.

Roast the tomatoes over the flame with the peppers or in the oven for about 15 minutes. Scrape off the peels and cut them into cubes.

Combine the onions, eggplant, peppers, and tomatoes in a large salad bowl. Pour the dressing over the mixture and toss gently to coat. Add salt and pepper to taste and sprinkle the parsley on top. Serve at room temperature.

This salad gives off liquid as it sits, so you may want to dress it or refresh the dressing at serving time.

ALTERNATE DRESSINGS:
No need to keep this dish just in Spain—
cross the Gibraltar waters to North Africa
and try **charmoula** (page 326),
harissa (page 328),
or **preserved lemon dressing** (page 299).

moroccan pepper and tomato salad
MISHWIYA

THIS CLASSIC NORTH AFRICAN SALAD can be served as a starter or as an accompaniment to meat and fish dishes. Tunisians might turn it into a quasi-Niçoise by garnishing it decoratively with chunks of tuna, oil-cured olives, and sliced hard-boiled eggs.

6 ripe tomatoes
3 green bell peppers
3 to 4 cloves garlic, minced
1 teaspoon sea salt
1/2 teaspoon freshly ground black pepper
1/2 cup preserved lemon dressing (page 299)
2 tablespoons chopped fresh flat-leaf parsley or cilantro
1 small hot chili pepper, seeded and finely minced (optional)

Heat the oven to 400 degrees F.

Place the tomatoes and peppers on baking sheets and bake until the skins are wrinkled, about 20 minutes. Or roast the peppers on a rack in a broiler or over a direct flame, turning often with tongs, until they are charred on all sides. Place them in a plastic container or a paper or plastic bag and close. Allow the peppers to steam inside the container for about 20 minutes. When they are cool enough to handle, peel off the skin with your fingers and scrape off any stubborn pieces of peel with a knife blade. A few flakes of peel are acceptable. If possible, do not wash the peppers. Cut them in half, remove the seeds and ribs, and cut the peppers into small dice.

Peel the tomatoes with a knife. Remove the seeds and cut the tomatoes into small dice.

Place the peppers and tomatoes in a large bowl, add remaining ingredients, and mix well. Serve at room temperature.

ALTERNATE DRESSINGS:
charmoula vinaigrette (page 326),
anchovy garlic vinaigrette (page 286).

moroccan green pepper salad with preserved lemon dressing

BECAUSE RED AND YELLOW PEPPERS ARE SWEET, they can handle a tart vinegar-based dressing. Green peppers are more assertive and have a sharper, more intense and earthy flavor, so for this salad from Marrakech, I prefer to use lemon juice rather than vinegar, which makes them taste bitter.

3 large green bell peppers (1 to 1 1/2 pounds)
1/2 cup preserved lemon dressing (page 299)
Chopped fresh flat-leaf parsley or cilantro, for garnish
Oil-cured olives or strips of anchovy, for garnish (optional)

Roast the peppers on a rack in a broiler or over a direct flame, turning often with tongs, until they are charred on all sides. Place them in a plastic container or a paper or plastic bag and close. Allow the peppers to steam inside the container for about 20 minutes. When they are cool enough to handle, peel off the skins with your fingers and scrape off any stubborn pieces of peel with a knife blade. A few flakes of peel are acceptable. If possible, do not wash the peppers. Cut them in half, remove the seeds and ribs, and cut the peppers into strips about 1/2-inch wide.

Place the pepper strips in a large bowl and drizzle the dressing over them. Toss to mix. Sprinkle with chopped parsley or cilantro and garnish with olives or anchovy if you like. Serve at room temperature.

ALTERNATE DRESSING:
toasted cumin citrus dressing (page 301).

tunisian roasted pepper salad
SLATA FILFIL

ALL OVER THE MEDITERRANEAN, platters of roasted peppers are a classic appetizer, but leave it to the Tunisians to add harissa heat. As in Italy and France, this pepper salad is garnished with strips of anchovy and preserved lemon peel and with olives.

2 red bell peppers
2 yellow bell peppers
2 hot chili peppers
About 1/3 cup harissa dressing (page 329)

GARNISHES
3 ounces oil-cured black olives
12 anchovy fillets
Thinly sliced preserved lemon peel

Roast the peppers on a rack in a broiler or over a direct flame, turning often with tongs, until they are charred on all sides. Place them in a plastic container or a paper or plastic bag and close. Allow the peppers to steam inside the container for about 20 minutes. When they are cool enough to handle peel off the skins with your fingers and scrape off any stubborn pieces of peel with a knife blade. A few flakes of peel are acceptable. If possible, do not wash the peppers. Cut them in half, remove the seeds and ribs, and cut the peppers into strips about 1/2-inch wide.

Place the pepper strips in a large bowl and toss with the dressing. Decorate with olives and strips of anchovy and preserved lemon.

VARIATION:
Some versions of this salad add chopped fresh tomatoes.

ALTERNATE DRESSINGS:
caper and garlic citrus dressing (page 291),
or cut back on the anchovy fillets and use
anchovy garlic vinaigrette (page 286).

facing page: tunisian roasted pepper salad
with harissa dressing and a garnish of
anchovies, preserved lemon peel, and olives

roasted peppers and onions
with anchovy garlic vinaigrette

ROASTING BRINGS UP THE SWEETNESS in both the peppers and the onions. For texture contrast, serve them on a bed of bitter greens.

> **2 medium red onions**
> **Olive oil**
> **2 large red bell peppers**
> **4 large handfuls of arugula (about 1/3 pound)**
> **About 1/2 cup anchovy garlic vinaigrette (page 286)**

Heat the oven to 400 degrees F.

Rub the unpeeled onions with a little olive oil and place them in a baking pan. Roast until they are tender but not mushy, 1 hour or a bit longer. Let stand until cool enough to handle, then peel and slice 1/2-inch thick.

Roast the peppers on a rack in a broiler or over a direct flame, turning often with tongs, until they are charred on all sides. Place them in a plastic container or a paper or plastic bag and close. Allow the peppers to steam inside the container for about 20 minutes. When they are cool enough to handle, peel off the skins with your fingers and scrape off any stubborn pieces of peel with a knife blade. A few flakes of peel are acceptable. If possible, do not wash the peppers. Cut them in half, remove the seeds and ribs, and cut the peppers into strips about 1/2-inch wide.

Toss the arugula with about half the vinaigrette and place it on a platter or divide among 4 salad plates. Toss the peppers and onions with some of the remaining vinaigrette and place on top of the arugula. Drizzle with the remaining vinaigrette. Serve immediately.

ALTERNATE DRESSINGS:
garlic vinaigrette (page 269),
charmoula vinaigrette (page 326),
tapenade vinaigrette (page 322).

roasted pepper and celery salad
with tomato vinaigrette

THIS IS A STUDY IN TEXTURES, with crisp celery and soft, fleshy roasted peppers. The celery offers a clean, refreshing taste, but if you want additional sweetness to echo the sweetness of the peppers, you can use fennel instead. If you are a fan of salt, top this salad with strips of anchovy or shavings of *bottarga*, the air-dried roe of tuna or mullet.

3 large red bell peppers
6 small handfuls of assorted salad greens (1/4 pound or less)
About 1/2 cup tomato vinaigrette (page 282)
6 stalks celery, strings removed, thinly sliced on the diagonal, or 2 bulbs
fennel, cut in half, trimmed, cored, and very thinly sliced
Anchovy fillets or shavings of *bottarga*, for garnish (optional)

Roast the peppers on a rack in a broiler or over a direct flame, turning often with tongs, until they are charred on all sides. Place them in a plastic container or a paper or plastic bag and close. Allow the peppers to steam inside the container for about 20 minutes. When they are cool enough to handle, peel off the skin with your fingers and scrape off any stubborn pieces of peel with a knife blade. A few flakes of peel are acceptable. If possible, do not wash the peppers. Cut them in half, remove the seeds and ribs, and cut the peppers into strips about 1/2-inch wide.

Toss the greens with some of the vinaigrette and divide among 6 salad plates. Toss the peppers and celery in a large bowl with the remaining vinaigrette. Distribute them over the lightly dressed greens.

Top with anchovies or *bottarga* if desired and serve immediately.

ALTERNATE DRESSINGS:
catalan vinaigrette (page 278),
charmoula vinaigrette (page 326),
or omit the anchovies and *bottarga* and use
anchovy garlic vinaigrette (page 286).

roasted peppers filled with herbed goat cheese

THESE PEPPER ROLLS ARE a fine addition to an hors d'oeuvre or antipasto assortment. They are intense in flavor and dramatic in appearance. You might want to pair them with the eggplant rolls on page 89.

6 large red bell peppers or pimiento peppers
1 pound fresh goat cheese (about 2 cups)
2 cloves garlic, finely minced
4 tablespoons chopped fresh chives
4 tablespoons chopped fresh flat-leaf parsley, plus
    more for garnish (optional)
3 tablespoons chopped fresh basil
2 teaspoons chopped fresh thyme
1/2 teaspoon freshly ground black pepper
Heavy cream or extra-virgin olive oil, as needed
About 1 cup tapenade vinaigrette (page 322)

Roast the peppers on a rack in a broiler or over a direct flame, turning often with tongs, until they are charred on all sides. Place them in a plastic container or a paper or plastic bag and close. Allow the peppers to steam inside the container for about 20 minutes. When they are cool enough to handle, peel off the skin with your fingers and scrape off any stubborn pieces of peel with a knife blade. A few flakes of peel are acceptable. If possible, do not wash the peppers. Cut them in half and remove the seeds and ribs. Try to keep the peppers in unbroken halves.

In a large bowl, combine the cheese, garlic, and herbs and add the black pepper. Add a bit of cream or olive oil if the cheese mixture is very stiff and difficult to mix.

Spread the cheese mixture onto the pepper halves and roll them into cylinders. Chill the rolls in the refrigerator, covered with plastic wrap, for a few hours so the filling can firm up.

At serving time, cut the pepper rolls crosswise into rounds. Arrange them on a platter and drizzle with the tapenade dressing and a little chopped parsley if desired.

ALTERNATE DRESSINGS:
anchovy garlic vinaigrette (page 286),
pesto vinaigrette (page 320),
charmoula vinaigrette (page 326).

zucchini with mint and vinegar
CONCIA

CONCIA IS SERVED ALL OVER ITALY, from the Veneto down to Sicily, and has been adopted as a signature dish by the Roman Jewish community. Other names for the dish are *scapece, zucchini all'aceto,* and *zucchini all'agro.* Most often served as part of an antipasto platter or as an accompaniment for meat dishes, especially *bollito* (boiled beef), *concia* is a wonderful topping for crostini and makes a tangy sandwich filling.

4 to 6 small zucchini (about 1 1/2 pounds)
Sea salt
3 to 4 tablespoons extra-virgin olive oil
2 large cloves garlic, minced
1/2 cup mint vinaigrette (page 280)

Cut the zucchini crosswise into 1/4-inch-thick slices, or, to prepare it in the Veneto fashion, cut it lengthwise into 1/4-inch-thick slices. Sprinkle with salt and let stand in a colander for 30 minutes to drain off any bitter juices. Rinse and pat dry.

Warm the olive oil in a sauté pan over medium-high heat. Add the zucchini and cook, in batches, turning as needed, until golden on both sides, 4 to 5 minutes. Transfer to a shallow serving dish and sprinkle with some of the garlic and some of the vinaigrette. Repeat with the rest of the zucchini, garlic, and vinaigrette. Let rest at room temperature for 1 to 2 hours, basting the zucchini occasionally with the dressing that pools in the bottom. Serve at room temperature.

NOTE: *You can bake or grill the slices of zucchini, instead of sautéing them.*

ALTERNATE DRESSINGS:
garlic vinaigrette (page 269),
yogurt dressing (page 306).

zucchini and eggplant with yogurt dressing

YOU HAVE A CHOICE of cooking method here. Whichever you choose, the vegetables should be tender and cooked through, translucent and lightly colored. The chili enlivens the yogurt and brightens this simple meze dish. You may want some garlic in the dressing too.

> **1 pound small zucchini (about 4)**
> **1 pound small eggplants (about 4 Japanese or 2 globe)**
> **Sea salt**
> **Extra-virgin olive oil**
> **1 hot chili pepper, chopped**
> **1 clove garlic, finely minced**
> **1 cup yogurt dressing (page 306)**

Cut the ends off the zucchini and eggplants. Cut them on the diagonal into long 1/2-inch-thick slices. Lay them on paper towels or on a wire rack on a baking sheet and sprinkle with salt. Let rest for 20 minutes, then rinse and pat dry.

If grilling, heat a gas grill or make a charcoal fire. Brush the zucchini and eggplant with oil. Grill over medium-high heat for 3 to 5 minutes per side, or until tender. Arrange the slices on a platter.

If baking, heat the oven to 450 degrees F. Brush the vegetables with oil on both sides and place on baking sheets. Bake until tender, about 25 minutes, turning once halfway through and brushing with a bit more oil. Arrange the slices on a platter.

If frying, heat 2 to 3 tablespoons oil in a large sauté pan and fry the vegetable slices in batches, adding oil as needed, turning once, for 5 to 6 minutes. Arrange the slices on a platter.

Fold the chili and garlic into the yogurt dressing and spoon it over the warm cooked vegetables. Serve immediately.

ALTERNATE DRESSINGS:
tomato vinaigrette (page 282),
sun-dried tomato vinaigrette (page 283),
tahini dressing (page 303).

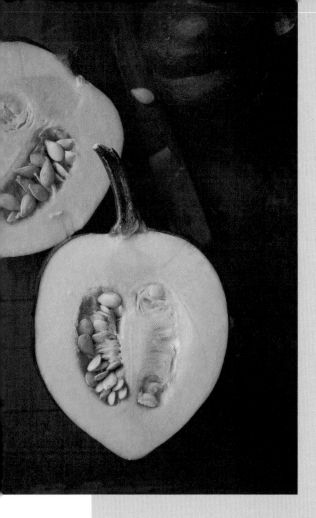

PEELING AND CUTTING WINTER SQUASH

Be warned: peeling a winter squash, with its round contours and slick exterior, then scooping out the seeds and fibers and trying to cut uniform slices, is challenging even for experienced cooks. My advice is to buy a butternut squash with the longest neck possible; it is easier to peel than other types and has the greatest yield of solid flesh. Just cut the squash where the round, seed-filled bottom part joins the neck, ideally with a heavy cleaver or a cleaver aided by a mallet. Peel the neck and cut it crosswise with a cleaver or knife (it is easier to cut when peeled). If you like, you can discard the bottom, because after you scrape out the seeds and trim the thin, rounded walls, you don't have much flesh left. If you feel daring with your knife skills, try this with wedges of kabocha squash: cut the squash in half with the cleaver and mallet, scoop out the seeds, and then cut it into wedges. Then peel the wedges with a sharp knife.

sweet-and-sour winter squash
ZUCCA GIALLA IN AGRODOLCE

MEATY WINTER SQUASH DRESSED WITH mint vinaigrette resembles a famous Sicilian dish called *fegato ai sette cannoli,* which translates fancifully as "liver of the seven spouts." It takes its name from a fountain in Palermo that has seven spouts. As few people in that poverty-stricken neighborhood could afford to eat meat in the past, they cooked inexpensive pumpkin, which has so much body that they likened it to liver. Use Hubbard, kabocha, butternut, or another large yellow hard-skinned winter squash for this dish.

2 pounds butternut or other hard winter squash
1/2 cup olive oil, plus more if needed
2 to 3 large cloves garlic, sliced paper-thin
4 tablespoons sugar
Pinch of ground cinnamon
About 1 cup mint vinaigrette (page 280)
Sea salt and freshly ground black pepper
Thinly slivered fresh mint, for garnish

Peel the squash, discard the seeds and fibers, and cut the flesh into 1/3-inch-thick slices.

Warm half the olive oil in a large sauté pan over medium heat. Add enough squash slices to fit without crowding and sauté, adding oil as needed and turning to color both sides lightly, until tender, 6 to 8 minutes. Using a slotted spatula, transfer to a serving platter, trying to keep the slices in one layer. Sprinkle with garlic slivers. Repeat with the remaining slices, working in batches.

Add the sugar and cinnamon to the mint vinaigrette. Pour into the warm sauté pan, stirring in any remaining oil. Simmer over medium heat until the vinaigrette thickens, about 5 minutes. Pour the hot vinaigrette over the squash and season to taste with salt and pepper.

Ideally, this dish should sit for about 2 hours so the squash absorbs the dressing. Garnish with additional mint and serve at room temperature.

VARIATION:
You may bake the squash instead of frying it. Brush the slices with oil and arrange in a single layer on oiled baking sheets. Bake in a 400-degree F oven for 20 minutes, then turn the slices over, brush with oil, and cook until tender, another 10 to 15 minutes.

ALTERNATE DRESSINGS:
Use **catalan vinaigrette** (page 278) or **sherry vinaigrette** (page 270) and garnish with chopped toasted Marcona almonds, or use **basic balsamic vinaigrette** (page 276) and garnish with chopped toasted almonds or hazelnuts.

facing page: sweet-and-sour winter squash garnished with almonds and sherry vinaigrette

winter squash with ricotta salata and anchovy garlic vinaigrette   ZUCCA ALLA RICOTTA FORTE

THIS DISH IS A SPECIALTY OF THE SEAPORT town of Brindisi in the Italian region of Puglia. Allow enough time for the squash to absorb the dressing. If you can't find ricotta salata, use a sharp or salty cheese like pecorino or Ragusano, or even feta.

> 4 tablespoons olive oil
> About 1 1/2 pounds butternut squash, peeled, seeded, and cut into
>   1-inch pieces
> Sea salt and freshly ground black pepper
> 2 large stalks celery, chopped
> 1 onion, chopped
> 2 tablespoons salt-packed capers, rinsed and chopped
> 1/4 cup oil-cured black olives, pitted
> About 1/2 cup anchovy garlic vinaigrette (page 286)
> 1/4 pound ricotta salata cheese
> Toasted bread

Heat 2 tablespoons olive oil in a large sauté pan over medium heat. Add the squash and sauté, in batches if necessary, tossing the squash from time to time, until tender and lightly colored, 8 to 10 minutes. Remove to a bowl and sprinkle with salt and pepper.

Warm the remaining 2 tablespoons olive oil in a clean large sauté pan over medium heat. Add the celery and onion and sauté until the onions are translucent, about 8 minutes.

Add the squash along with the capers and olives and stir in the vinaigrette. Cook over low heat for about 5 minutes to blend the flavors. Remove the pan from the heat and let sit for 30 minutes for the squash to absorb the vinaigrette.

Transfer the squash to a serving bowl or platter. Grate the cheese on the large holes of a box grater, or make shavings with a potato peeler. Top the squash with the ricotta salata and serve warm or at room temperature, with toasted bread.

NOTE: *You may roast the diced squash instead of frying it. Heat the oven to 400 degrees F. On a baking sheet, toss the squash with 2 tablespoons oil and salt and pepper to taste. Roast until tender, about 30 minutes.*

acorn squash

roasted winter squash with bitter greens

CONTRAST IS THE THEME OF this autumn dish: sweet versus bitter, soft versus crunchy. While I like a creamy Middle Eastern dressing here, the squash is equally delicious with the alternate dressings.

> 1 1/2 pounds butternut squash, peeled, seeded, and cut into 1-inch pieces
> 1/4 cup extra-virgin olive oil
> Sea salt and freshly ground black pepper
> 3 small bunches of arugula or 4 large handfuls of assorted bitter greens or
>   mesclun (about 1/3 pound)
> 1/2 cup thin tahini dressing with cumin (page 303)
> 2 tablespoons toasted sesame seeds, pine nuts, or walnuts, for garnish

Heat the oven to 400 degrees F.

On a baking sheet, toss the squash with the olive oil and salt and pepper to taste. Roast until tender, about 30 minutes. Let cool.

Toss the arugula with some of the dressing and divide among 6 salad plates. Top with the squash and drizzle the rest of the dressing on top. Sprinkle each serving with sesame seeds or nuts and serve.

ALTERNATE DRESSINGS:
walnut vinaigrette (page 273),
orange balsamic vinaigrette (page 277),
or use pomegranate seeds and
pomegranate citrus dressing (page 297).

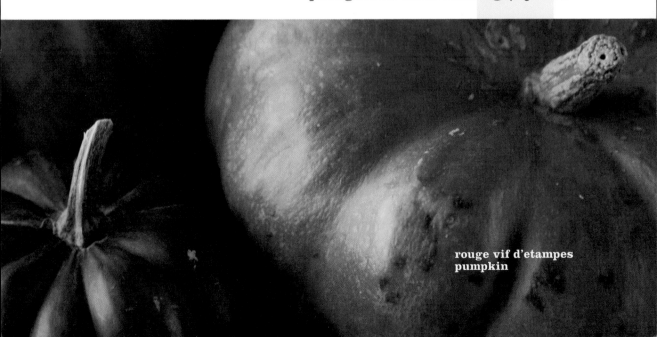

rouge vif d'etampes
pumpkin

tunisian squash puree
AJLOUK DE POTIRON

AJLOUK IS A TUNISIAN NAME for a mashed or chopped vegetable dish. (The term *zahlouk* is used in Morocco.) It usually is served as part of a meze assortment at the start of the meal. (In Tunisia this assortment is called *aadou;* in Algeria it's *kemia.*) You can make this with mashed cooked butternut squash, corn squash, carrots, or zucchini. Some cooks boil the vegetable on the stovetop, but I prefer the deeper flavor that roasting imparts. Other versions of this recipe add a small mashed potato for additional body.

1 1/2 pounds butternut squash or other hard winter squash
3 tablespoons olive oil
1 teaspoon caraway seeds, toasted
1 teaspoon ground coriander
2 cloves garlic, minced
About 1/3 cup harissa dressing (page 329)
Sea salt

Heat the oven to 400 degrees F.

Place the squash on a baking sheet and roast until it is soft. It could take over an hour. When it is cool enough to handle, remove the seeds, peel, and mash coarsely.

Heat the oil in a small sauté pan. Add the caraway seeds and coriander and stir over low heat until fragrant. Add the mashed squash, garlic, and harissa dressing and heat until warm through. Season with salt to taste. Serve at room temperature, with bread.

ALTERNATE DRESSINGS:
mint vinaigrette (page 280),
hot pepper citrus dressing (page 295).

artichoke and fennel salad with citrus dressing
CARCIOFI E FINOCCHIO ALLE AGRUMI

YOU MAY HAVE READ SOME ITALIAN RECIPES that call for sliced raw artichokes. No, it's not a misprint—in Italy it is possible to buy young, garden-fresh artichokes that lack a fuzzy choke and are tender enough to be eaten raw. Unfortunately, most of our artichokes spend too much time in cold storage before they get to market. During this period they dry out and become less supple and even tough. Unless you buy artichokes at a farmers' market, young, tender, and freshly picked, you'll probably want to cook them.

I love the contrast of the slightly bitter artichoke with sweet fennel, but if you can't find fennel, celery cut on the bias will work nicely. To increase the sweetness factor, you can add a few chopped toasted almonds or hazelnuts. And please use Parmigiano Reggiano for the garnish. If you love anchovies and other fishy flavors, add thin shavings of *bottarga* instead of the cheese. *Bottarga* is dried preserved tuna or mullet roe. It adds a scent of the sea to whatever it adorns.

> 1 lemon
> 4 to 6 medium artichokes
> About 3/4 cup basic citrus dressing (page 290) or one made with part
>   Meyer lemon juice (page 288)
> Water
> 2 bulbs fennel
> Shavings of Parmigiano Reggiano cheese or *bottarga*, for garnish
> 1/4 cup toasted almonds or hazelnuts, for garnish (optional)

Fill a large bowl with cold water and squeeze the juice of the lemon into it. If the artichoke stems are tender, trim them to 2 inches and peel. If not, cut the stems off close to the base. Remove the tough outer leaves, trim the tops of the artichokes with a sharp knife, and pare away all the dark green parts until you reach the pale green leaves. Carefully scoop out the choke with a melon baller or a small pointed spoon. Cut the artichokes into 1/4-inch-thick slices. As each artichoke is trimmed, drop the slices into the lemon water.

If you have been lucky enough to get fresh, tender baby artichokes, remove the stiff outer leaves and slice them thin on a mandoline. Keep in lemon water for a short time so they do not discolor. Pat dry, or slice them at the very last minute.

(continued on next page)

Drain the artichoke slices. In a sauté pan, warm 1/2 cup dressing over low heat. Add the artichokes and just enough water to barely cover them. Simmer, stirring occasionally, until the artichoke slices are cooked through (they will be translucent) but are not too soft and most of the water has evaporated, 10 to 15 minutes. Remove from the heat and let cool in the pan.

Cut the bulbs of fennel in half and cut away the cores. Discard any tough or discolored outer leaves. Slice the fennel very thin. Toss with 2 tablespoons of the dressing.

Arrange the artichokes and fennel on a platter or divide them among individual salad plates. Drizzle with the last bit of dressing and garnish with the cheese shavings or *bottarga*. Top with chopped nuts if desired. Serve immediately.

VARIATION:
To move this salad to North Africa,
use **preserved lemon dressing** (page 299),
charmoula citrus dressing (page 326),
or **harissa dressing** (page 329) and garnish with olives and chopped fresh cilantro or mint rather than cheese, *bottarga,* or nuts.

ALTERNATE DRESSING:
caper and garlic citrus dressing (page 291),
but do not add nuts.

three artichoke and orange salads

THERE IS SOMETHING MAGICAL about the combination of artichokes and oranges. The mild acidity in the orange juice tames the odd bittersweetness of the artichoke. Add some lemon and hot pepper and you have a most interesting dish. Artichokes cooked in citrus juices appear in recipes from Morocco, Turkey, and Sicily. In the three recipes that follow, the artichokes are cooked in the citrus dressing. In the second, they are then layered with fresh orange segments and drizzled with the remaining dressing.

serves 6

turkish-style artichokes and orange with hot pepper dressing

6 large artichokes
1 1/2 cups hot pepper citrus dressing (page 295)
1/2 cup fresh orange juice
Water
6 thick slices (1/2 inch) orange, with peel
12 thick slices (1/2 inch) yellow or white onions
Sea salt

Remove the stems and any tough outer leaves from the artichokes. Trim the pointy tops by about 2 inches. Arrange the artichokes upright in a saucepan just wide enough to hold them. Add the hot pepper citrus dressing, orange juice, and enough water to come halfway up the sides of the pan. Top with the orange and onion slices. Cover the pan and simmer over low heat until the bottoms can be pierced easily with a sharp knife, about 45 minutes.

Remove the artichokes and orange and onion slices from the pan and reserve them. Taste the pan juices and season with salt to taste. If you want a thicker sauce, boil the pan juices to reduce them a bit. Let the sauce cool completely.

Cut the artichokes in half and remove the fuzzy chokes with a spoon. Put the artichokes in a bowl, top with the orange and onion slices, and pour the sauce over the top. Serve at room temperature.

moroccan artichoke and orange salad

IN THIS SALAD the artichokes are cooked in citrus dressing and then paired with fresh orange segments. The radish slivers add a bit of crunch and punch to the mix.

1 lemon plus 1 tablespoon fresh lemon juice
3 artichokes
About 1 cup basic citrus dressing (page 290)
Water
3 navel oranges
1 large head butter, oak leaf, or red leaf lettuce or 2 Little Gem lettuces
Sea salt and freshly ground black pepper
6 to 8 red radishes, thinly sliced
3 tablespoons chopped fresh flat-leaf parsley
3 tablespoons thinly sliced fresh mint

Fill a bowl with cold water and squeeze the juice of the lemon into it. Working with 1 artichoke at a time, remove all the leaves until you reach the tender pale green leaves. Pare away any dark green parts from the base and the stem. (If the stem does not seem fresh, cut it off flush with the base.) Cut the artichoke in half lengthwise and use a sharp-edged spoon or a melon baller to remove the choke from each half. Cut each half lengthwise into 1/4-inch-thick slices and place the slices in the lemon water. Repeat until all the artichokes are trimmed.

In a sauté pan, warm 1/2 cup dressing over low heat. Drain the artichoke slices and add to the pan with just enough water to cover. Simmer, stirring occasionally, until the artichokes slices are cooked through (they will be translucent) but are not too soft and most of the water has evaporated, about 15 minutes. Remove from the heat and let cool.

Working with 1 orange at a time, cut a thin slice off the top and bottom to reveal the flesh. Stand the orange upright and remove the peel in wide strips, cutting downward and following the contour of the fruit. Holding the orange over a bowl, cut along both sides of each segment, releasing the segments from the membrane and letting them drop into the bowl. Use the knife tip to pry any seeds from the segments. Squeeze the membrane over the bowl to collect extra juice, which you can add to the dressing at serving time if you like.

In a large bowl, sprinkle the lettuce leaves with salt and pepper to taste and toss in a bit of the dressing. Place them on a platter or divide among 6 salad plates. Top the lettuce with alternating artichoke slices, orange segments, and radish slices, and dress with the remaining dressing. Sprinkle with the herbs and serve immediately.

ALTERNATE DRESSINGS:
catalan vinaigrette (page 278),
mixed citrus dressing I (page 293),
hot pepper citrus dressing (page 295).

facing page: moroccan artichoke and orange salad with basic citrus dressing

sicilian artichokes braised
in mixed citrus dressing

I LOVE THE WILD Sicilian/Arabic palate, which has sweet, sour, salty, and fishy components, all combined in perfect, crazy harmony. It sounds weird, but trust me, these artichokes will be a hit. They are a stellar addition to an antipasto assortment.

  1 lemon
  6 artichokes
  1/2 cup plus 1 tablespoon olive oil
  3 onions, cut in half and thinly sliced
  1 cup mixed citrus dressing I (page 293)
  Water
  1 teaspoon sea salt
  2 tablespoons salt-packed capers, rinsed
  4 anchovy fillets, finely minced
  2 tablespoons sugar, or to taste
  Thinly slivered fresh mint, for garnish (optional)

Fill a large bowl with cold water and squeeze the juice of the lemon into it. If the artichoke stems are tender, trim them to 2 inches and peel. If not, cut the stems off close to the base. Remove the tough outer leaves and trim the tops of the artichokes with a sharp knife. Pare away all the dark green parts until you reach the pale green leaves. Cut the artichokes in half. Carefully scoop out the chokes with a melon ball scoop or a small pointed spoon. As each artichoke is trimmed, drop it into the lemon water.

In a Dutch oven, heat 1/2 cup olive oil over low heat. Add the onions and stir over medium heat for about 5 minutes. Drain the artichoke halves and add them along with the mixed citrus dressing and just enough water to barely cover the artichokes. Sprinkle with the salt. Cover the pan and cook very slowly, over low heat, until the artichokes are tender, 25 to 35 minutes. With a slotted spoon, carefully remove the artichokes to a serving bowl.

Add the capers to the juices remaining in the pan and reduce the sauce over high heat until thickened, 10 to 15 minutes.

In a small sauté pan or saucepan, warm the anchovies in the remaining 1 tablespoon oil over low heat. When they have dissolved, add them to the sauce, along with the sugar. Cook for 5 minutes longer and adjust the sweetness if necessary.

Spoon the sauce over the artichokes and garnish with slivered mint if you like. Serve at room temperature.

moroccan cooked carrot salad

THIS SWEET SALAD MIGHT BE served alongside a contrasting one that is tart or hot. It also makes a nice accompaniment for broiled or roast chicken. You can also prepare this dish with cooked beets.

> **1/2 cup mixed citrus dressing I (page 293)**
> **1/8 teaspoon cayenne**
> **1/2 teaspoon toasted cumin seed, ground**
> **3 tablespoons sugar**
> **1 pound carrots (about 8 medium carrots)**
> **Sea salt**
> **Thinly slivered fresh mint, for garnish (optional)**

In a small bowl, mix the dressing with the spices and sugar.

Trim the carrots and cut them into thin slices or julienne strips. Cook in boiling salted water until just tender, 5 to 8 minutes. Drain quickly and toss with the dressing mixture. Season with salt to taste.

Place the carrots in a serving dish and garnish with fine slivers of fresh mint if you like. Serve warm or at room temperature.

moroccan salad of raw grated carrots
with citrus cinnamon dressing

THINLY SHAVED OR GRATED CARROTS are added to raw leafy salads mostly to contribute a note of color and contrasting texture. For carrots with a bit more body and texture, you need to cook them briefly, as they are not porous enough to absorb the flavors of a salad dressing. For optimum flavor, dress carrots while they are warm. You may warm the grated carrots in the dressing or serve them as is.

> 4 large carrots
> 1/4 cup citrus cinnamon dressing (page 294)
> Chopped walnuts or almonds (optional)

Grate the carrots on the large holes of a box grater. Toss with the dressing, top with chopped walnuts or almonds if desired, and serve.

CARROT SALADS

Carrots are remarkably versatile and take to any number of dressings.

BASIC CITRUS DRESSING (page 290): Add chopped parsley or mint to the dressing along with some strips of orange zest. Or top with plumped raisins and toasted pine nuts for an Arabic accent, or use citrus cinnamon dressing.

MINT VINAIGRETTE (page 280): Add a bit more sugar or honey to punch up the sweetness of the carrots.

TOASTED CUMIN CITRUS DRESSING (page 301): Top with crumbled feta cheese.

CHARMOULA CITRUS DRESSING (page 326): Add a bit of cinnamon to the charmoula dressing to accent the sweetness of the carrots.

TAHINI DRESSING (page 303): Garnish with toasted pine nuts and chopped mint or dill.

YOGURT DRESSING (page 306): Top with toasted walnuts and maybe a few plumped raisins.

HOT PEPPER CITRUS DRESSING (page 295): Use chopped parsley as a garnish.

CATALAN VINAIGRETTE (page 278): Top with chopped parsley.

facing page: moroccan salad of raw grated carrots with golden raisins, toasted pine nuts, and citrus cinnamon dressing

tunisian carrot salad

MZOURA

YOU MAY KEEP the carrots in slices or cook and mash them. If they are mashed, the salad is called *om houriya*.

> 1 pound carrots (about 8 medium carrots)
> About 1/2 cup harissa dressing (page 329)
> 1 tablespoon toasted caraway seeds, for garnish (optional)
> 3 tablespoons chopped fresh cilantro, for garnish (optional)
> Extra-virgin olive oil

Slice the carrots and cook them in boiling salted water until tender, 5 to 8 minutes. Drain and place in a serving dish. Dress the carrots with the harissa dressing and garnish with the caraway seeds or chopped cilantro. Drizzle the top with olive oil. Serve with pita or toasted bread.

ALTERNATE DRESSING:
hot pepper citrus dressing (page 295).

moroccan carrot salad
with cumin

CARROTS AND CUMIN ARE A TRADITIONAL Mediterranean flavor combination. If you want to keep the carrots in pieces, you have the choice of cutting them into rounds or julienne strips and parboiling them until they are tender-crisp. Or you can cook them until they are soft enough to mash. Top the carrots with crumbled feta, or with cheese and toasted walnuts, if you like—these garnishes are not authentically Moroccan, but they work well.

1 pound carrots (about 8 medium carrots)
1 clove garlic, smashed
About 1/2 cup toasted cumin citrus dressing (page 301)
Sea salt
1/4 pound feta cheese, crumbled, for garnish (optional)
1/4 cup toasted walnuts, for garnish (optional)

Cut the carrots into thin slices or narrow strips. Cook in boiling salted water along with the garlic until tender, 5 to 7 minutes. Drain and place in a serving dish. While warm, toss with the dressing and season with salt to taste. If you like, top with crumbled feta or feta and walnuts. Serve warm or at room temperature.

VARIATIONS:
For an Algerian version, increase the garlic to 3 cloves, add a pinch of ground caraway, and use vinegar instead of lemon. You may prepare cooked beets with the same dressing.

ALTERNATE DRESSINGS:
mint vinaigrette (page 280),
mixed citrus dressing I (page 293),
charmoula citrus dressing (page 326),
harissa dressing (page 329).

carrots and celery root
with creamy tarator dressing

ASSEMBLING THIS SALAD IS FAST and easy, but you need a little patience to cut the carrots and celery root into lovely uniform strips. A mandoline is helpful in getting perfect thin slices. Then all you have to do is cut the slices crosswise into strips, blanch, and toss with the dressing.

> 6 medium carrots
> 1 large celery root
> 1/2 cup hazelnut tarator dressing (page 305)

Peel the vegetables. Slice about 1/4-inch thick, preferably using a mandoline (use the finger guard!) and then cut into thin strips about 1/4-inch wide. If you are using a knife, slice the celery root crosswise into 1/4-inch slices, then stack a few slices and cut into 1/4-inch-wide strips. Repeat until you have cut all the slices. Cut the carrots in half lengthwise, place them cut side down, and cut into 1/3-inch-wide strips.

Cook the vegetables in boiling salted water until just tender, 4 to 5 minutes. Drain well and place in a serving dish. Toss with the dressing. Serve warm.

ALTERNATE DRESSINGS:
yogurt dressing mixed with 4 ounces
chopped toasted hazelnuts (page 306),
tahini dressing (page 303),
tarragon mustard cream dressing, (page 310),
remoulade mayonnaise dressing (page 316).

beet salads

BEET SALADS ARE VERY popular all over the Mediterranean. Most are dressed simply with olive oil and red wine vinegar or fruit vinegar, or with a citrus dressing to pick up on the sweetness of the beets.

You can choose red, gold, or striped Chioggia beets for these salads. In general, the smaller beets will be the sweetest. Try to buy beets with their greens still attached. Some supermarkets remove all the greens, which means you have no way of knowing how old the beets may be. Yellow, limp, tired leaves are a giveaway, and crisp, bright greens are a good indication of freshness. Besides, you can steam the greens and serve them with the beets as a bonus for your salad.

There are two methods of cooking beets, boiling and baking. Some cooks prefer the earthier, deeper flavor of roasted beets.

TO BOIL: Scrub the beets and cut off the greens, but leave an inch of root attached so the beet doesn't bleed its color into the water. Put the beets in a saucepan and cover with cold water. Bring to a boil over high heat, then turn the heat to low and simmer, partially covered, until tender, 20 to 30 minutes. Drain. When the beets are cool enough to handle, cut off the roots and rub off the peel with your fingers.

TO BAKE: Heat the oven to 400 degrees F. Place the scrubbed beets in a baking pan with about an inch of hot water, cover tightly with foil, and bake until tender, 45 minutes to 1 hour, depending on the size of the beets. Cool a bit and then rub off the peel. Slice or quarter the beets, depending on their size.

If the beet greens are fresh and green, steam them in boiling salted water until tender. Drain and then refresh with cold water to set the color. Use them as a bed for the salad.

BEET SALADS

Simple beet salads can take many of the same dressings recommended for carrot salads.

BASIC CITRUS DRESSING (page 290) or **CITRUS CINNAMON DRESSING** (page 294): Add chopped parsley or mint to the citronette along with some strips of orange zest or orange segments. Toasted pine nuts or almonds make a good garnish.

MINT VINAIGRETTE (page 280): Add a bit more sugar or honey to punch up the sweetness.

TOASTED CUMIN CITRUS DRESSING (page 301): Top with crumbled feta cheese.

CHARMOULA VINAIGRETTE (page 326): Add a bit of cinnamon to the charmoula dressing to accent the sweetness of the beets.

TAHINI DRESSING (page 303): Garnish with toasted pine nuts and chopped fresh mint or dill. You can serve this on top of wilted beet greens too.

TARATOR DRESSING (page 305): Top with chopped walnuts and dill.

GORGONZOLA CREAM DRESSING (page 313): Top with chopped walnuts.

ROMESCO VINAIGRETTE (page 325): Pair with cooked asparagus or green beans.

beets, oranges, and greens with tapenade vinaigrette

THIS PRETTY SALAD BECOMES DRAMATIC when topped with a dark slash of tapenade dressing. The sweetness of the beets and the tart sweetness of the oranges hold their own against the rich olive dressing. If you want to play up the sweetness even more and add crunch, garnish the salad with toasted almonds.

1 large bunch watercress, stems trimmed, or cooked beet greens
    from 2 small bunches beets
About 1/2 cup tapenade vinaigrette (page 322)
4 large or 8 small beets, cooked and sliced
2 oranges, peeled and cut into segments or cut crosswise into
    1/4-inch slices
Toasted slivered almonds (optional)

Toss the greens with 1/4 cup of the dressing and arrange on 4 salad plates. Top each serving with alternating beets and oranges and drizzle the remaining dressing on top. Garnish with almonds if you like and serve immediately.

ALTERNATE DRESSINGS:
mint vinaigrette (page 280),
basic citrus dressing (page 290),
mixed citrus dressing I (page 293),
citrus cinnamon dressing (page 294),
charmoula citrus dressing (page 326).

beets, goat cheese, and arugula with walnut vinaigrette

IN FRANCE, BEETS ARE OFTEN tossed with walnut vinaigrette and topped with chopped toasted walnuts and crumbled goat cheese. In this classic crowd-pleaser, sweet beets, bitter walnuts and arugula, and tart, salty goat cheese are held in balance by the rich walnut dressing. If you like, add slivers of tart-sweet apple for even greater complexity.

> 4 large or 8 small beets, cooked
> About 2/3 cup walnut vinaigrette (page 273)
> 1/2 cup walnuts, toasted
> 2 small bunches arugula
> Slivers of tart apple (optional)
> 1/2 cup crumbled goat cheese
> 2 tablespoons slivered fresh mint, chopped fresh dill, or chopped fresh
>   flat-leaf parsley (optional)

Place the beets in a large bowl with 1/4 cup vinaigrette and toss. In a small bowl, toss the walnuts with 1/4 cup vinaigrette. For maximum flavor, let both marinate for 15 to 30 minutes.

In a large bowl, toss the arugula with the beets and walnuts and the apple slivers if using. If the salad seems a bit dry, drizzle on a little more vinaigrette. Arrange the salad on 4 salad plates. Top with crumbled cheese and with herbs if you like.

ALTERNATE DRESSINGS:
gorgonzola cream dressing (page 313),
with slivers of apple.
tahini dressing (page 303),
tarator dressing (page 305),
or **yogurt dressing** (page 306),
omitting the cheese and apple.

facing page: beets, goat cheese, and arugula with walnut vinaigrette

beets and greens
with yogurt dressing

THIS DISH IS A VISUAL BOMBSHELL because the beets tint the yogurt an electric pink. Of course, you also may use gold or Chioggia beets, which taste as good but are subtler in hue. For even more color contrast, add some cooked green beans.

1/4 teaspoon ground cinnamon
1 cup yogurt dressing (page 306)
6 large or 12 small beets, cooked and diced
1 large bunch watercress, mâche, or purslane, coarsely chopped
2 tablespoons chopped fresh dill
3 tablespoons walnuts, toasted, for garnish (optional)
Crumbled feta cheese, for garnish (optional)

Add the cinnamon to the yogurt dressing. In a large bowl, toss the beets and greens with the dressing. Top the salad with chopped dill and with walnuts or crumbled feta cheese if you like. Serve at room temperature.

ALTERNATE DRESSINGS:
tahini dressing (page 303),
tarator dressing (page 305).

beets

beet, celery, potato, and mâche salad with gorgonzola or roquefort cream dressing

serves 4

YOUR CHOICE OF CHEESE can take this salad to Italy or France. Roquefort is a bit saltier than Gorgonzola, so you may want to add more lemon to counteract the salt. Mâche is a perfect green for this salad, as it is slightly chewy and not too sharp in flavor. Peppery watercress adds another dimension and may call for a little more cream. Belgian endive or endigia, with its red-streaked leaves, looks very pretty and also may require more cream to temper its bitterness.

You can turn this into a chopped salad by cutting endive into 1/2-inch-wide strips and tossing it with the other ingredients. Mâche and watercress leaves are small, so there is no need to cut them.

> 4 cups mâche, watercress, Belgian endive, or other salad greens
>   (about 1/3 pound)
> Extra-virgin olive oil
> 2 cups diced cooked new potatoes
> 1 cup diced celery
> 1/2 cup walnuts, toasted and coarsely chopped
> 1 cup Gorgonzola or Roquefort cream dressing (page 313)
> 4 small beets, cooked and diced
> 4 tablespoons crumbled Gorgonzola dolce, for garnish (optional)

Toss the mâche with a little olive oil. If you like, distribute the greens among 4 salad plates.

Toss the potatoes, celery, and nuts in half the dressing and place on the greens. Sprinkle the beets on top. Drizzle with the rest of the dressing and add crumbled Gorgonzola dolce if you like. Serve immediately.

To make a chopped salad, chop the greens and combine them with the potatoes, celery, walnuts, and beets in a bowl and toss with the dressing. (The beets will turn everything pink unless you use gold or Chioggia beets, which will not bleed.)

ALTERNATE DRESSINGS:
lemon mustard cream dressing (page 308),
walnut cream dressing (page 312),
tuna mayonnaise dressing (page 316), omitting the nuts.

green beans and fennel with hazelnut cream dressing

DELICATE HARICOTS VERTS ARE SHOWN to advantage when paired with hazelnut cream dressing. The hazelnuts contribute sweetness and the green beans provide some mild earthiness. You can make this salad with walnuts and walnut cream, but you may want to increase the lemon juice to temper the nuts' bitterness.

1 pound slender green beans (haricots verts), trimmed
2 small bulbs fennel
1 head butter lettuce
About 1 cup hazelnut cream dressing (page 311)
1/2 cup hazelnuts, toasted, peeled, and coarsely chopped

Bring a large saucepan of water to a boil over high heat and add salt. Drop in the green beans and cook until tender-crisp, about 3 minutes. Drain and refresh in a bowl filled with ice water. When cold, drain again and pat dry. Place in a bowl.

Cut the bulbs of fennel in half and cut away the cores. Discard any tough or discolored outer leaves. Slice the fennel very thin and add to the bowl with the beans.

Arrange the lettuce leaves on a platter or on 4 salad plates. Drizzle the creamy dressing over the beans and fennel and toss to coat evenly. Place the vegetables on top of the lettuce leaves. Sprinkle with the hazelnuts and serve immediately.

VARIATIONS:
Slivers of fresh fig are a nice and surprising garnish for this salad. You can also add sliced beets to the beans and fennel.

ALTERNATE DRESSINGS:
Use walnuts instead of hazelnuts with
walnut cream dressing (page 312).
tarragon mustard cream dressing (page 310),
gorgonzola cream dressing (page 313).

poached leeks
with mustard vinaigrette

LEEKS ARE ASSERTIVE IN FLAVOR, so an equally forthright vinaigrette is needed to stand up to their presence. Mustard has enough inherent bitterness to keep these earthy onions in check.

24 thin small leeks or 16 medium leeks
1/2 cup mustard vinaigrette (page 271)
2 hard-boiled eggs, finely chopped
Chopped fresh flat-leaf parsley, for garnish (optional)

Cut most of the green tops from the leeks and trim the root ends but leave them intact. Slit each leek down the middle almost to the root end. Rinse them thoroughly by sloshing them around in a sink full of cold water.

Heat a large pot of water to simmering. Add the leeks and simmer gently until tender, 5 to 10 minutes, depending on size. Test by pinching the root end of a leek with your fingers; if it cracks slightly, it is done. Test each one, because they differ in thickness. When they are cooked, refresh in a bowl filled with ice water to stop the cooking and set the color. Drain well and gently squeeze dry.

Arrange the leeks on a platter or on 6 salad plates.

Pour the mustard vinaigrette over the leeks. Allow them to marinate for 1 to 2 hours to develop the flavors. Garnish the leeks with the eggs and with parsley if you like. Serve at room temperature.

ALTERNATE DRESSINGS:
basic vinaigrette (page 268),
caper and garlic citrus dressing (page 291),
tomato vinaigrette (page 282).

grilled leeks
with walnut cream dressing

BECAUSE LEEKS HAVE A STRONG FLAVOR, bitter toasted walnuts balance them better than sweeter, milder hazelnuts. The only trick here is to cook the leeks until they are completely tender. Grilling adds a layer of complexity and echoes the toastiness of the nuts, but if you don't have time to grill the leeks, you can still use this dressing. You can also use spring onions for this dish.

> 24 small leeks or 12 to 18 medium leeks
> 1/2 cup walnut cream dressing (page 312)
> 1/2 cup walnuts, toasted and chopped, for garnish
> 2 tablespoons chopped fresh flat-leaf parsley or mint, for garnish

Cut most of the green tops from the leeks and trim the root ends but leave them intact. Slit each leek down the middle almost to the root end. Rinse them thoroughly by sloshing them around in a sink full of cold water.

Heat a large pot of water to simmering. Add the leeks and simmer gently until tender, 5 to 10 minutes, depending on size. Test by pinching the root end of a leek with your fingers; if it cracks slightly, it is done. Test each one, because they differ in thickness. When they are cooked, refresh in a bowl filled with ice water to stop the cooking and set the color. Drain well and gently squeeze dry.

If you like, briefly mark the leeks on a charcoal or gas grill or in a cast-iron grill pan on the stovetop. Grill or broil the leeks for just a few minutes to char the outside.

Divide the leeks among 6 salad plates. Make the dressing just before serving, and spoon it over the leeks. Sprinkle with the walnuts and fresh parsley. Serve warm or at room temperature.

VARIATION:

A combination of leeks and baby beets makes a rather dramatic-looking salad. If possible, use both yellow and red or Chioggia beets and arrange them attractively with the leeks on the plates. This is a good salad for a buffet, as the leeks and beets will not become limp or soggy as they sit in the dressing.

ALTERNATE DRESSINGS:
tarragon mustard cream dressing (page 310),
lemon mustard cream dressing (page 308).

grilled leeks and asparagus
with romesco vinaigrette

WHEN *CALÇOTS*, OR WILD GREEN ONIONS, APPEAR at Barcelona's famed Boqueria Market, it's the signal for the locals to fire up the grill for a romesco party. I cannot find authentic *calçots* here, but I rely on my market to provide baby leeks or spring bulb onions. Traditionally calçots are grilled two hours before serving and wrapped in plastic wrap or newspaper to steam. This resting period allows the burnt skin to loosen and the insides to become butter-soft. To assure tenderness, precook the leeks or spring onions thoroughly before grilling. For variety, steam some fat spears of asparagus to grill along with them.

16 baby leeks or spring onions, about 3/4 inch in diameter
16 large asparagus spears
4 tablespoons extra-virgin olive oil
Sea salt and freshly ground black pepper
About 3/4 cup romesco vinaigrette (page 325)

Cut most of the green tops from the leeks, leaving 3 to 4 inches of green, and trim the root ends, leaving them intact. Slit each leek down the middle almost to the root end. Rinse them thoroughly by sloshing them around in a sink full of cold water. If you are using spring onions, simply trim them and wash them whole.

Heat a large pot of water to simmering. Add the leeks or spring onions and simmer gently until tender, 5 to 10 minutes, depending on size. Test by pinching the root end of the leek or onion with your fingers; if it cracks slightly, it is done. Test each one, because they differ in thickness. When they are cooked, refresh in a bowl filled with ice water to stop the cooking and set the color. Drain well and gently squeeze dry.

Break off the tough part of the asparagus spears and peel the bottom halves. Cook in boiling salted water until firm, 2 to 3 minutes. Drain and rinse immediately with cold water. Drain again and dry well.

Soak 4 long wooden skewers in water for about 20 minutes so they do not burn on the grill. Arrange 4 leeks and 4 asparagus spears on each skewer.

Make a charcoal fire or heat a gas grill. Brush the leeks and asparagus with the oil and sprinkle with salt and pepper to taste. Grill, turning halfway through, until well browned and a little charred, 5 or 6 minutes. Place on a platter and drizzle with romesco vinaigrette. Serve immediately.

ALTERNATE DRESSINGS:
tarragon mustard cream dressing (page 310),
hazelnut cream dressing (page 311),
mustard shallot vinaigrette (page 271),
gorgonzola cream dressing (page 313),
lemon mayonnaise dressing (page 316).

asparagus

SPRING HAS OFFICIALLY arrived when local asparagus appears at the market. I eat it every day until the season is over. I have a few different ways of cooking the spears, depending on their size. Thin pencils are best steamed quickly and left a bit al dente. Fatter spears can be roasted, sautéed, or steamed.

Snap off the tough ends of the asparagus spears and then trim the spears so they are even in length and look symmetrical on the plate. If they are very thick, peel the bottom half with a vegetable peeler.

TO STEAM: If you have a vertical steamer, add an inch or so of water to the bottom of the pot and bring to a boil. Place the steamer basket with the asparagus inside, so the stems are in the water and the tops are in the steam. Cover the pot and steam until tender, 3 to 6 minutes.

If you do not have a vertical steamer, bring a large saucepan of water to a boil; the pan should be wide enough for the asparagus to lie horizontally. Drop in the asparagus and cook until tender, 3 to 6 minutes. The cooking time will depend on the thickness of the spears.

Remove the asparagus from the water with tongs and rinse immediately with cold water to stop the cooking and set the color. (I use the sink spray attachment; I do not put them in a bowl of ice water, as I do not want them to become waterlogged and lose flavor.) Drain well, pat dry with a dish towel, and place on a serving platter or individual plates.

TO ROAST: Heat the oven to 450 degrees F. Arrange the spears in a single layer on a baking sheet with sides, leaving a little space between them. Drizzle with a few tablespoons of olive oil, roll them around to coat, and sprinkle with salt and freshly ground black pepper. Place the sheet in the oven and roast until tender, 7 to 10 minutes; the timing will depend on the thickness of the spears. Remove the asparagus from the oven and arrange on a serving platter or individual plates.

TO PAN-ROAST OR SAUTÉ: Heat 3 tablespoons oil or unsalted butter in a very large nonstick pan over low heat. Add the asparagus spears in a single layer and sauté them, turning often, until they are lightly browned and tender, about 8 minutes. Place on a serving platter or individual plates.

TO GRILL: Steam the spears for 2 minutes. Refresh with cold water and pat dry. Arrange the spears on soaked wooden skewers and then put them on a hot grill for 4 to 5 minutes to give them a hint of smokiness. Place on a serving platter or individual plates.

steamed asparagus
with tarragon mayonnaise dressing

THIS SMALL PLATE is a lovely and elegant start to a meal.

2 pounds asparagus, cooked
Sea salt and freshly ground black pepper
1/2 cup tarragon mayonnaise dressing (page 316)
2 tablespoons chopped fresh flat-leaf parsley or 1 tablespoon each chopped
   parsley and chopped fresh tarragon, for garnish
1 hard-boiled egg, finely chopped, for garnish (optional)

When the asparagus spears are cool, season to taste with salt and pepper. Then spoon the dressing over the asparagus. Garnish with the chopped parsley and with the egg if you like. Serve at room temperature.

ALTERNATE DRESSINGS:
balsamic vinaigrette (page 276),
tarragon mustard cream dressing (page 310),
hazelnut cream dressing (page 311),
lemon mustard cream dressing (page 308)
with chopped basil or mint as the garnish.
In his classic cookbook, *Auberge of the Flowering Hearth*, Roy de Groot wrote of a salad of warm steamed asparagus topped with 1 cup mayonnaise thinned with 1/2 cup dry red wine. Tasty!

green and white asparagus with hazelnut cream dressing

serves 6

THIS RECIPE CALLS FOR A COMBINATION OF green and white asparagus, but you can choose just one. Green asparagus is easier to prepare. Snap off the ends and peel the stems if the stalks are thick, and they are ready to be cooked. White asparagus is another story. The stalks are tougher and firmer and must be peeled completely to become tender. Simmer them in a mixture of water and milk until they are tender; this can take up to 25 minutes, depending on their thickness. White asparagus is not an ideal candidate for the grill or the oven.

1 pound green asparagus, cooked
1 pound white asparagus, cooked
Sea salt and freshly ground black pepper
About 1 cup hazelnut cream dressing (page 311)
1/4 cup chopped toasted hazelnuts, for garnish

Arrange the green and white asparagus attractively on a serving platter or 6 salad plates. When the spears are cool, season to taste with salt and pepper, then spoon the dressing on top. Garnish with the hazelnuts and serve immediately.

ALTERNATE DRESSINGS:
balsamic vinaigrette (page 276),
tarragon mustard cream dressing (page 310),
lemon mustard cream dressing (page 308),
tarragon mayonnaise dressing (page 316),
aioli dressing (page 316),
mustard shallot vinaigrette (page 271).
Or try catalan vinaigrette (page 278), omitting the nuts.

facing page: green and white asparagus with hazelnut cream dressing and slices of prosciutto

cauliflower zahlouk

IN MOROCCO, *ZAHLOUK* IS THE NAME for a chopped or mashed vegetable salad. It is most commonly associated with eggplant but can be applied to other vegetables as well. (In Tunisia, this kind of salad is called *ajlouk*.) Cauliflower can be too strong for some palates. Mashing it with charmoula seems to tame its aggressive, cabbagey nature. For contrast, I like to fold in some cubes of zucchini or green beans for color and cooked chickpeas for toothsome chewiness.

> 1 cauliflower (about 1 pound), cut into florets
> 4 cloves garlic
> 1 strip fresh lemon peel
> 1/2 cup charmoula thinned with lemon juice (page 326)
> 1 or 2 small zucchini, parboiled and cut into 1/2-inch dice, or 1/8 pound
>   green beans, parboiled and cut into 1/2-inch dice
> 1/2 cup cooked chickpeas
> A few oil-cured black olives, for garnish

Steam the cauliflower with the garlic and lemon peel in lightly salted water until very tender, about 8 minutes. Place the cauliflower and garlic in a large bowl and mash coarsely. Stir in the charmoula dressing. Alternatively, steam the cauliflower and garlic and transfer to a sauté pan. Add the dressing and sauté and mash in the pan.

Fold the zucchini or green beans and the chickpeas into the cauliflower. Place in a serving dish and garnish with olives. Serve immediately.

ALTERNATE DRESSINGS:
preserved lemon dressing (page 299),
harissa dressing (page 329).

facing page: cauliflower zahlouk
with charmoula

tunisian cauliflower, artichoke, and potato salad

CAULIFLOWER IS BOLDLY ASSERTIVE, artichokes are mildly bitter, and potatoes are mild and starchy, yet they all respond to a vinaigrette with the power to tame the cauliflower, mellow the artichokes, and enliven the potatoes. Harissa dressing does the trick for this chopped salad.

> 1 lemon
> 4 large artichokes
> 3 to 4 tablespoons olive oil
> Sea salt and freshly ground black pepper
> 1 cauliflower, broken into florets
> 8 little red potatoes or new potatoes
> 1/2 cup harissa dressing (page 329), plus more if needed
> A few oil-cured black olives, for garnish

Remove strips of zest from the lemon with a sharp potato peeler and set aside. Squeeze the juice of the lemon into a large bowl of water, reserving a little.

Trim the artichokes by cutting off the stems flush with the bottoms. Remove all the leaves, trim all the dark green from the hearts, scoop out the fuzzy chokes, and place the artichoke hearts in the lemon water.

Warm the oil in a large saucepan over medium heat. Add the artichokes, the remaining squeeze of lemon juice, and enough water to barely cover the artichokes. Sprinkle with salt and pepper to taste and simmer, covered, for 20 to 25 minutes. Check the liquid from time to time, adding a little water if necessary.

Meanwhile, heat a large pot of water to boiling. Lightly salt the water, add the cauliflower and the reserved lemon zest, and cook over medium-high heat until the cauliflower is crisp-tender, 4 to 5 minutes. Drain. Refresh in cold water and drain again. Transfer to a large bowl.

Heat another pot of water to boiling, lightly salt, and add the potatoes. Simmer over medium-low heat until the potatoes are cooked through but still firm, 8 to 12 minutes. Drain and rinse with cold water to stop the cooking. When the potatoes are cool enough to handle, cut them into bite-sized chunks that are about the same size as the cauliflower florets and add them to the bowl.

When the artichokes are cooked, cut them into pieces about the same size as the potatoes and cauliflower and add them to the bowl.

Toss the vegetables with the harissa dressing and let sit. After an hour, readjust the seasoning, as the potatoes will absorb most of the salt. Place the salad in a serving bowl and garnish with olives if desired. Serve at room temperature.

ALTERNATE DRESSINGS:
hot pepper vinaigrette (page 272),
tapenade vinaigrette (page 322),
preserved lemon dressing (page 299),
charmoula vinaigrette (page 326),
anchovy garlic vinaigrette (page 286).

broccoli, olive, and ricotta salata
with sun-dried tomato vinaigrette

WITH ASSERTIVE VEGETABLES LIKE BROCCOLI, cauliflower, and pale green broccoflower, you need a full-flavored dressing with strong acidity. For balance and contrast, the sun-dried tomatoes are raisiny and sweet. I add shavings of tart, salty ricotta salata, but pecorino works well too (I mean the sharp pecorino from Rome or Sardinia, not the nutty aged Tuscan variety). The cheese is a garnish, so the vinegar-based dressing does not fight with it and upset the balance. Even a few slices of fresh mozzarella or burrata on the side would not be assaulted by the dressing, as these cheeses are sweet, mild, and creamy.

Do not dress the salad until ready to serve or the broccoli will discolor.

> 2 cloves garlic, finely minced
> About 3/4 cup sun-dried tomato vinaigrette (page 283)
> Sea salt and freshly ground black pepper
> 1 large head broccoli, trimmed into florets, thick stems peeled
> 1/4 cup sun-dried tomatoes packed in oil, cut into thin slivers
> 1 cup oil-cured black olives, pitted and halved or sliced, for garnish
> Ricotta salata, pecorino Sarde, or pecorino Romano cheese, for garnish

Add the garlic to the sun-dried tomato vinaigrette. Season to taste with salt and pepper.

Bring a large pot of salted water to a boil. Add the broccoli and cook until crisp-tender, about 6 minutes. Drain carefully and refresh in ice water to set the color. Drain well and pat dry. Place in a serving bowl. To serve, toss the broccoli with the vinaigrette and the sun-dried tomato. Sprinkle with olives. With a sharp potato peeler, remove long strips of cheese and place atop the broccoli. Serve warm or at room temperature.

ALTERNATE DRESSINGS:
anchovy garlic vinaigrette (page 286),
hot pepper vinaigrette (page 272).

facing page: broccoli, olive, and ricotta salata with sun-dried tomato vinaigrette

broccoli and potato salad with tapenade vinaigrette

A STRONGLY FLAVORED DRESSING HELPS tame assertive vegetables and enhance ingredients that are mild and neutral. Broccoli and potatoes are good candidates for tapenade dressing. For another note of color and added sweetness, I add fresh red bell pepper or roasted pepper.

1 large head broccoli, trimmed into florets, thick stems peeled
1 pound new or Yukon Gold potatoes
1 red bell pepper, cut into large dice
About 1 cup tapenade vinaigrette (page 322)
2 hard-boiled eggs, finely chopped, for garnish

Bring a large pot of salted water to a boil. Add the broccoli and cook until crisp-tender, about 6 minutes. Drain carefully and refresh in ice water to set the color. Drain well and pat dry.

Bring another pot of salted water to a boil and cook the potatoes until tender but not soft, 15 to 20 minutes. Drain and rinse with cold water to stop the cooking. When the potatoes are cool enough to handle, cut them in halves if small, quarters if large.

Arrange the broccoli, potatoes, and red bell pepper on a platter or individual salad plates and drizzle with the dressing. Garnish with the hard-boiled eggs. Serve warm or at room temperature.

ALTERNATE DRESSINGS:
anchovy garlic vinaigrette (page 286),
hot pepper vinaigrette (page 272),
hot pepper citrus dressing (page 295),
sun-dried tomato vinaigrette (page 283).

celery and potato salad
with remoulade mayonnaise dressing

CRISP, CLEAN-TASTING CELERY and bland potatoes need a dressing
with a distinct and full-flavored personality. While the creamy mayonnaise
coats and binds the ingredients, the capers, cornichons, and minced onions
in the dressing add brininess and a hint of bitterness to liven the mix. Serving
the salad on a bed of watercress increases the flavor dynamics.

2 bunches watercress
1 to 2 tablespoons extra-virgin olive oil
4 cups diced cooked new potatoes (about 1 pound)
1 1/2 cups diced celery
1/2 cup finely chopped green onions or scallions
1 cup remoulade mayonnaise dressing (page 316)

Toss the watercress with a little olive oil and divide among 4 salad plates.
Toss the potatoes, celery, and green onions with the dressing, place on
the watercress, and serve.

ALTERNATE DRESSINGS:
tarragon mayonnaise dressing (page 316),
tarragon mustard cream dressing (page 310).

celery root remoulade

THIS CLASSIC FRENCH SALAD is worth having in your repertoire.
Celery root remoulade is traditionally served as part of an hors d'oeuvres
assortment. Just allow enough time for the celery root to soften in the
dressing and the flavors to meld.

> 1 medium celery root (about 1 pound)
> 1/2 cup remoulade mayonnaise dressing (page 316)
> Chopped fresh flat-leaf parsley, for garnish

Trim the celery root, cutting away the leaves and the dark brown outer
peel. Using a mandoline with care, slice it thin and then cut the slices into
thin strips. Place in a bowl, toss with the dressing, and let sit for about
1 hour to allow the flavors to develop.

To serve, place the celery remoulade in a serving bowl or divide among
4 salad plates and top with the chopped parsley.

ALTERNATE DRESSING:
lemon mayonnaise dressing (page 316).

fresh fava bean salad with sherry vinaigrette
ENSALADA DE HABAS

THIS IS A CLASSIC MEDITERRANEAN SPRINGTIME salad, made when fresh favas are at their tender best. In Portugal, the herb of choice is cilantro, but in Spain, mint is used to punch up the flavor. Look for tender young pods and try to tune into the meditative process of peeling the beans.

3 cups shelled fresh fava beans (about 3 pounds in the pod)
1/2 cup sherry vinaigrette (page 270)
1 large head romaine lettuce, shredded
3 tablespoons chopped fresh mint
2 spring onions, chopped (white and green parts)
1/2 cup slivered Serrano ham

Cook the fava beans in boiling salted water for 2 minutes. Drain and refresh in cold water. Using your fingers, carefully remove the outer peel from each bean. It may take a little time, but you'll get faster at this the more you do it.

Place the peeled favas in a salad bowl. Dress them with half the vinaigrette and let them marinate for about 30 minutes.

When ready to serve, toss the lettuce, mint, and spring onions with the rest of the dressing and place on a serving platter. Top with the favas and slivered ham.

VARIATION:
For an Italian version, use prosciutto instead of Serrano ham.

ALTERNATE DRESSING:
mint vinaigrette (page 280).

cucumber salad
with yogurt dressing

KNOWN AS *CACIK* IN TURKEY, *tzatziki* in Greece, *khiar bil Laban* in the Arab nations, and *mast va khiar* in Iran, this cooling salad is equally at home in Albania, Lebanon, and the countries that used to be Yugoslavia. In Bulgaria, walnuts are added and it is called *tarator* (not to be confused with the sesame tarator or teradot sauce). In Iran, raisins and walnuts may be added, or sour cherries, walnuts, and dill, or pomegranate seeds, walnuts, mint, and rose petals. *Tzatziki* is used as a dip for pita bread or as a sauce for fried eggplant, zucchini, fish, or meat, especially kebabs. Mint or dill is the herb of choice. Occasionally *cacık* is thinned with water and served as a chilled summer soup.

Please keep in mind that cucumbers give off quite a bit of water and many yogurts are quite liquid. So you don't end up with a soupy mess, it's wise to place the yogurt in a cheesecloth-lined strainer set over a bowl in the refrigerator for a few hours to thicken it before making the dressing. Salt the cucumbers and let them drain for 30 minutes to rid them of excess water. Squeeze them and dry them well before adding them to the yogurt.

> 2 cloves garlic, minced
> Olive oil, if needed
> 2 cucumbers, peeled, seeded, and cut into small dice or
>   coarsely grated on the large holes of a box grater
> 1 cup yogurt dressing (page 306)
> Sea salt and freshly ground black pepper
> 1/4 cup chopped fresh mint or dill

If the garlic is "hot," cook it in a little olive oil over low heat for a minute or two, just to soften the bite. The garlic kick never bothers me, as I think the yogurt cools it down, but some people complain about the burn.

Combine all of the ingredients in a bowl and refrigerate. Serve at room temperature or lightly chilled.

VARIATIONS:

If you like, add 1/3 cup plumped raisins, sour cherries, or toasted and chopped walnuts to the salad.
Or fold in the seeds from 2 small pomegranates, 1/3 cup walnuts, and some fresh rose petals (be sure they have not been sprayed with pesticide).

facing page: cucumber salad with pomegranate seeds and yogurt dressing

three persian salads with yogurt dressing

The following three salads are part of a group of Persian salads called *borani*. I love to serve these together, accompanied with pita bread for dipping. All of these salads serve 4.

persian mushroom salad BORANI GARCH

3 tablespoons unsalted butter
1 small onion, chopped
1 pound cremini or white mushrooms, coarsely chopped or
    cut into small pieces
Sea salt
1 cup yogurt dressing (page 306)
2 tablespoons slivered fresh mint, for garnish

Melt the butter in a medium sauté pan over moderate heat. Add the onion and cook for 5 minutes. Add the mushrooms and cook until tender, about 5 minutes. Season lightly with salt. Remove this mixture from the heat and let cool.

Place the cooled mushroom mixture in a serving bowl, toss with the yogurt dressing, and top with the mint. Serve at room temperature with pita bread.

persian spinach salad BORANI ESFANAJ

1 pound fresh spinach
3 tablespoons unsalted butter
1 small onion, minced
1/2 teaspoon ground cinnamon (optional)
2 cloves garlic, minced (if you do not add garlic to the dressing)
1 cup yogurt dressing (page 306)
Sea salt and freshly ground black pepper
3 tablespoons walnuts, toasted and chopped, for garnish
1 tablespoon slivered fresh mint, for garnish

Remove the stems from the spinach, wash well, drain, and coarsely chop the leaves.

Melt the butter in a large sauté pan. Add the onion and cook over medium heat until translucent, about 5 minutes. Add the cinnamon if using, the garlic, and the spinach and cook until the spinach is wilted, about 5 minutes, stirring often. Drain well and let cool.

Place the cooled spinach in a serving bowl, toss with the yogurt dressing, and season to taste with salt and pepper. Sprinkle with the walnuts and mint. Serve at room temperature with pita bread.

persian eggplant salad BORANI BADEMJAN

2 globe eggplants
Sea salt
Olive oil
1 cup yogurt dressing (page 306)
2 cloves garlic, minced (if you do not add garlic to the dressing)
1/4 cup chopped fresh flat-leaf parsley

Cut the eggplants in half lengthwise, then slice them crosswise into 1/2-thick slices. Sprinkle with salt and set them aside to drain for 30 minutes. Pat dry with paper towels.

Heat a film of olive oil in a large skillet over medium heat. Add the eggplant slices in batches and fry, turning once and adding oil as needed. Cook until the slices are tender and translucent, about 3 minutes per side. They do not need to be golden. Drain on paper towels.

To assemble the salad, spread a layer of yogurt dressing on a serving plate, add a layer of eggplant and some minced garlic, then a layer of dressing. Continue layering until all the ingredients have been used. Sprinkle with parsley and serve warm or at room temperature, with pita bread.

potato and egg salad with yogurt dressing

THIS YUMMY POTATO SALAD offers respite from those sweet mayonnaise-drenched versions found in delicatessens. It is tangier, lighter, and truly refreshing. The greens add some color to the otherwise white mixture. Purslane leaves are chewy and tart, so if they are not to your taste, or if you can't find them, use watercress or mâche. You may also add sliced radishes to the salad.

1 pound small fingerling, Bintje, or Yukon Gold potatoes
Sea salt
4 green onions thinly sliced (white and green parts), or
   1 spring bulb onion cut in thin rings
2 tablespoons salt-packed capers, rinsed
2 hard-boiled eggs, cut in quarters
1 cup torn watercress, mâche, or purslane leaves
1/2 cup diced celery (optional)
About 2/3 cup yogurt dressing (page 306)
2 tablespoons chopped fresh dill, for garnish

Place the potatoes in a large saucepan and cover with cold water. Bring to a boil, add salt, and reduce the heat to low. Simmer until just tender, about 15 minutes. Drain and rinse with cold water to stop the cooking. When the potatoes are cool enough to handle, cut them into thick slices or chunks and transfer to a serving bowl.

Add the green onions, capers, eggs, watercress, and celery if using. Mix the ingredients gently with the yogurt dressing. Your hands may be the best tool here, as hard utensils can crush the potatoes and the eggs. Sprinkle with dill and serve at room temperature.

ALTERNATE DRESSINGS:
tarragon mustard cream dressing (page 310),
anchovy or remoulade mayonnaise dressing (page 316).

fruit salads

WHEN YOU ARE SHOWCASING fruit in a salad, the acid component in the dressing is the key to successful balance. Of course, the salad oil needs to be mild or simply neutral. Dark green peppery oils will overpower and obscure the fruit's flavor. Mild and fruity olive oils such as those from Liguria or the French Riviera, or neutral oils such as canola and grapeseed, are best. If nuts are a component in the salad, you can add toasted nut oil to the dressing.

By their nature, most citrus fruits contribute ample acidity and need to be held in check so the salad is not overly tart. Adding orange juice or a pinch of sugar or honey can balance the dressing and highlight both the fruit and the greens. Sweeter fruits like pears, apples, persimmons, and figs require a bit more acidity in the dressing for their sweetness to shine. Lemon juice may predominate, or the dressing can be made with a sweet fruit-based vinegar, balsamic vinegar, or a combination of citrus and balsamic vinegar to bring out the best in the fruit.

Don't forget that the rich and creamy avocado is a fruit. It needs acid and salt for us to appreciate its goodness. The tomato is also a fruit, even though we are used to thinking of it as a vegetable, so we forget that its sweetness is a factor in a salad.

Here are some salads that feature fruit as a major ingredient or the star. Most of the accompanying dressings are citrus-based or have tart-sweet pomegranate or use one of the sweet vinegars.

melon, cucumber, watercress, and goat cheese salad with mint vinaigrette

ON MY FIRST TRIP TO TURKEY, I ordered a meze assortment, and one of the small plates was a slice of sweet melon paired with a chunk of tart white cheese. I am accustomed to serving fruit and cheese after dinner, but I found this combination a refreshing way to stimulate the palate at the start of a meal. I wanted to turn this into a full-fledged salad on its own, so I combined the melon and the cheese with cucumbers, watercress, and mint. While you can use a simple citrus dressing, I think you will find that the mint vinaigrette adds another level of coolness to this delightful summer salad.

> 2 or 3 bunches watercress, stems well trimmed
> 24 mint leaves, cut in half if large
> 1/2 to 3/4 cup mint vinaigrette (page 280)
> 1 small ripe cantaloupe or 1/2 ripe Crenshaw melon, cut into
>   large cubes or thin 2-inch wedges
> 2 small cucumbers, peeled, seeded, and diced or sliced
> 1/2 to 3/4 cup feta or goat cheese

Toss the watercress and mint leaves in a bowl with enough dressing to coat. Distribute the greens on salad plates.

Toss the melon and cucumbers with the remaining dressing and place them on the greens. Top with crumbled feta or goat cheese. Serve immediately.

ALTERNATE DRESSINGS:
yogurt dressing without garlic (page 306),
lemon cream dressing (page 308).

orange, onion, and olive salad with hot pepper citrus dressing

THIS SALAD, WITH MINOR VARIATIONS, appears in Greece, Sicily, Spain, and North Africa. Sometimes mint, lemon balm, dill, or parsley is chopped and strewn on top of the salad at the last minute. In Spain, cooks may add about 4 ounces of flaked cooked salt cod, canned tuna, or anchovies or top this salad with thin slices of *mojama*, or salt-cured, air-dried tuna (see "Mojama," below).

> 3 large navel oranges
> 1 small red onion, sliced paper-thin
> 1/3 cup oil-cured black olives, pitted
> 1/4 cup hot pepper citrus dressing (page 295)
> A few slices *mojama*, for garnish

Working with 1 orange at a time, cut a thin slice off the top and bottom to reveal the flesh. Stand the orange upright and remove the peel in wide strips, cutting downward and following the contour of the fruit. Make sure to remove all the white pith. With a serrated knife, cut the orange crosswise into 1/4-inch-thick slices. With the tip of a knife or a toothpick, push out all of the seeds.

In a large bowl, layer the orange slices with the onion slices and let sit for at least 15 minutes, so the orange juice softens the onion and reduces its sharpness.

Sprinkle the salad with the olives and dress with the hot pepper citrus dressing. Garnish with *mojama* if you like and serve immediately.

ALTERNATE DRESSINGS:
mint vinaigrette (page 280),
mixed citrus dressing I (page 293),
toasted cumin citrus dressing (page 301).

MOJAMA

The name is Arabic, from **musama**, which means "to dry," but it was the Phoenicians who perfected the technique of filleting tuna, cutting it into pieces, salting them, washing them, and hanging them out to dry in the sea air. **Mojama** is packaged in chunks or bars. Slice it at the last minute or it will become too dry, or cover it with olive oil or a damp cloth to hold it for a short while. You can find **mojama** at some specialty markets or order it from www.spanishtable.com or www.tienda.com.

peach and tomato salad

IN SPAIN, ADVENTUROUS YOUNG CHEFS have been playing with novel fruit combinations: gazpacho made with melon and tomato, salads of melon and tomato or peach and tomato. It is fun to try these new pairings, but be sure to taste the fruit before you dress the salad. (Remember that the tomato is a fruit too.) Some peaches are tart; others are quite sweet and lacking in acid. If peaches are not at their best, use melon. Cantaloupe, Galia, and other muskmelons tend to be sweet, with hardly any acidity. If you opt for watermelon, it is always sweet. Tomatoes also vary in flavor. They can be quite tart or mildly acidic. All of these are factors in determining the amount of lemon to use in the dressing.

As I did not want this salad to be too sweet, I thought I'd try a citrus and black pepper dressing and add a little onion. This mélange would also be a great accompaniment for roast chicken or pork. You have the option of expanding the Spanish theme by adding crunchy ingredients such as toasted Marcona almonds or strips of Serrano ham.

4 large ripe tomatoes, peeled, seeded, and cut into large dice
2 large peaches, peeled and cut into large dice
1/2 a small red onion, finely minced or cut into thin slivers
About 1/3 cup citrus and black pepper dressing (page 295)
3 tablespoons thinly slivered fresh mint or basil, for garnish

Combine all the ingredients in a salad bowl and gently toss with the dressing. Garnish with the mint and serve.

ALTERNATE DRESSINGS:
mint vinaigrette (page 280),
catalan vinaigrette (page 278),
orange balsamic vinaigrette (page 277).

facing page: peach and tomato salad with roast chicken breast and citrus and black pepper dressing

spanish orange and fennel salad
with mixed citrus dressing

PAIRING ORANGES WITH ANISE-SCENTED FENNEL is a traditional
Sicilian flavor marriage. For many years Sicily was controlled by Spain, so
taking this salad to the Iberian peninsula with greens, almonds, and a few
strips of Serrano ham is not really off the mark. For a more Italian accent, use
pistachios and prosciutto.

> **4 Valencia or blood oranges**
> **3 small bulbs fennel, trimmed, cored, and very thinly sliced**
> **1/2 to 3/4 cup mixed citrus dressing II (page 293)**
> **6 large handfuls of assorted greens (try baby spinach, mizuna,**
> **   whole mint leaves, watercress; a scant 1/2 pound)**
> **1 cup slivered almonds, toasted**
> **4 to 6 thin slices Serrano ham, cut in 1/4-inch-wide strips**

Working with 1 orange at a time, cut a thin slice off the top and bottom
to reveal the flesh. Stand the orange upright and remove the peel in wide
strips, cutting downward and following the contour of the fruit. Make sure
to remove all of the white pith. Holding the orange over a bowl, cut along
both sides of each segment, releasing the segments from the membrane
and allowing them to drop into the bowl. Using the knife tip or a toothpick,
pry out any seeds. Squeeze the membrane over the bowl to collect extra
juice, which you can add to the dressing at serving time.

Place the fennel in a bowl, add a few tablespoons of the dressing, and
toss to coat evenly.

In another bowl, toss the greens with most of the remaining dressing.
Divide the greens and fennel evenly among individual salad plates.
Using a slotted spoon, remove the orange segments from their bowl and
distribute evenly over the fennel. Top each serving with almonds and strips
of Serrano ham and serve immediately.

ALTERNATE DRESSINGS:
mint vinaigrette (page 280),
or cut back on the amount of nuts
and use **catalan vinaigrette** (page 278).

figs, almonds, greens, and cabrales cheese

RIPE FIGS, SLIGHTLY CRACKED AND BURSTING with sweet juices, are the sexiest Mediterranean fruit. Black Mission, green Adriatic, Brown Turkey—I love them all and eat them out of hand; sometimes I just nibble alternating bites of sweet fig and salty cheese. I love to serve figs draped in prosciutto, with a squeeze of lime juice and some cracked black pepper, or grilled in a prosciutto or pancetta wrap. Ripe figs are the stars of this salad. As a little note of contrast, you might want to add some whole mint leaves to the salad greens. Cabrales is a blue-veined Spanish cheese. You may use any mild blue cheese in its place.

6 large handfuls of assorted mild greens or chicory (about 1/2 pound)
1/2 cup slivered almonds, toasted
About 1/2 cup pomegranate citrus dressing (page 297)
12 ripe figs, cut in quarters
1/4 pound Cabrales or another creamy blue cheese, crumbled

Place the greens and almonds in a salad bowl. Toss with half the dressing. Arrange on 6 salad plates. Top with the figs and crumbled cheese and drizzle with the remaining dressing. Serve immediately.

ALTERNATE DRESSINGS:
lemon cream dressing (page 308),
mint vinaigrette (page 280),
orange balsamic vinaigrette (page 277),
or use hazelnuts instead of almonds
and pomegranate and nut oil dressing (page 298).

figs, greens, and prosciutto with gorgonzola cream dressing

MANY YEARS AGO, RICHARD OLNEY, in his seminal book, *Simple French Cooking*, had a recipe for an appetizer of figs cut almost in quarters, topped with fine strips of prosciutto, and drizzled with a mint-infused lemon cream. I still prepare this wonderful dish to serve along with a glass of Prosecco. I love the classic combination of figs and prosciutto and have noticed that some young chefs in Italy are using crunchy fried prosciutto to dress salad greens. This recipe takes the fig and prosciutto duo more into the salad realm by adding greens and turning the cheese into a Gorgonzola cream dressing. You can serve the strips of prosciutto at room temperature or briefly warm them in olive oil until they are slightly crunchy.

6 handfuls of salad greens, including arugula, radicchio, and a
    few mint leaves, torn into bite-sized pieces (about 1/2 pound)
6 ripe figs, cut in quarters
Sea salt and freshly ground black pepper
About 1 cup Gorgonzola cream dressing, not too thick (page 313)
3 to 4 tablespoons extra-virgin olive oil
4 ounces sliced prosciutto, cut into strips about 1 1/2 inches long
    and 1/4 inch wide

Place the salad greens and the figs in a large bowl. Season to taste with salt and pepper and toss with enough dressing to coat.

If you want to cook the prosciutto, warm the olive oil in a small sauté pan, over medium-high heat. Add the prosciutto strips and sauté, stirring to ensure even cooking, until they are a bit crunchy, 3 to 5 minutes. Using a slotted spoon, transfer the prosciutto to the salad. Or toss the salad greens and figs with the dressing and top with strips of uncooked prosciutto. Serve immediately.

ALTERNATE DRESSINGS:
mint vinaigrette (page 280),
lemon cream dressing (page 308),
or add hazelnuts and use **hazelnut vinaigrette** (page 273) or
hazelnut cream dressing (page 311).

facing page: figs, greens, and prosciutto
with gorgonzola cream dressing

persian pomegranate and cucumber salad

IT TAKES A BIT OF PATIENCE to remove the seeds from a pomegranate. You have to cut the ends off the fruit and tap it hard on a counter to loosen the seeds, then run a knife down the sides to cut it into segments, crack it open, and pick out the seeds. You can also cut the pomegranate into segments, bop them hard on a countertop or with a heavy spoon, and let the seed packets fall into a bowl of cold water. Pick out the seeds and discard the membrane. Happily, today we can buy pomegranate seeds in the refrigerated section of the produce department. If frozen, they keep for up to a year.

This is a very pretty and dramatic salad. If you find it too intense, you may serve it tossed with chopped mild lettuces.

> 1 English cucumber, seeded and chopped, or 2 or 3 Persian or
>   Japanese cucumbers, chopped
> 1 small onion, chopped
> Sea salt
> 2 small lemons, peeled and pith removed, finely chopped
> A handful of mint leaves, torn or thinly slivered
> Seeds of 4 large pomegranates (about 2 cups)
> 1/4 cup pomegranate citrus dressing (page 297)

Combine the cucumber and the onion in a bowl and sprinkle with salt. Let rest for 10 minutes, then rinse and dry. Combine in a large bowl with the lemons, mint, and pomegranate seeds. Toss with the dressing and serve immediately.

ALTERNATE DRESSING:
mint vinaigrette (page 280).

persimmon and pomegranate salad with butter lettuce

AUTUMN ON A PLATE! The persimmons I refer to here are not the pointy Hachiyas, which must be fully soft to be edible; those are the pudding persimmons. What I want for the salad are the squat round ones called Fuyu. They are bright orange and have a semi-firm texture with just a little give if you push on them. Some may have seeds, which you will want to cut away. Pomegranate seeds, called arils, can be found in the refrigerator case in some markets, near the bottled juice, or you can cut open a pomegranate and pick out your own (see headnote, page 158). Oak leaf or red leaf lettuce will work well here too.

2 heads butter lettuce, leaves separated

3 ripe Fuyu persimmons, peeled and cut into wedges

Seeds of 1 large pomegranate (about 1 cup)

1/2 cup pomegranate and nut oil dressing made with hazelnut oil (page 298)

1/4 cup toasted hazelnuts, coarsely chopped, for garnish

Combine the lettuce, persimmons, and pomegranate seeds in a large bowl and toss with the dressing. Place on 6 salad plates and top with the toasted nuts. Serve immediately.

VARIATION:

Slivers of cooked chicken or duck breast are a fine addition to this salad. Just increase the dressing by 1/2 cup.

ALTERNATE DRESSING:

mixed citrus dressing I (page 293).

grapefruit and avocado salad
with leafy greens

THIS DISH SHOWCASES TWO OF ISRAEL'S major food exports: grapefruit and avocado. If cost is not a factor, you can make the salad more elegant and the flavors more complex by adding cooked shellfish, such as crabmeat, scallops, or shrimp. Not exactly kosher, but quite delicious.

2 small grapefruits
2 avocados
3/4 to 1 cup mixed citrus dressing I (page 293)
6 handfuls of assorted mild, sweet leafy greens, such as butter,
    oak leaf, or red leaf lettuce (a scant 1/2 pound)
1/2 pound crabmeat, shrimp, or scallops (optional)

Working with 1 grapefruit at a time, cut a thin slice off the top and bottom to reveal the flesh. Stand the grapefruit upright and remove the peel in wide strips, cutting downward and following the contour of the fruit. Holding the grapefruit over a bowl, cut along both sides of each segment, releasing the segments from the membrane and allowing them to drop into the bowl. Using the knife tip or a toothpick, pry out any seeds. Squeeze the membrane over another bowl to release the juice. Repeat with the remaining grapefruit. You should have about 1/2 cup juice.

Cut the avocados in half and remove and discard the pits. With a large spoon, scoop the avocado from the peel. Cut the flesh into 1/4-inch slices. Drizzle with 1/4 cup dressing.

Toss the greens with 1/4 cup dressing. Distribute among 4 salad plates or arrange on a large platter. Top with avocado slices and grapefruit segments and drizzle with the remaining dressing.

If you are adding crabmeat, just toss it with the citrus dressing and pile it on top, or place it in the center of a circle of avocado slices and grapefruit segments.

If you like, you may add cooked shrimp or scallops to this salad. Sprinkle the seafood with salt and pepper. Place 1/4 cup citrus dressing in a large sauté pan along with the reserved grapefruit juice and bring to a boil. Add the shellfish to the pan and cook, turning once, until they are barely cooked through, about 4 minutes, depending on the size of the shellfish. Remove the pan from the heat and arrange the shellfish on top of the

facing page: grapefruit and avocado salad with leafy greens and seared scallops

(continued on next page)

greens, alternating them with the grapefruit and avocado. Drizzle with the remaining citrus dressing.

Serve immediately.

VARIATION:

Orange and avocado salad: If you combine creamy, rich avocado with tart-sweet orange segments and mild lettuces, you need a dressing that has salt, acidity, and textural contrast. **catalan vinaigrette** (page 278) fits the bill perfectly. The anchovies and capers add salt, the sherry vinegar adds acidity, and the toasted almonds add crunch, bringing the salad into balance.

ALTERNATE DRESSINGS:
mint vinaigrette (page 280),
hot pepper citrus dressing (page 295),
citrus and black pepper dressing (page 295).

israeli chopped salad with avocado

ALONG WITH CITRUS FRUITS, Israel is known for its avocados. This savory salad is one of my favorites and a perfect fit for toasted cumin dressing. As the ingredients are hardy and will not wilt, you can assemble this salad ahead of time, which makes it a prime candidate for the buffet table.

2 ripe avocados, cut into 1-inch chunks
1 cup walnuts, toasted and very coarsely chopped
1 1/2 cups diced celery, cut 1/2-inch thick
1 1/2 cups diced seeded cucumber, cut 1/2-inch thick
1/2 cup finely chopped red onion
About 1 cup toasted cumin citrus dressing (page 301)

Combine all of the ingredients in a salad bowl and toss. If you like, you can serve this on a bed of greens, with the same dressing. Serve at room temperature.

ALTERNATE DRESSING:
preserved lemon dressing (page 299).

farro

couscous

bulgur

classic and modern grain, bread, and pasta salads

MOST GRAIN SALADS, WHETHER based on bulgur, farro, wheat berries, or rice, are bland and starchy, so they need a full-flavored dressing. With the Middle Eastern tabbouleh, made with fine bulgur wheat, lemon juice traditionally is preferred over vinegar, as the grain is tiny. Farro is larger and chewier than bulgur, and wheat berries are even more toothsome, so a vinaigrette penetrates the grain more fully than a lighter citronette. Rice salads can be dressed with vinaigrette or citrus dressing, and in Spain they are often tossed with a mayonnaise-based dressing.

I have included couscous and pasta salads in this chapter, as both are made from wheat. Modern deli creations, couscous and pasta salads are not "authentic," but I have come to the realization that they are here to stay. They are endlessly popular with diners and so must be given some attention. My begrudging acceptance of their genre does not mean that I haven't formed strong opinions about them. I don't like either of these salads burdened with too much "stuff." I prefer light citrus dressings on couscous salads. I do not like mayonnaise on pasta salads (or macaroni salad, a truly American creation)—I find it way too heavy.

Bread salads are traditional in the Mediterranean, and I have included them in this chapter because bread is made with wheat flour. Because bread is dense, salads based on bread are best dressed with vinaigrettes. Keep in mind that bread is bland and porous and will absorb much of the dressing, so the vinaigrette must be strong enough to cut through the starch and still accent the accompanying components without overwhelming them.

Although Americans are of course familiar with bread, rice, and pasta, I've found that they confuse many of the traditional grains of the Mediterranean with one another or don't understand exactly what they are. Here is a brief introduction to the important salad grains of the Mediterranean.

BULGUR is wheat that has already been cooked. The cooked wheat is dried, then cracked and sieved. It is available in four sizes. Extra-coarse is used for steaming and soups. Coarse is used for pilafs. Medium is used for stuffing grape leaves and other vegetables. Fine is used in salads such as tabbouleh or kisir and to make kibbe. Bulgur is a common ingredient in Turkish, Armenian, Arab, Greek, Assyrian, and Sephardic Jewish cooking.

CRACKED WHEAT is made from wheat berries and is uncooked. Many recipes confuse cracked wheat and bulgur. Bulgur only needs soaking, whereas cracked wheat must be cooked. Both, however, will produce a grain that can be used in salads. If you buy your grain from a bin in the health food store or market, check to see whether it is labeled bulgur or cracked wheat. (Of course, the store staff might not know either.) Bulgur most often comes packaged. To keep it from becoming mushy, work in some salt with the water.

FARRO is an old variety of wheat, sometimes erroneously labeled spelt. (Farro, *Triticum dicoccum*, is related to spelt, *Triticum speltum*. A similar grain in France called *épeautre* is *Triticum monococcum*.) Farro is primarily cultivated around Lucca, in the Garfagnana region of Tuscany, and in the Abruzzo and Umbria. In the old days you had to clean the grain carefully, removing debris and stones, then soak it overnight and cook it for 2 hours! I can cheerfully report that today this is unnecessary. Packaged farro is well cleaned and abraded (semiperlato or pearled) and is tender in about 25 minutes. It has a lighter mouth feel than wheat berries. With its nutty taste and texture, farro resembles barley more than wheat. Start testing for doneness after 15 minutes; you want it tender but chewy. Drain it when it has achieved the proper texture.

Farro used to be hard to find at the market, but most Italian delicatessens now carry it, and you can order it by mail from agferrari.com or indianharvest.com. It is also imported by Rustichella. Be suspicious of places that offer this Italian grain in bulk; it is probably spelt, which is darker and less sweet, has a firmer texture, and takes much longer to cook. Farro comes from Italy, usually in small bags or packages, and is not (yet) produced in America. The proof will be in the cooking. Farro, which has been abraded or pearled, will cook in 25 to 30 minutes, while the tougher spelt requires at least an hour.

COUSCOUS is not a grain, although it looks like one. It's a granular pellet made by rolling semolina with water and pushing it though a screen. In North Africa, couscous is steamed over hot water, broth, or a stew. Repeated steaming makes it fluffier and more tender and increases its volume.

Do not confuse couscous with a round pasta called "Israeli couscous," which is much heavier and chewier in texture and is neither Israeli nor couscous. It is made from semolina pasta balls called *berkukis* or *magrebiyya* ("from the Magreb") and was probably introduced to Israel by Sephardic Jews.

Most of the salads in this chapter are rather filling and too heavy for a starter course, but they make a satisfying meal.

cracked wheat salad with garden vegetables

serves 4

GRANO PESTATO E VERDURE

IN THE SOUTHERN ITALIAN REGION of Puglia, cooks pound *grano*, or wheat berries, to break the outer casing, an impromptu way to get cracked wheat. They add vegetables and then dress the salad with vinegar. You can save the elbow grease and use cracked wheat, or cook farro or whole wheat berries for a chewier grain salad. Wheat berries take about 1 1/2 hours to cook; farro takes 25 to 30 minutes.

2 cups cracked wheat

8 medium tomatoes, peeled, seeded, and diced (3 to 4 cups)

2 carrots, peeled and diced

2 cucumbers, peeled, seeded, and diced

1 large handful of arugula, coarsely chopped

3 tablespoons salt-packed capers, rinsed

1 small hot chili pepper, minced (omit if using hot pepper vinaigrette)

About 3/4 cup garlic vinaigrette (page 269)

Sea salt and freshly ground black pepper

Wash the grain. Place it in a saucepan with boiling salted water and cook over medium heat until tender, about 15 minutes. Drain well and transfer to a large bowl.

Add the tomatoes, carrots, cucumbers, arugula, capers, and chili pepper to the grain. Toss with the dressing. Season with salt and pepper to taste and serve at room temperature.

ALTERNATE DRESSING:
hot pepper vinaigrette (page 272).

lebanese bulgur wheat salad

TABBOULEH

TABBOULEH'S SUCCESS IS DEPENDENT ON good tomatoes, so this grain-based salad is best in the summer. In Turkey, this salad is called *keser* or *kisir*, and chopped green peppers are added. The technique for softening the grain varies: some cooks pour boiling salted water over the bulgur, while others soak it in salted cold water. If all the water has not been absorbed but the grain is tender and still a bit crunchy, just drain it in a strainer. Measurements for tabbouleh need not be exact. More tomato, less parsley—it will still be delicious and refreshing.

1 to 1 1/2 cups fine bulgur
2 to 3 cups finely chopped fresh flat-leaf parsley
2 to 3 cups chopped ripe tomatoes (about 4 medium tomatoes)
1 cup chopped fresh mint
1/2 cup chopped green onions (about 1 bunch; green and white parts)
1 cup basic citrus dressing (page 290)
Sea salt and freshly ground black pepper
Romaine leaves, for serving

In a bowl, soak the bulgur in salted cold or hot water for 20 to 30 minutes and then place in a strainer to drain. Transfer to a salad bowl and add the parsley, tomatoes, mint, and green onions. Whisk the citrus dressing and toss it with the salad. Season with salt and pepper to taste. Serve with romaine leaves as scoops.

VARIATIONS:

Add 2 teaspoons Aleppo pepper to the dressing.

Use **tahini dressing** (page 303) or **walnut tarator dressing** (page 305) to make the Turkish grain salad called *batirik*.

ALTERNATE DRESSING:

mint vinaigrette, but reduce fresh mint in the salad to 1/2 cup (page 280).

wheat salad with vegetables
INSALATA DI FARRO

I LOVE GRAIN SALADS: Lebanese tabbouleh (page 168), Spanish rice salad (page 174), Pugliese pounded wheat called *grano pestato* (page 167). But my all-time favorite grain for salads is farro; I am crazy for its nutty taste and texture. Don't overcook the grain. You want it tender but still chewy. Start testing for doneness after 20 minutes, and drain it when it has achieved the proper texture.

2 1/2 to 3 cups water
Sea salt
1 cup farro
2 tablespoons extra-virgin olive oil
About 3/4 cup mint vinaigrette (page 280)
Freshly ground black pepper
1/2 cup chopped red onion
1/2 cup chopped celery or fennel
1 cup peeled, seeded, and chopped cucumber (1 regular or 1/2 English)
4 small tomatoes, seeded and chopped (optional)
A large handful of arugula leaves, tough stems removed, leaves coarsely
    chopped (optional)
1/4 cup chopped fresh flat-leaf parsley
1/4 cup chopped fresh mint
Oil-cured black olives for garnish (optional)

To cook the farro, bring the water to a boil over high heat and salt it lightly. Add the farro, reduce the heat to low, cover, and simmer, checking for doneness after 20 minutes. When cooked, the grain will be tender but will still have some firmness at the center. If the farro is ready but not all the water has been absorbed, drain the grain in a sieve. (Each brand absorbs water slightly differently.)

Place the drained farro in a bowl, toss with the olive oil, and let cool. When cooled, toss the farro with half the dressing and salt and pepper to taste. Fold in the onion, celery, cucumber, tomatoes, arugula, if using, parsley, mint, and remaining dressing and toss again. Taste and adjust the seasoning. Garnish the salad with olives, if desired. Serve at room temperature.

ALTERNATE DRESSINGS:
garlic vinaigrette (page 269),
red wine vinaigrette (page 268).

syrian wheat salad
BAZERGAN

BAZERGAN IS A SYRIAN JEWISH VERSION of tabbouleh. Its name means "of the bazaar." Some versions incorporate chopped hazelnuts or pine nuts. The dressing is often enhanced with tamarind paste, but pomegranate syrup works well too. Both have a tart and sweet quality that, along with the lemon juice, accents the spices. At serving time, adjust the spices, saltiness, and tartness, adding more lemon juice if needed.

2 cups fine bulgur
Sea salt
3 teaspoons ground cumin, toasted
2 teaspoons ground coriander
1/2 teaspoon allspice
1/4 teaspoon cayenne, or to taste
3 tablespoons tomato paste
2 tablespoons fresh lemon juice
1/2 cup pomegranate dressing from concentrate (page 298)
1 cup walnuts, toasted and coarsely chopped
1/4 cup chopped fresh flat-leaf parsley
1/4 cup toasted pine nuts (optional)
1/4 to 1/2 cup pomegranate seeds (optional)

Put the bulgur in a bowl and cover with lightly salted water. Let soak for 20 to 30 minutes, until tender. Drain well and transfer to a large bowl.

Whisk together the salt, spices, tomato paste, and lemon juice, then whisk this mixture into the pomegranate dressing. Taste and adjust the seasoning. You may want more lemon or a bit more oil.

Toss the dressing with the bulgur. Fold in the walnuts, parsley, and pine nuts, if using, and mix well. Let the salad marinate for 4 to 5 hours or as long as overnight for the flavors to develop. To serve, bring the salad to room temperature. Taste and adjust the seasoning. If you have pomegranate seeds, you might want to add a few for color.

VARIATION:
Add 3/4 cup finely chopped red onion.

ALTERNATE DRESSING:
mint vinaigrette (page 280).

facing page: syrian wheat salad with pomegranate seeds and pomegranate dressing

paella rice salad

EVERYONE IS ENAMORED of the Valencian classic paella, so I've transformed this signature dish into a rice salad. Instead of using short-grain Spanish rice, however, I prefer to use fragrant basmati, which stays firm a great deal longer than short-grain rice or any other long-grain rice, especially in a vinaigrette. Paella rice salad makes a wonderful lunch dish or light summer supper.

6 small boneless, skinless chicken breast halves

1 1/2 to 2 cups oregano garlic vinaigrette (page 284)

3 1/4 cups water, plus more for shrimp

1/2 teaspoon crushed saffron filaments

2 cups basmati rice

Sea salt

2 bell peppers, red or green or both, cut in 1/4-inch dice

1 red onion, finely diced

1 cup peeled, seeded, diced tomatoes

Freshly ground black pepper

30 medium shrimp, shelled and deveined

White wine

1/2 cup olives, for garnish (optional)

Marinate the chicken in 1/2 cup vinaigrette for at least 4 hours or overnight. Broil or grill for about 3 minutes per side. When cool, cut the chicken into strips that are about 2 inches long and 1/2 inch wide. Set aside.

Put 1/4 cup water and the saffron in a small saucepan and bring to a simmer over high heat. Remove the pan from the heat and set aside to steep.

Wash the rice, drain it, and place it in a medium saucepan. Cover with 3 cups water and the saffron infusion and bring to a boil over high heat. Add salt to taste, lower the heat, and cover the pan. Cook over low heat for 12 to 15 minutes, until all the water is absorbed.

When the rice is cooked and still warm, toss it in a large bowl with most of the remaining vinaigrette. Add the bell peppers, onion, and tomatoes and toss well. Season to taste with salt and pepper.

In a large skillet over medium-high heat, poach the shrimp in wine or water to cover until they turn pink, about 3 minutes. Or brush with vinaigrette and grill.

Toss the chicken and shrimp with the remaining vinaigrette.

Distribute the rice salad among 6 plates or place on a large platter. Top with chicken and shrimp and garnish with olives if desired. Serve warm or at room temperature.

ALTERNATE DRESSING:
garlic vinaigrette (page 269).

facing page: paella rice salad with prawns

spanish rice salad
ENSALADA DE ARROZ

RICE SALADS ARE SERVED in Italy, France, and Spain, often embellished with cooked tuna or shellfish. In Spain, mayonnaise is often the dressing of choice. Vinaigrette is more popular in Italy and France and is a little less rich.

1 cup rice, preferably basmati

1 1/2 cups water

Sea salt

2 tablespoons extra-virgin olive oil, plus more if needed

About 1 1/2 cups tarragon mayonnaise dressing (page 316)

1/2 cup finely minced red onion

1/2 cup diced roasted red pepper (pimientos or red bell peppers)

1/4 cup chopped fresh flat-leaf parsley

Freshly ground black pepper

7 ounces canned tuna, packed in oil, or 1/2 pound cooked squid, prawns, or mussels

Put the rice, water, and 1 teaspoon salt in a saucepan and bring to a boil over high heat. Reduce the heat to low, cover the pan, and simmer until the rice absorbs the water, about 15 minutes. Transfer to a bowl and toss with the olive oil to prevent clumping. Let the rice cool.

When the rice is lukewarm or cool, toss it with 2/3 cup of the tarragon mayonnaise dressing. Add the onion, pepper, and parsley, mix well, and season with salt and pepper to taste.

Toss the tuna or cooked shellfish with the remaining dressing. Top the rice with the seafood and serve immediately.

ALTERNATE DRESSINGS:
tuna mayonnaise dressing (page 316),
remoulade mayonnaise dressing (page 316),
saffron mayonnaise dressing (page 316).

couscous salad
with grilled shrimp

WHILE NOT AUTHENTICALLY MOROCCAN, this couscous salad comes to life with charmoula dressing and the contrasting crunch of shrimp, celery, and almonds.

1 cup charmoula citrus dressing (page 326)
32 medium to large shrimp, peeled and deveined
1/4 teaspoon saffron threads, crushed
1 1/8 cups water
2 cups couscous
2 tablespoons extra-virgin olive oil
1 teaspoon sea salt
1/2 teaspoon cumin
1 red onion, finely minced
4 stalks celery, chopped
1 cup slivered almonds, toasted
Moroccan oil-cured olives, for garnish

In a shallow container, toss 1/4 cup charmoula dressing with the shrimp. Roll the shrimp around in the dressing and marinate for 1 hour. Meanwhile, soak 16 wooden skewers in water. When the shrimp have marinated, heat a charcoal grill or a gas grill.

Arrange the shrimp on the skewers, using 2 parallel skewers for every 4 shrimp (this prevents them from turning on a single skewer). Brush the shrimp with the olive oil and grill for 2 to 3 minutes per side. Set them aside. Or grill the shrimp after you have made the couscous salad and serve them warm.

In a small saucepan, combine the saffron with 1/8 cup water and bring to a simmer. Remove the pan from the heat and steep for 15 minutes.

Place the couscous in a 9-inch square baking pan with sides. In a saucepan, combine the remaining 1 cup water, saffron infusion, olive oil, salt, and cumin and bring to a boil. Pour over the couscous and cover the pan. Let sit for 10 minutes, then fluff with a fork.

In a salad bowl, toss the onion, celery, almonds, couscous, and 1/2 cup charmoula dressing. Top with the grilled shrimp, drizzle with more charmoula and garnish with olives. Serve warm or at room temperature.

ALTERNATE DRESSINGS:
basic citrus dressing (page 290),
preserved lemon dressing (page 299),
mint vinaigrette (page 280).

couscous salad
with almonds, raisins, and saffron onions

WHILE NOT TRADITIONAL in North Africa, couscous salads have become a deli standard—no surprise, as the results are similar to salads made with bulgur, rice, and farro. All packaged couscous can be steamed for greater fluffiness, but that is not necessary for this salad. Follow the instructions below.

Individual plating of this salad is an aesthetic issue. For the sake of presentation and neatness, some chefs try to contain the couscous by jamming it into a ring mold. Couscous was not meant to be compacted, because it becomes gummy. It needs to be free, fluffy, and flowing. I suggest serving it mounded on a platter, surrounded by slices of fresh fruit and mint leaves or watercress—or, very simply, in a salad bowl.

> 1 cup raisins
> 4 1/8 cups water
> 1/4 teaspoon saffron
> 2 tablespoons extra-virgin olive oil
> 1 medium onion, diced
> Freshly grated zest of 1 orange
> 2 cups couscous
> 1 cup fresh orange juice
> 1 teaspoon ground cinnamon
> 1 teaspoon ground ginger
> 1/2 teaspoon cumin
> 1 teaspoon sea salt
> 1 cup slivered almonds, toasted
> About 1/2 cup basic citrus dressing (page 290)
> Chopped fresh flat-leaf parsley or mint, for garnish

Put the raisins in a small bowl, cover with 3 cups hot water, and set them aside to plump.

In a small saucepan, combine the saffron with 1/8 cup water and bring to a simmer over high heat. Remove from the heat and steep for 15 minutes.

Heat the olive oil in a medium sauté pan and cook the onion over medium heat until tender and translucent, about 7 minutes. Add the saffron infusion and orange zest and simmer 3 minutes. Drain and set aside.

Place the couscous in a 9-inch baking pan or Pyrex baking dish.

Combine 1 cup water and the orange juice, spices, and salt in a saucepan and bring to a boil over high heat. Pour over the couscous and cover the pan tightly with foil. Let sit for 10 minutes, then fluff with a fork.

Drain the raisins well. Toss the raisins, onion, almonds, and citrus dressing with the couscous. Adjust the seasoning and add salt to taste. Place on a platter or in a bowl and top with parsley or mint. You may garnish this with slices of melon or other fresh fruits or lettuce leaves if you like.

VARIATION:
Chopped dried apricots may be added to or replace some of the raisins in the salad. They too need to be plumped in hot water.

ALTERNATE DRESSINGS:
mint vinaigrette (page 280),
citrus cinnamon dressing (page 294).

couscous salad with almonds,
raisins, and saffron onions with
basic citrus dressing

179

pasta salad
with pesto vinaigrette

FOR ALL PASTA SALADS, it is very important to use dried pasta that will not gradually disintegrate after it is dressed. Hard durum wheat pasta is essential, and I recommend De Cecco—of all the brands I have tried, it holds up the longest after cooking. You should stop cooking the pasta when it is a bit harder than al dente, as it continues to soften as it sits. Also be sure to add the right amount of ingredients that give off water, as too much liquid causes the pasta to break down.

My preference for dressing pasta salad is a light vinaigrette, or in this instance pesto vinaigrette, which adds more concentrated herb flavor than simply tossing in some chopped basil leaves does.

> 1/2 pound dried pasta such as penne, farfalle, or fusilli
> (preferably De Cecco brand)
> 2 tablespoons extra-virgin olive oil
> 1 cup chopped celery or fennel
> 1 cup diced fresh mozzarella cheese
> 1 or 2 red or yellow bell peppers, diced
> 1/2 cup minced red onion
> About 1/2 cup pesto vinaigrette (page 320)
> 1 pound cooked tuna or shrimp (optional)

In a large saucepan, cook the pasta in boiling salted water for about 7 minutes. Bite a piece; it should be quite firm but starting to become tender on the outside. Look at the bitten cross-section: you want to see a small amount of the white uncooked center. Drain, rinse with cold water, and toss with the olive oil. Set aside to cool.

When the pasta has cooled to room temperature, place it in a salad bowl and toss with the remaining ingredients. You will need more dressing if you wish to use tuna or shrimp. Serve immediately.

VARIATIONS:
The same ingredients can be used in a rice salad.

My favorite Genovese cooked pasta dish combines pesto with green beans and potatoes, so they are obvious candidates for a pasta salad. Toss cooled pasta as above with 1/2 pound cooked new potatoes, diced, and 1/2 pound cooked green beans cut into 1-inch pieces. Add a few toasted pine nuts or walnuts for texture.

ALTERNATE DRESSINGS:
red wine vinaigrette (page 268),
garlic vinaigrette (page 269),
oregano garlic vinaigrette (page 284).

facing page: pasta salad with penne
and pesto vinaigrette

tuscan bread salad
PANZANELLA

WHAT FOLLOWS IS A PERSONAL and contemporary interpretation of the Tuscan panzanella salad. The bread should be from a firm Italian or French loaf trimmed of hard crust and may be a day old. In the classic version, the bread is soaked in water and crumbled, then mixed with the tomatoes. I find the texture of cubed bread more to my liking, and I think it looks much more attractive on the plate. Sometimes I even toast the bread lightly to help it retain texture as the tomatoes add their juices to the salad. It should go without saying, but I will say it anyway: great tomatoes are essential. Remember to salt the vegetables before adding them to the bread mixture.

4 to 5 cups cubed bread (1-inch cubes, from 1 large loaf with
   crust removed)
1/3 cup fruity extra-virgin olive oil, plus more if toasting the bread
3 tablespoons red wine vinegar
3 cups diced ripe tomatoes, cut 1/2-inch thick (about 6 medium tomatoes)
2 cups diced cucumbers, peeled and seeded if necessary, cut 1/2-inch thick
   (1 English or 2 regular cucumbers)
1/2 cup finely diced red onion
About 1 cup pesto vinaigrette (page 320)
Sea salt and freshly ground black pepper
Slivered fresh basil, for garnish (optional)

If you like, toss the bread cubes with a bit of olive oil and toast in a 400-degree F oven for about 15 minutes. This is not essential, but it is a nice touch.

Toss the bread cubes (toasted or not) in a salad bowl with the 1/3 cup oil and the vinegar and let them absorb this preliminary dressing for about 30 minutes. Add the remaining ingredients, including salt and pepper to taste, and quickly toss together. Garnish with slivered basil if you want a dramatic presentation. Serve at room temperature.

ALTERNATE DRESSINGS:
red wine vinaigrette (page 268),
garlic vinaigrette (page 269),
tomato vinaigrette (page 282),
oregano garlic vinaigrette (page 284).

facing page: tuscan bread salad with oregano garlic vinaigrette

fattoush

FATTOUSH WAS THE MOST REQUESTED summer salad at my restaurant, Square One. Not just our customers but our staff too would start requesting it in late June. I'd say, "Please be patient. We have to wait until the tomatoes are perfect—ripe and perfumed."

Fattoush is a Lebanese variation of tabbouleh, the classic Middle Eastern wheat salad (see page 168), but instead of using bulgur, it uses toasted pita bread. I love the textures in this salad and suggest that for the full crunch effect, you dress it just before serving, so the bread does not become soggy. Like tabbouleh, it typically takes a lemon and olive oil dressing, usually enhanced with tart sumac and lots of fresh mint and parsley. Adding the fleshy purslane and ground sumac is optional, as they are not readily found in many markets. They are, however, worth seeking out. Purslane is now considered a gourmet weed and is sold at many farmers' markets. Sumac is available at stores that specialize in Middle Eastern food or online from websites such as Penzeys.com and Vannsspices.com.

While the ingredients are not authentic, you can extend this salad by adding strips of cooked chicken or lamb, or even a few shrimp if you want to turn it into a full meal. Under the pan-Mediterranean umbrella, where ingredients from any region may be used, proprietary to the recipe or not, you'll find feta cheese added to fattoush—again, not authentic but tasty.

4 large or 8 small pita breads
1 to 1 1/2 cups basic citrus dressing (page 290)
2 teaspoons ground sumac (optional)
Sea salt and freshly ground black pepper
2 1/2 to 3 cups diced tomatoes, cut 1/2-inch thick (3 medium tomatoes)
2 cups diced cucumbers, peeled and seeded if necessary, cut 1/2-inch thick
    (2 small cucumbers)
1/2 cup very finely diced red onion
6 tablespoons finely chopped green onions (white and green parts)
1 cup chopped fresh flat-leaf parsley
1/2 cup thinly slivered fresh mint
2 cups chopped purslane (optional)
4 cups loosely packed romaine strips, cut 1 inch wide

Heat the oven to 350 degrees F. Place the pita breads on a baking sheet and bake until they are dry, about 15 minutes. Remove from the oven. When cool enough to handle, break the bread into large bite-sized pieces.

In a small bowl, whisk together the dressing and sumac, if using, and add salt and pepper to taste.

In a large salad bowl, combine the tomatoes, cucumber, red onion, green onion, parsley, and mint, then add the pita pieces, the purslane if using, and the romaine, and toss with the remaining dressing. Serve immediately.

ALTERNATE DRESSING:
mint vinaigrette (page 280).

gazpacho bread salad

THE WORD *GAZPACHO* is Arabic for "soaked bread." In the days before Columbus, gazpacho was a mixture of water-soaked bread, olive oil, vinegar, and garlic. Over time, as tomatoes and peppers from the New World entered the culinary repertoire, they were added to this dish, and it evolved into the cold summer soup we know today. One day, while I was making panzanella for the hundredth time, I thought of adding gazpacho ingredients and a tomato vinaigrette. This makes a lively bread salad.

> 6 cups cubed French or Italian bread (1/2-inch cubes, from 1 large loaf with crust removed)
> About 1 1/2 cups tomato vinaigrette (page 282)
> 3 cups peeled, seeded, and diced tomatoes (3 to 4 medium tomatoes)
> 2 cups diced cucumbers, peeled and seeded if necessary (1 English or 2 regular cucumbers)
> 1 cup diced red bell pepper
> 1 cup diced green bell pepper
> 3/4 cup finely minced red onion
> 1/2 cup chopped fresh flat-leaf parsley
> Sea salt and freshly ground black pepper

Toss the bread cubes in a large bowl with half the vinaigrette and marinate for 30 minutes. Add the chopped vegetables and the remaining vinaigrette, salt and pepper to taste, and serve.

ALTERNATE DRESSINGS:
toasted cumin citrus dressing (page 301),
mint vinaigrette (page 280),
pesto vinaigrette (page 320),
oregano garlic vinaigrette (page 284).

bean salads

BECAUSE OF THEIR STARCHY and substantial texture, salads made with dried beans are best dressed with vinaigrettes. Most of the time vinegar works better than lemon juice to cut through the beans' richness. Occasionally you'll want a combination of vinegar and lemon, especially if delicate seafood is a component in the salad. (With fresh shell beans, however, you want light, less intense dressings, because fresh beans are not as starchy as dried ones.) I want the beans to absorb some of the dressing rather than just being coated with it, so I prefer to dress these salads while the beans are still warm.

In the Mediterranean, many of the same ingredients are used from country to country. It is in the choice of spices and herbs that national differences emerge. So you can prepare a basic bean salad from this chapter with any number of the vinaigrettes in this book and move about the Mediterranean at will. (Please note that I'm not talking about green bean salads here, which are in the Raw and Cooked Vegetable Salads chapter.)

cooking dried beans

WHEN YOU BUY DRIED BEANS at the store, you have no idea how old they are. But age affects their absorbency, so cooking time varies wildly from batch to batch. That's why I advise you not to combine different batches of beans in one container, because some of the fresher beans may cook quickly while older beans remain hard. You do not want to be picking bean after bean from the pot—life is way too short for that.

As the beans cook, check on them from time to time so they don't overcook. Start testing for doneness after about 20 minutes and then bite a bean every 5 to 10 minutes. Also, some beans firm up a bit after chilling, so don't panic if you think you cooked them a bit too long. After the beans cool for a while, they may surprise you by being perfect instead of too soft.

to soak or not to soak

IN A PERFECT WORLD, YOU will remember to soak the beans in water to cover overnight. If you have forgotten or need cooked beans in a hurry, you can use the quick-soak method: Put the beans in a saucepan with water to cover generously and place over high heat. Bring to a boil, boil for 2 minutes, then remove from the heat. Cover and let stand for 1 hour, then drain. (Although you can use this method for chickpeas and favas, it will not shorten their cooking time by much.)

Whatever method you use for soaking, drain the beans and put them in a saucepan. Cover with enough fresh water to come about 2 inches over them. Bring to a gentle boil over medium-high heat; if you like, add a sachet of aromatics, such as a few whole cloves of garlic, an onion, some sage leaves or a bay leaf. Reduce the heat to low, skim off any foam that accumulates on the surface, partially cover the pan, and simmer gently until the beans are tender, 40 to 60 minutes. (The timing will depend on the age and variety of the beans; chickpeas and favas can take up to 1 1/2 hours even if the quick-soak method has been used.) Add 1 to 2 teaspoons salt after the first 10 to 15 minutes of cooking.

When the beans are done, discard the aromatics. If you will be using the beans in another dish, store them in their cooking liquid until needed. For salads, drain the beans and dress them while still warm with a few tablespoons of olive oil and some salt and pepper or some of your chosen dressing.

to salt or not to salt

ACCORDING TO ASSORTED grandmothers and old wives, and even chefs, you dare not salt beans until they are fully cooked or they will never become tender. The salt supposedly toughens the skins and makes the beans split. *Los Angeles Times* food wine columnist Russ Parsons, who writes on the subject of beans and salt in his book *How to Read a French Fry*, has disproved this notion quite nicely.

I usually salt beans after they have been simmering for 10 to 15 minutes. There is no point in salting the cooking water after the beans are cooked, because they will never absorb it—and they need salt.

What causes splitting is cooking beans too rapidly. The water must bubble quietly. Some cooks add a pinch of baking soda to the soaking water to soften the skins. I have done this with chickpeas, but I do not think it is necessary with other beans, except perhaps dried favas that have not been peeled.

white bean salad
PIYAZ

PARSLEY AND ONION SALADS ARE POPULAR in Turkish cuisine, and this recipe provides an interesting variation on the typical bean salad. Rather than tossing chopped raw onions in with the cooked beans, you use the onion-parsley mixture as a garnish. Hard-boiled eggs are an enrichment, and in summer, sliced tomatoes adorn the beans. In other words, the simple bean salad is the center of the plate and the onions, eggs, and tomatoes are satellites around it. When tomatoes are not in season, a sprinkling of toasted walnuts adds richness and complexity. The salad also takes beautifully to a topping of *boquerones* (page 211).

My preference here is for a dressing made with almost equal parts of oil and vinegar. I suggest you start with a classic red wine vinaigrette and then add more vinegar to taste. Sumac heightens the tartness of the already tart dressing.

> 2 cups cannellini or Great Northern beans, soaked overnight
> 1 teaspoon sea salt
> About 1 cup red wine vinaigrette (page 268)
> 2 small onions, cut in half and sliced paper-thin
> 1/2 cup chopped fresh flat-leaf parsley
> 1/4 cup walnuts, toasted and chopped (optional)
> 3 hard-boiled eggs, quartered
> 3 ripe tomatoes, sliced or quartered (optional)
> Sumac (optional)

Drain the soaked beans and cover them with fresh cold water. Bring to a boil and simmer until tender, about 40 minutes, adding the salt after 15 minutes. Drain and transfer to a bowl or a deep platter. Pour most of the vinaigrette over the beans while they are still hot and toss well.

Place the remaining vinaigrette in a bowl with the onions and parsley and macerate for 15 to 20 minutes, until the onions soften and lose their bite. If you like, add the walnuts to the onion and parsley mixture.

Surround the bean salad with the onion-parsley mixture. Arrange the eggs and the tomatoes, if using, over and around the beans. Sprinkle on some sumac if you like and serve.

ALTERNATE DRESSING:
oregano garlic vinaigrette (page 284).

cannellini beans
with sun-dried tomato vinaigrette

CANNELLINI SALADS ARE OFTEN PART of an antipasto assortment, but they can be served as a course in themselves, as they are rather filling. The most popular version of this salad is the classic combination of oil-packed canned tuna and white beans topped with lots of chopped red onion and parsley and dressed with basic red wine vinaigrette. This version features deeply flavored sun-dried tomato vinaigrette with sweet basil. Of course, if you love the classics, you may use tuna, or even squid, in place of shrimp. Sybarites top simple white bean salads with dollops of caviar; in that delightful and extravagant case, use only lemon and omit the herbs and tomatoes. If you want to play with textural contrasts, serve either the seafood or the bean salad warm.

2 cups cannellini or Great Northern beans
2 quarts (8 cups) water
Sea salt
About 1 1/3 cups sun-dried tomato vinaigrette (page 283)
Freshly ground black pepper
2/3 cup finely chopped red onion
1/2 cup chopped oil-packed sun-dried tomatoes
2 tablespoons finely minced garlic
1 pound medium shrimp, shelled and deveined, or 1 pound tuna fillet,
    or 1 1/2 to 2 pounds squid
1/4 cup thinly slivered fresh basil

To prepare the beans, pick them over, rinse well, place them in a bowl with water to cover generously, and soak overnight. The next day, drain the beans and place in a saucepan with about 2 quarts water. Bring to a boil over medium-high heat. Reduce the heat to low, cover, and simmer until the beans are tender but not soft, about 40 minutes, adding 2 teaspoons salt after 15 minutes of cooking. Remove from the heat; you should have about 3 cups cooked beans.

Drain the beans and transfer to a bowl. While they are still warm, toss with 1/2 cup of the dressing and salt and pepper to taste. Let the beans cool and absorb the flavor of the dressing. When cool, add the onion and more of the remaining dressing, leaving some to drizzle on the seafood.

(continued on next page)

facing page: cannellini beans with
oregano garlic vinaigrette and shrimp

In a saucepan, warm the remaining 1/2 cup dressing with the sun-dried tomatoes and garlic over low heat for just a minute or two to blend the flavors. Add the shrimp and cook in the dressing until they turn pink, turning once, 3 to 5 minutes.

If you are using tuna, brush the fillet lightly with some of the sun-dried tomato vinaigrette and broil for 4 minutes on each side, until cooked but not dry. Cool, then break up into pieces.

If you are using squid, pull the heads from the bodies. Cut off the tentacles just above the eyes and set aside. Push out the little round hard piece (the "beak") in the middle of the tentacles and discard. With a flat side of a knife, push down on the body of the squid to push out the squooshy innards. Discard them and then reach into the cavity, pull out the inner bone, and discard it. Scrape away the skin and wash the bodies well. Pat them dry and cut into 1-inch rings. If the tentacles are large, cut them in half. Bring a pot of lightly salted water to a boil. Drop in the squid, and when they turn white, in about 1 minute, drain them immediately. Then toss them in the warm dressing.

Just before serving, fold the basil into the beans and top with cooked seafood and the last of the sun-dried tomato vinaigrette. Serve warm or at room temperature.

VARIATIONS:

Use 12 ounces canned olive-oil-packed tuna, drained and broken into good-sized pieces, in place of the shrimp. Top the salad with 1/4 cup chopped or shaved red onion.

A similar salad can be prepared with cooked chickpeas.

ALTERNATE DRESSINGS:

In summer you may want to add fresh chopped tomatoes, so skip the sun-dried tomato vinaigrette and dress the beans with **oregano garlic vinaigrette** (page 284), **charmoula vinaigrette** (page 326), **pesto vinaigrette** (page 320), or **red wine vinaigrette** (page 268).

tunisian-inspired chickpea salad
with peppers, capers, and harissa dressing

I LIKE THE CONTRAST OF CRUNCHY chickpeas and velvety roasted peppers in this salad. Because the beans are so neutral, they can work with any number of vinaigrettes: For this salad try garlic vinaigrette (page 269), sherry vinaigrette (page 270), tomato vinaigrette (page 282), oregano garlic vinaigrette (page 284), hot pepper vinaigrette (page 272), charmoula vinaigrette (page 326), or, in this recipe, harissa dressing (page 329). Choose olives that work well with your selected dressing: Spanish arbequinos, oil-cured Moroccan or Italian olives, or Niçoise olives. If you like, you can serve this salad on a bed of bitter greens. You may also top it with grilled tuna or anchovies, drizzling some dressing over the fish.

1 1/2 cups chickpeas, soaked overnight
1 small onion
2 bay leaves
2 cloves garlic
1 teaspoon sea salt
1/4 cup extra-virgin olive oil
3 large red bell peppers, roasted, peeled, and seeded
1/3 cup salt-packed capers, rinsed
1 cup harissa dressing (page 329), plus more if needed
1/2 cup ripe Moroccan black or green olives, for garnish
2 or 3 hard-boiled eggs, quartered, for garnish
Chopped fresh cilantro, for garnish (optional)

Drain and rinse the chickpeas, place in a medium saucepan, and cover with fresh cold water. Put the onion, bay leaves, and garlic in cheesecloth to make a sachet, add, and bring the water to a boil. Reduce the heat and simmer, covered for about 15 minutes. Add the salt and continue to cook for another 20 minutes, or until the chickpeas are done. Drain the beans and discard the sachet. Transfer the beans to a bowl and toss with the olive oil.

Cut the peppers into large dice.

Add the peppers and capers to the beans and toss with the dressing to coat. Garnish the salad with the olives and eggs and with the cilantro, if desired. Serve warm or at room temperature.

ALTERNATE DRESSINGS:
See the headnote for suggestions.

chickpeas with squid and chorizo

THE COMBINATION OF SQUID AND CHORIZO is typical of the Iberian table. Add them to cooked beans—in this case the beloved chickpea, or garbanzo (or you can use white beans)—and you have a dish with a decidedly Spanish flair. It is good if both the chorizo and squid are warm and even better if you warm the beans too.

Do not confuse Spanish chorizo with Mexican chorizo; they are seasoned quite differently. Mexican chorizo is soft and uncooked, flavored with garlic, spices, and red vinegar. Spanish chorizo is dry (like salami or pepperoni) or semidry and flavored with garlic and hot or sweet pimentón, a smoky paprika. Either Spanish chorizo will work with the mild and starchy beans, but the semidry variety is less chewy.

1 cup chickpeas, soaked overnight
1 small onion
1 bay leaf
2 cloves garlic
1 teaspoon sea salt, plus more as needed
About 1 cup tomato vinaigrette (page 282)
2 pounds squid (about 1 pound after cleaning)
4 to 5 ounces semidry Spanish chorizo, sliced 1/4-inch thick
1 red onion, minced
2 red bell peppers, or 1 red and 1 green, diced
Chopped fresh flat-leaf parsley, for garnish

Drain and rinse the chickpeas, place in a medium saucepan, and cover with fresh cold water. Place the onion, bay leaf, and garlic in cheesecloth to make a sachet, add, and bring the water to a boil. Reduce the heat and simmer, covered, for about 15 minutes. Add the 1 teaspoon salt and continue to cook for another 20 to 30 minutes, or until the beans are done. Drain the beans and discard the sachet. Transfer the beans to a bowl and toss with 1/4 cup tomato vinaigrette.

To clean the squid, pull the heads from the bodies. Cut off the tentacles just above the eyes and set aside. Push out the little round hard piece (the "beak") in the middle of the tentacles and discard. With a flat side of a knife, push down on the body of the squid to push out the squooshy innards. Discard them and then reach into the cavity, pull out the inner bone, and discard it too. Scrap away the skin and wash the bodies well.

(continued on next page)

facing page: chickpeas with squid,
chorizo, and tomato vinaigrette

Pat them dry and cut into 1-inch rings. If the tentacles are large, cut them in half.

Bring a pot of lightly salted water to a boil. Drop in the squid, and when they turn white, in about 1 minute, drain immediately. Transfer them to a bowl and toss with 1/4 cup vinaigrette while they are warm. Set aside.

Warm 1/4 cup vinaigrette in a small sauté pan over low heat and add the chorizo. Simmer a few minutes so it releases its flavor into the dressing. If you are using dry chorizo, it will take a little more time to soften.

Combine the chickpeas, red onion, peppers, squid, and chorizo in a large bowl and toss with the remaining vinaigrette if needed. Garnish with the chopped parsley. Serve warm.

ALTERNATE DRESSINGS:
oregano garlic vinaigrette (page 284),
hot pepper vinaigrette (page 272).

lentil salad

serves 4

UNLIKE CHICKPEAS AND CANNELLINI BEANS, lentils require no soaking. I recommend using green lentils, because they hold their shape after cooking. Brown or red lentils are trickier. They can become soft and mushy in a matter of moments. That's fine if you are making soup but not so great for salads, where toothsome texture is important. The best green lentils are from Le Puy in France or from the Italian region of Umbria.

Just by your choice of dressing or garnish, you can take this salad in many different directions. Mint vinaigrette is often my first choice, but see the alternate dressings for delicious options.

> 2 cups green lentils, rinsed
> Sea salt
> 3 tablespoons olive oil
> 1 1/2 cups diced onions
> 1/2 cup diced carrots
> 1/3 cup diced celery
> 1 teaspoon minced garlic
> Freshly ground black pepper
> About 1 cup mint vinaigrette (page 280)
> 1/4 pound feta cheese, crumbled (optional)

Place the lentils in a saucepan with water to cover them by 2 inches. Bring to a boil, reduce the heat, and simmer gently, covered, until tender but not soft, adding 2 teaspoons salt after the lentils have begun to simmer. You want them to be tender but not mushy. Timing will vary according to their age; they can take 25 to 45 minutes to become tender.

While the lentils cook, heat the olive oil in a sauté pan or skillet over medium heat. Add the onion, carrots, and celery and cook until tender, 8 to 10 minutes. Add the garlic and cook a minute or two longer. Remove the pan from the heat and let cool.

When the lentils are cooked, drain and place in a salad bowl. Add the cooled vegetable mixture and toss to combine. Season with salt and pepper to taste and dress the salad while the lentils are still warm. Top with the feta cheese if desired and serve immediately.

(continued on next page)

ALTERNATE DRESSINGS:

For a flavor of Turkey and the Middle East, use **toasted cumin citrus dressing** (page 301) and garnish with tomato wedges, oil-cured black olives, and crumbled feta cheese.

For a Greek accent, use **oregano garlic vinaigrette** (page 284), 1/2 cup oil-cured olives, and 2 tablespoons capers, rinsed.

For a French flavor, use **red wine vinaigrette** (page 268) or **garlic vinaigrette** (page 269) and goat cheese instead of feta.

For a Spanish accent, use **sherry vinaigrette** (page 270) and add diced pancetta or chopped chorizo sausage to the vegetables when sautéing.

bean puree with toasted cumin dressing
BESSARA

IN THE MEDITERRANEAN, beans are not only used for salads but also mashed or pureed and used as spreads. This North African bean dip is meant to be eaten with crackers or pita bread.

1 1/2 cups dried fava or large white beans, soaked overnight
A few garlic cloves, peeled
1/4 to 1/2 cup toasted cumin citrus dressing (page 301)
Sea salt
Sesame seeds, for garnish (optional)

After soaking the favas, remove the wrinkly skins. (Some dried favas come peeled, so shop carefully; you could save some time here.) Drain them, put in a saucepan, and cover with fresh water. Add the garlic cloves and bring to a boil. Reduce the heat to low and simmer until the beans are very, very tender. This can take 1 hour or longer.

Drain the beans and mash or pulse in a food processor. Add the cumin dressing gradually as you mash. Salt the puree to taste and place in a serving dish. Sprinkle sesame seeds on top if you like and serve with pita bread.

VARIATIONS:

In Greece, people serve pureed yellow split peas (which they call fava) the same way. Cook and puree the split peas and serve topped with **basic citrus dressing** (page 268). Garnish with shaved red onions and maybe some chopped fresh dill. You can also cook fresh favas and puree them. Serve with chopped cooked greens on grilled bread.

Or mash the beans with **oregano garlic vinaigrette** (page 284) and spread on grilled bread. Top with a slice of prosciutto or salami if you like.

ALTERNATE DRESSING:
charmoula vinaigrette (page 326).

chickpeas with tahini dressing
HUMMUS BA TAHINI

HUMMUS IS A CLASSIC BEAN SPREAD, popular as a meze in Syria, Lebanon, Egypt, and Israel. It has become a staple on supermarket food-to-go shelves and is often "enhanced" with other ingredients, such as roasted peppers, spinach, and tomatoes. I prefer to make my own so I can control the texture and the amount of tartness and garlic. Commercial versions are never tart enough for me and often have a sludgy consistency. Serve hummus with pita bread or with cucumbers, radishes, carrots, and green onions.

1 cup dried chickpeas, soaked overnight
Sea salt
1 cup tahini dressing (page 303), plus more if needed
Cayenne

OPTIONAL GARNISHES
2 tablespoons extra-virgin olive oil
3 tablespoons chopped fresh flat-leaf parsley
3 tablespoons pomegranate seeds
1/2 teaspoon ground cumin
1/4 teaspoon cayenne or 1/2 teaspoon Aleppo pepper

Drain and rinse the chickpeas, place in a large saucepan, and cover with cold water. Bring to a boil, then reduce the heat to low and simmer, covered, until the beans are very soft, 1 hour or longer. Add 1 teaspoon salt after the chickpeas have simmered for about 15 minutes. When they are soft, transfer them to the container of a food processor, reserving the cooking liquid.

Pulse the chickpeas with 1/4 cup cooking liquid to make a puree. Add the tahini dressing and puree again. Add enough cold water to achieve a spreadable consistency and season with salt and a pinch of cayenne.

If you are serving the hummus right away, spoon it onto a shallow plate and smooth it with a spoon or spatula. Sprinkle with your choice of olive oil, parsley, pomegranate seeds, cumin, or cayenne. Serve with pita bread.

NOTE: *To store the hummus, transfer it to a container and refrigerate. Before serving, whisk with a fork. It probably will have thickened, so thin it with reserved cooking liquids or water. Then spread it on a shallow plate and serve as above. Hummus keeps for 3 or 4 days in the refrigerator.*

chickpea croquettes
FALAFEL

FALAFEL ORIGINATED IN EGYPT, but today they are popular street food in Syria, Lebanon, and Israel. Tuck these crunchy croquettes into warm pita bread along with chopped tomato and cucumber and add a good drizzle of tahini dressing. Some recipes say all you need to do is soak the chickpeas but not cook them; others say to cook them partway so they are tender but still firm. That's the way I like them.

2 cups partially cooked chickpeas
1 slice firm white bread, crust removed
2 tablespoons flour, plus more for dipping
1/2 teaspoon baking soda
3 cloves garlic, finely minced
1 egg, lightly beaten
3 tablespoons chopped fresh flat-leaf parsley
1 teaspoon cumin seeds, ground and toasted
1 teaspoon ground coriander
1/2 teaspoon freshly ground black pepper
1/2 teaspoon cayenne
1/2 teaspoon turmeric
Sea salt
Water as needed to bind the mixture
Olive oil
8 pita breads, warmed
2 cups diced tomatoes (2 medium tomatoes)
2 cups peeled, seeded, and diced cucumbers (2 regular or 1 English cucumber)
1 cup tahini dressing (page 303)

Grind the chickpeas with the coarse blade of a meat grinder or pulse in a food processor until coarsely ground. Place in a large bowl and add the bread, 2 tablespoons flour, baking soda, garlic, egg, parsley, spices, and salt to taste. Mix well. If the mixture does not hold together, add a little water to bind the ingredients. Form the mixture into balls that are 1 1/2 inches in diameter, and flatten them slightly with your hand.

Pour olive oil to a depth of 3 inches into a wok or a deep saucepan and heat to 365 degrees F.

(continued on next page)

Dip the falafel into flour and deep-fry in batches until golden and crunchy, about 4 minutes. Drain on paper towels.

To serve, warm the pita breads in a microwave oven for 50 seconds. (I keep them in the plastic bag.) Microwaving gives the bread a distinctive chewy texture. You also can wrap the breads in foil and steam them in the top of a double boiler until warm, about 5 minutes. You can warm them in the oven, but they will not be chewy.

Cut each bread in half crosswise. Push your finger gently into the cut side of each half to open the pocket. Spoon in about 2 tablespoons each of chopped tomatoes and cucumber and some of the tahini dressing. Then slip in a falafel. You may want to spoon a little more tahini over the falafel. Serve warm.

from the sea

SEAFOOD IS FOUND IN abundance in Mediterranean waters and on the Mediterranean table. In this chapter you'll find fish and seafood in many modes: raw, marinated, and cooked.

The first recipes include raw seafood in the form of carpaccio, tartare, and *crudo*. In Italy, years before the now ubiquitous fish tartares and fish carpaccios hit every fashionable restaurant menu, there was simply *pesce crudo*, or sliced raw fish. Italian fishermen and home cooks often served thin slices of impeccably fresh swordfish, bass, hake, turbot, tuna, or mackerel drizzled with extra-virgin olive oil and lemon juice. Today, plates of artfully dressed raw fish are a hot item in our restaurants. Called *crudo*, they have been give new life and attention, bathed in the exotic Japanese aura of "*susci*."

Next are dishes of cooked or marinated oily fish with tart vinegar-based dressings. Oily fish, sometimes called "blue fish" (not the same as the East Coast fish of the same name), are prized in the Mediterranean. Some American diners find them . . . ahem, kind of fishy and prefer mild white fish that taste like chicken. But if you try these recipes, you will become a convert. While most delicate seafood salads do best with a citrus dressing, when it comes to assertive-tasting oily fish, vinaigrette is better to tame the richness and strong flavors.

Recipes for warm shellfish dishes, as well as those served lightly chilled, follow. Composed fish and seafood plates are also included. For example, I combine cooked salmon or shrimp with baby green beans and roasted new potatoes in a garlicky pesto vinaigrette, but you might easily choose tarragon mayonnaise or lemon mustard cream dressing instead. Depending on your mood, you might dress a plate of cooked tuna, green beans, cherry tomatoes, and potatoes with mint vinaigrette, remoulade mayonnaise, or anchovy, garlic, tapenade, or charmoula vinaigrette. Spring asparagus served with seafood and potatoes might be dressed with lemon or tarragon mustard cream or Catalan or romesco dressing. In winter, a plate of tuna or shrimp with broccoli and potatoes might be topped with sun-dried tomato vinaigrette, oregano garlic vinaigrette, tapenade, or anchovy garlic vinaigrette.

You will also find in this chapter a few hot seafood and fish dishes that use salad dressings as marinades and finishing sauces. As many chefs and home cooks have discovered, salad dressings are not just for salads. With their bright acidity, citrus dressings and vinaigrettes add liveliness when drizzled over a piece of grilled fish or a bland chicken breast. They are also superb marinades for kebabs, for fish, and for poultry and lamb. After a few hours in a citrus dressing or vinaigrette, the protein is tender and infused with flavor. Just grill and serve with a drizzle of reserved vinaigrette.

Vinaigrettes and citrus dressings are lighter in body than most pan sauces. With diners seeking healthy dietary alternatives yet still demanding full flavor intensity, one solution is to use vinaigrettes as sauces. No need to reduce a pan sauce or thicken it with butter when you can spoon on a bit of emulsified salad dressing for an illusion of richness.

fish carpaccio

CARPACCIO DI PESCE

serves 4

MOST OF US ASSOCIATE the term *carpaccio* with thin slices of raw beef. Beef carpaccio was created at Harry's Bar in Venice in 1950, the year of a major exhibition of the works of the famed Venetian painter Vittore Carpaccio, whose paintings adorn the church of San Giorgio degli Schiavoni. Legend has it that the dish was created for a frequent guest whose doctor had placed her on a diet forbidding cooked meat. So today sliced raw beef is commonly called by the more modern name carpaccio instead of *carne cruda*. Carpaccio di pesce follows a similar concept but is prepared with thin slices of fish, *pesce crudo*.

Some fish need to spend a bit of time in a marinade to partially "cure" and become fork-tender. Tuna is almost always my first choice for carpaccio, as it doesn't need to marinate, but buttery slices of Alaskan halibut or salmon are good too, as are shrimp and scallops. They just need a little extra time to absorb the dressing.

> Four (1/3-inch thick) slices ahi tuna, Alaskan halibut, or
>   salmon (3 ounces each)
> 2 bunches watercress or young, tender arugula, tough stems removed
> About 1/2 cup mustard shallot citrus dressing (page 292)
> 10 to 12 black or red radishes or 1/2 daikon, sliced paper-thin
> Sea salt or fleur de sel
> 2 tablespoons chopped fresh chives, for garnish

Place each slice of tuna between 2 sheets of lightly oiled parchment paper or plastic wrap and pound very gently, smoothing the fish with a circular motion, to a uniform thickness of 1/8 inch. The fish is already tender, so don't be too exuberant. You don't want to make holes. Refrigerate, still in oiled paper, until needed.

To serve, toss the watercress or arugula in a bowl with a few spoonfuls of the dressing. Arrange the greens in a circular pattern on 4 salad plates. Arrange the radish slices on the greens, placing them at the outer edges of each plate. Take the fish out of the refrigerator and peel away the top sheet of paper from each slice. Invert the fish carefully onto the greens. Push the fish down onto each plate with the heel of your hand. Peel away the second sheet of oiled paper and drizzle the remaining dressing on top. It is crucial to sprinkle the fish lightly with good salt, or it will taste flat; plus the salt delivers a delightful crunch. Sprinkle with the chopped chives and serve immediately.

(continued on next page)

ALTERNATE DRESSINGS:
caper and garlic citrus dressing (page 291),
preserved lemon dressing (page 299),
hot pepper citrus dressing (page 295).

NOTE: *For halibut or salmon, pound as directed, remove the parchment or plastic, and put the fish on the serving plates without any greens or radishes. Marinate the fish in some of the vinaigrette for about 15 minutes to partially cure it. Then tuck the dressed radishes and greens around the fish just before serving.*

arugula

scallop carpaccio
with meyer lemon dressing

I LOVE SCALLOPS BARELY COOKED, so a carpaccio treatment, where they briefly cure in a citrus dressing, suits my palate. For a sexy contrast in texture I like to add creamy slices of avocado to this dish. While you don't really need the greens, they do add textural contrast. In modern chefs' style they would be perched on the scallops like a curly green hat, but you can place them on the side.

> 6 to 8 large sea scallops (see page 217)
> 3 green onions (white and green parts) or 1 small spring bulb onion, sliced crosswise paper-thin
> 1/2 cup basic citrus dressing (page 290) made with Meyer lemons (see page 288)
> 1 avocado, halved, pit removed, peeled, and thinly sliced
> Sea salt or fleur de sel
> 1/2 cup microgreens or 1 cup mesclun

Remove the foot muscle from each scallop and then cut the scallops crosswise into slices about 1/8-inch thick. Arrange the slices on individual plates, in a single layer if possible, and top with the slices of onion.

Spoon 3 to 4 tablespoons of the dressing on top, dividing it equally among the servings, and cover the plates with plastic wrap. Chill for 2 to 3 hours.

Remove the plates from the refrigerator and place the avocado slices around the scallops. Drizzle lightly with half of the remaining dressing and sprinkle with salt.

Toss the microgreens or mesclun with the last of the dressing. Place a little on each plate with the scallops. Top the scallops with a pinch of sea salt just before serving and serve cold.

VARIATION:

Alternate scallop slices with very thin slices of orange and drizzle with **hot pepper citrus dressing** (page 295). Refrigerate for 2 to 3 hours.

tuna tartare

TAKING ITS NAME FROM STEAK TARTARE, raw fish cut into tiny cubes is called fish tartare. It is presented the same way as the beef, mounded on a plate and accompanied by a few crostini or pieces of toast.

> 1 pound top-quality raw tuna, cut into 1/4-inch dice
> 2 tablespoons minced green onion (white and green parts)
> 1/4 cup finely minced red onion
> 1 1/2 tablespoons minced hot chili or to taste (optional)
> 1/2 cup basic citrus dressing (page 290) or caper and garlic citrus dressing (page 291)
> Sea salt and freshly ground black pepper

In a bowl, mix the tuna with the green and red onions and the chili, if using. Add the citrus dressing, toss, and season the mixture amply to taste with salt and coarsely ground black pepper.

Mound the tartare on a serving plate. Surround it with crostini, toast, or crisp flatbread and a lemon wedge, if you like.

VARIATION:
You can make this dish with salmon instead of tuna.

ALTERNATE DRESSINGS:
lemon mayonnaise dressing (page 316),
or **hot pepper citrus dressing** (page 295),
omitting the chili pepper in the recipe.

marinated anchovies
BOQUERONES

BOQUERONES ARE A PART of almost every tapas assortment. These fresh small anchovies are marinated in a tart vinaigrette and served as is, on a plate or with a lettuce salad, or on croutons. If you don't want to make them from scratch, you can find them in plastic packs in delicatessen cold cases. They are perfect placed on a salad of roasted peppers or on grilled bread.

1 pound fresh anchovies
Kosher salt
About 3/4 cup garlic vinaigrette (page 269)
1 red onion, sliced paper-thin
3 tablespoons chopped fresh flat-leaf parsley
Freshly ground black pepper

Sprinkle the anchovies with kosher salt and leave in the refrigerator overnight.

Remove the fish from the refrigerator and use a sharp knife to slit them up the belly. Remove the bones and heads and discard. Place the anchovies in a shallow container and cover with vinaigrette. Marinate for 45 minutes at room temperature.

Place the onion slices in a bowl, spoon some of the remaining vinaigrette on top, and let sit for 15 minutes.

Divide the onions among 4 serving plates. Place the anchovies on top and sprinkle with the parsley and pepper. Serve immediately.

marinated fish
ESCABECHE

ESCABECHE IS A CLASSIC STARTER DISH in Portugal and Spain. Its name is derived from the Arabic *sikbaj*, or vinegar stew. In Italy it may be called *scapece*. In the days before refrigeration, *escabeche* was usually prepared with meat. (In Piedmont, I tasted an *escabeche* made with chicken, and because the chicken had no real fat, the dish was dry.) Today it has evolved into a dish of pickled fish. Small oily fish such as sardines and small mackerel are traditional, as they take to the marinade particularly well and develop a smooth, velvety texture. Fatty tuna is also an option. You can substitute fillets of a firm white fish, although they will take the marinade in a totally different manner and will not achieve a voluptuous texture. For maximum flavor, let the fish marinate for a day before serving.

1 1/2 pounds oily fish fillets or 12 to 18 sardines, cleaned and deboned
Kosher salt
1/3 cup extra-virgin olive oil
2 or 3 white onions, sliced paper-thin
2 carrots, peeled and grated (optional)
2 or 3 cloves garlic, smashed
2 small bay leaves, torn up
3/4 cup basic vinaigrette made with 1/4 cup oil and 1/2 cup white vinegar
   (page 268)
2 teaspoons sea salt
Freshly ground black pepper
1 teaspoon paprika (optional)
Paper-thin slices of lemon (optional)
Chopped fresh cilantro (optional)

Sprinkle the fish with kosher salt and let sit for about 15 minutes.

Heat 2 tablespoons olive oil in a large skillet and sauté the fish in batches over moderate heat, turning once, until it is golden and is done when probed with a knife, about 8 minutes total (sardines will take less time). Repeat, adding 2 more tablespoons oil, until all the fish is cooked. Set the fish aside and wipe out the pan.

Heat the remaining 2 tablespoons of oil over medium-high heat and cook the onions until limp, about 5 minutes. Add the carrots, if using, and the garlic, bay leaves, vinaigrette, sea salt, pepper to taste, and paprika, if using, and let bubble for a minute or two. Remove from the heat and let cool. Toss in the lemon and cilantro if you like.

Arrange the fish and the onion mixture in alternating layers on a deep platter. Cover with plastic wrap and chill for 2 days. Serve cold.

catalan salt cod and pepper salad
ESQUEIXADA

INSTEAD OF USING STRONG-TASTING fresh fish, this wonderful salad is based on dried salt cod. Most traditional versions of the recipe tell you to soak the cod but not cook it. For this to succeed, you need top-quality salt cod, which is easy to find in the markets of Spain and Portugal (even presoaked!) but rarely available in our Italian delicatessens, where it is called *baccala*, or our supermarkets. Most of the salt cod at our markets comes from Canada. Whether crammed into little wooden boxes or stored in plastic bags, it has neither uniform thickness nor pure whiteness of color. My solution is to cook the cod and select the best parts.

This recipe is a cross between the traditional *esqueixada* and a chopped salad called *rin ran* from the town of Jaen in Andalusia, which combines cooked salt cod, potatoes, peppers, and olives. Some versions use roasted peppers instead of fresh ones, and others replace the salt cod with canned tuna. In the Basque provinces and in Portugal, grilled sardines are placed on a similar salad of green or red peppers and potatoes and garnished with sliced tomatoes.

1 pound salt cod
1 pound little new potatoes
2 large red bell peppers, seeded and diced
1 cup green olives, pitted and coarsely chopped
1 small red onion, minced (optional)
1/2 cup sherry vinaigrette (page 270)
Sea salt and freshly ground black pepper
4 tablespoons coarsely chopped fresh flat-leaf parsley, for garnish

Soak the cod in cold water for 2 days, changing the water at least 4 times. Drain and place in a small saucepan and cover with fresh cold water. Bring slowly to a simmer and cook gently for 10 to 15 minutes, or until the cod is very tender. Drain, and when the cod is cool enough to handle, shred it with your fingers, discarding any hard pieces, skin, and bone. You will probably end up with 1/2 to 3/4 pound of fish. Place in a bowl and set aside.

In a large saucepan, cook the potatoes in lightly salted water, over medium heat until they are just done, tender but firm enough to slice, 20 to 25 minutes. Rinse with cold water to stop the cooking. Cool the potatoes, then peel and dice them.

Combine the cod, diced potatoes, diced peppers, olives, and onion, if using, in a salad bowl. Dress the salad with the vinaigrette, season to taste with salt and pepper, and garnish with parsley.

ALTERNATE DRESSINGS:
garlic vinaigrette (page 269),
toasted cumin citrus dressing (page 301).

smoked trout, carrots, and cucumbers

ALTHOUGH SMOKED TROUT IS FORWARD in flavor, it does well with creamy or citrus-based dressings rather than more assertive vinaigrettes. This recipe is inspired by one from the Veneto. Sweet, smoky, and bitter flavors come together in a most amazing way because of the citrus dressing. If fennel is in season, you may use it in place of the cucumbers. You may also use avocado slices in place of the carrots. They add a creamy element and do well with the citrus dressing.

Slice the carrots and cucumbers or fennel with a mandoline for uniformly thin slices. If you want the carrots to curl, soak them in ice water. You can also add slices of black radish to the mix.

> 2 small bunches watercress, stems removed
> 1/2 cup mixed citrus dressing I (page 293)
> 2 cups very thinly sliced carrots
> 2 cups thinly sliced cucumbers
> 2 smoked trout, skin and bones carefully removed
> Fresh fennel fronds or chopped fresh flat-leaf parsley, for garnish

Toss the watercress with some of the dressing and distribute among 4 salad plates. Toss the carrots and cucumbers with some of the dressing and place them over the watercress. Break the smoked trout into pieces and arranged them on top. Drizzle with the remaining vinaigrette. Sprinkle with the fennel fronds or chopped parsley and serve.

ALTERNATE DRESSINGS:
lemon cream dressing (page 308),
caper and garlic citrus dressing (page 291).

smoked trout salad
with lemon cream dressing

THIS VARIATION ON TROUT with a basic horseradish cream comes from Treviso in the Veneto. Here the beets are sweet, the radicchio and horse-radish add the bitter element, and the neutral potatoes set off the smokiness of the trout, all tied together harmoniously by the lemon cream dressing. If you want to play up the sweetness, add a few pieces of apple. And if you want another bitter accent and some crunch, add toasted walnuts.

> 1/4 cup very finely minced white onion
> 2 tablespoons finely pureed fresh horseradish
> 1/2 cup lemon cream dressing (page 308)
> 1/4 cup diced tart apple (optional)
> 1/4 cup walnuts, toasted (optional)
> Sea salt and freshly ground black pepper
> 3 heads Treviso radicchio, leaves separated or cut into fine shreds
> 2 smoked trout, skin and bones carefully removed
> 8 little new potatoes, cooked and sliced
> 4 small beets, cooked and sliced

In a small bowl, stir the onion and horseradish into the lemon cream dressing. Add apple or walnuts if desired and season to taste with salt and pepper.

In a large bowl, toss the radicchio with some of the dressing. Divide among 4 salad plates. Break the trout into fillets and arrange with the potatoes and beets on top of the dressed greens. Drizzle with the remaining dressing and serve.

ALTERNATE DRESSING:
Omit the horseradish and use
lemon mustard cream dressing (page 308).

NOTE: *To obtain 2 tablespoons finely pureed horseradish, take 1/4 cup of small chunks of horseradish, peeled and sliced across the grain, and puree in a food processor with 1/4 cup distilled white vinegar. If you have a large processor, you may have to process more to get enough. Masochists can grate the horseradish by hand with a fine grater. Or use bottled horseradish to taste.*

warm scallop, orange, and fennel salad with peppery citrus dressing

serves 4

WITH WARM SALADS, it's all about texture and contrast. Here we play cool greens and fruits against warm shellfish. This classic dish combines crunchy anise-flavored fennel and sweet-tart oranges with sweet scallops. Hot pepper citrus dressing adds a subtle bite to enliven the sweet components. You can try tangerines instead of oranges, but they are a bit more difficult to cut into segments as the membrane is tougher.

> 3 navel oranges
> 2 bulbs fennel
> About 3/4 cup hot pepper citrus dressing (page 295)
> 1 pound sea scallops (3 to 4 per person; see page 217)
> 1 head butter lettuce
> Extra-virgin olive oil (optional)
> 1 cup dry white wine (optional)

Working with 1 orange at a time, cut a thin slice off the top and bottom to reveal the flesh. Stand the orange upright and remove the peel in wide strips, cutting downward and following the contour of the fruit. Cut the flesh crosswise into 1/4-inch-thick slices and remove the seeds with a toothpick or the tip of a paring knife. Or, working over a small bowl, cut between the membranes with a sharp knife to separate the orange into segments, letting them fall into the bowl. Squeeze the membranes over the segments to collect any extra juice, which you can add to the dressing.

Cut the bulbs of fennel in half and cut away the tough bottom part of the cores. Discard any tough or discolored outer leaves. Slice the fennel very thin with a mandoline. Toss with 1/4 cup of the dressing.

Remove the foot muscle attached to the side of each scallop. You have a choice of cooking technique: grilling, sautéing, or poaching. To grill or broil the scallops; arrange them on skewers and brush with olive oil. Grill about 2 minutes per side. To sauté, cook the scallops in olive oil over high heat, turning once, until pale gold, about 2 minutes per side. To poach, bring dry white wine or part wine and part water to a simmer in a shallow saucepan. Slip in the scallops and simmer gently until just barely cooked, about 2 minutes. Drain.

Tear the lettuce into bite-sized pieces. Place them in a large salad bowl and toss with 1/4 cup of the dressing, then distribute them among 4 salad plates. Top with the fennel. Then distribute the orange slices or segments and the warm scallops on top and drizzle with the remaining 1/4 cup dressing. Serve immediately.

VARIATION:
You can use shrimp instead of scallops.

ALTERNATE DRESSINGS:
Because the scallops and oranges are sweet, for a note of contrast you may want to add a few leaves of bitter greens such as Belgian endive or chicory along with the butter lettuce and use **catalan vinaigrette** (page 278). Or use **citrus and black pepper dressing** (page 295).

BUYING SCALLOPS

Fresh sea scallops are sweet and rich, with a sensual, almost fleshy texture. When shopping, try to buy scallops that have not been soaked in a solution of sodium tripolyphosphate (STP). This practice is not illegal, but it loads the scallops with extra water; scallops that have been soaked in STP feel slippery and lose their sweet smell, and they sit in a milky white liquid. High-quality unsoaked scallops, in contrast, have a fresh sheen and are creamy white to beige in color, and any surrounding liquid is clear.

warm salad of scallops, mushrooms, and catalan vinaigrette

SCALLOPS ARE SWEET AND RICH, with a sensual, almost fleshy texture. Contrast them with mild crisp mushrooms and bitter arugula in a warm dressing enriched with sweet toasty almonds and you have a very complex and seductive salad. The first few times I made this, I sautéed the mushrooms along with the scallops, but I found that the softened mushrooms lost presence. I decided to keep them crisp, in contrast with the tender scallops.

To make the balance work, you need a note of citrus in the vinaigrette; here the sweetness of orange plays up the sweetness of the scallops. Citrus is not deep enough, however, to hold the arugula in check. For this you need the deeper acidity that nutty sherry vinegar provides. It also echoes the toasted almonds. Even though the dressing has anchovies and capers, be sure to salt this salad enough or it will fall flat.

> 1 1/2 cups thinly sliced white or cremini mushrooms
> 3/4 cup Catalan vinaigrette (page 278)
> About 4 handfuls of arugula, small leaves preferred (about 1/3 pound)
> Sea salt
> 16 large or 24 small sea scallops (see page 217), foot muscles removed

Toss the mushrooms in a bowl with about 1/4 cup of the vinaigrette.

Place the arugula in a large salad bowl. Salt it lightly.

Sprinkle the scallops with salt. Warm 1/2 cup vinaigrette in a large sauté pan and cook the scallops quickly, until they become opaque but are still quite soft and tender, even quivery, about 3 minutes.

Add the mushrooms to the arugula and toss well. Arrange on 4 salad plates. Top with the warm scallops and their vinaigrette. Serve while the scallops are still warm.

ALTERNATE DRESSING:
hazelnut vinaigrette (page 273),
adding a few chopped hazelnuts.

shrimp and artichokes
with romesco vinaigrette

I LIKE TO SERVE THIS SALAD when both the shrimp and the artichokes are still warm. The crunchy shrimp are a fine contrast to the creamy artichokes, and both are brightened by the piquant romesco vinaigrette.

3 lemons
6 artichokes
1/2 cup olive oil
2 cloves garlic, minced
4 tablespoons chopped fresh flat-leaf parsley
Water
Sea salt and freshly ground black pepper
1 pound large shrimp, peeled and deveined
About 3/4 cup romesco vinaigrette (page 325)

Have ready a large bowl of water to which you have added the juice of 1 lemon. Trim the artichokes by cutting off the stems flush with the bottoms. Remove all the leaves from the artichokes, scoop out the fuzzy chokes with a melon ball scoop, and place the artichoke hearts in the lemon water.

Warm 4 tablespoons olive oil in a large saucepan over medium heat.

In a small bowl, mix together the garlic and parsley. Place the artichoke hearts, facing up, on a flat surface and fill the centers with the garlic and parsley mixture. Scrub 1 lemon (preferably small) and cut it into 6 pieces. Place 1 piece on top of each artichoke and place the artichokes carefully in the saucepan. Add the juice of the remaining lemon and enough water to just cover the artichokes. Sprinkle with salt and pepper to taste, turn the heat to low, and simmer, covered, for about 25 minutes. Check the liquid from time to time, adding a bit of water if necessary. When the artichokes are tender, carefully remove them from the cooking liquid and distribute among 6 salad plates.

Heat the remaining 4 tablespoons olive oil in a large sauté pan and sauté the shrimp quickly, tossing them over medium heat, until they turn pink, about 2 or 3 minutes.

When the shrimp are cooked, arrange them over the artichoke hearts. Spoon on the romesco vinaigrette and serve immediately.

ALTERNATE DRESSINGS:
tarragon mustard cream dressing (page 310),
lemon mayonnaise dressing (page 316),
catalan vinaigrette (page 278),
preserved lemon dressing (page 299).

grilled squid stuffed with rice and shrimp

NOW THAT SQUID ARE KNOWN as calamari, it's much easier to sell them to the American public. Granted, these are not battered and fried, but they are truly delicious. All of the Mediterranean countries have recipes for stuffed squid. Bread is usually used in Italy and France, and rice is the basis of the filling in Greece and Turkey.

There is no middle ground when cooking squid. You either cook them in a matter of moments or you cook them a long time; otherwise they will be tough and rubbery. For this dish you want to grill them quickly. Allow 2 or 3 small squid per person, and if you like, serve them on a bed of *horta* (page 67). Avoid large squid, because they will not be really tender.

> 1 1/2 pounds small to medium squid
> 5 tablespoons olive oil
> 1/2 pound small shrimp, shelled, deveined, and coarsely chopped
> 1/2 cup diced yellow onion
> 1 teaspoon minced garlic
> 1/2 cup long-grain rice, such as basmati
> 1 cup hot water
> 1/8 teaspoon crushed saffron filaments steeped in 2 tablespoons white
>   wine
> 2 tablespoons toasted pine nuts
> 2 or 3 tablespoons currants, plumped in hot water (optional)
> Freshly grated zest of 1 large lemon
> 2 tablespoons chopped fresh flat-leaf parsley
> 1 to 2 tablespoons chopped fresh dill
> Sea salt and freshly ground black pepper
> 1/2 cup caper and garlic citrus dressing (page 291)

To clean the squid, pull the heads from the bodies. Cut off the tentacles just above the eyes, and set aside. Push out the little round hard piece (the "beak") in the middle of the tentacles and discard. With a flat side of a knife, push down on the body of the squid to push out the squooshy innards. Discard them and then reach into the cavity, pull out the inner bone, and discard it. Scrape away the skin and wash the bodies well. Pat them dry. Chop the tentacles.

Warm 2 tablespoons olive oil in a medium sauté pan over moderate heat. Add the tentacles and chopped shrimp and sauté for 1 to 2 minutes. Remove from the pan and set aside.

Add 2 more tablespoons olive oil to the pan and sauté the onion until tender, about 8 minutes. Add the garlic and sauté for 1 minute. Add the rice, water, and saffron infusion, stir well, and bring to a boil. Reduce the heat to low and cook, covered, until the rice has absorbed all the liquids, about 20 minutes. Stir in the shrimp and tentacles, pine nuts, currants if using, lemon zest, parsley, and dill. Season with salt and pepper to taste. Cool the rice filling.

When the filling is cool, stuff it into the squid bodies and skewer them closed with toothpicks. You can do this a few hours before serving them and keep them in the refrigerator.

To serve, preheat a broiler or gas grill or make a fire in the charcoal grill. Thread the stuffed squid onto soaked wooden skewers.

Brush them with the remaining 1 tablespoon olive oil, sprinkle with salt and pepper, and grill quickly, until they turn white, a few minutes on each side. Place on a platter and drizzle with caper citrus dressing. Serve immediately.

ALTERNATE DRESSINGS:
oregano garlic vinaigrette (page 284),
hot pepper citrus dressing (page 295).

salt cod–stuffed peppers basque style
PIQUILLOS RELLENOS DE BACALAO

PIQUILLO PEPPERS ARE A SPECIALTY of the region of Navarra in Spain. They are roasted over wood fires and peeled by hand, never washed. Then they are hand-packed into jars or cans. Their name means "little beak," because they are pointy and triangular in shape. Piquillos are not spicy but have a rich, deep sweetness. Because of their size and shape, they are ideal for stuffing. I've eaten them filled with cheese, chorizo, blood sausage, and seafood. This dish of salt cod–stuffed peppers is from the Basque provinces. The peppers are often served warm, bathed in a savory mild tomato sauce, but they can be served at room temperature dressed with a tomato vinaigrette. You can also make the filling with regular cod or another tender white fish, or even crabmeat.

- 1 pound salt cod
- 6 tablespoons extra-virgin olive oil
- 2 large onions, finely chopped
- 3 cloves garlic, minced
- 1 cup bread crumbs, soaked in milk and squeezed dry
- Sea salt and freshly ground black pepper
- 2 egg yolks
- 1/4 cup chopped fresh flat-leaf parsley
- 16 roasted piquillo peppers or 8 large roasted pimiento peppers
- About 1 1/2 cups tomato vinaigrette (page 282)

Soak the cod in cold water for 1 or 2 days, changing the water 3 times. Drain, place in a skillet, and cover with cold water. Very slowly, over low heat, bring the water to a simmer. Remove the skillet from the heat when it comes to a boil and let cool. When the cod is cool enough to handle, break it into small pieces with your fingers. Discard any skin, bones, and tough and discolored pieces.

In another skillet, heat the olive oil and sauté the onion and garlic over moderate heat for about 8 minutes. Add the cod and then the milk-soaked bread crumbs. Season with salt and pepper to taste and cook gently, stirring from time to time until well mixed and softened. Remove from the heat. Let cool a bit and then stir in the egg yolks and 2 tablespoons chopped parsley. Cool the mixture completely.

Cut a slit on one side each of pepper and carefully remove the seeds. Stuff the peppers with the cooled cod mixture and press them closed. They will not need a toothpick to seal them, as they hold the filling unaided. If you like, briefly warm them over low heat in a sauté pan. Arrange on 8 salad plates or a platter, drizzle with tomato vinaigrette, and sprinkle with the remaining 2 tablespoon parsley. Serve warm or at room temperature.

ALTERNATE DRESSING:
lemon mayonnaise dressing (page 316).

shrimp salad with tarator dressing

SWEET SHRIMP ARE A LOVELY CONTRAST to crunchy cucumbers and greens, salty cheese, and bitter walnuts. If you find the bitter aspects of this dish too potent for your palate, you can omit the walnuts and increase the lemon juice in the dressing. If you want to highlight the sweetness, increase the mint and add a little salt.

1 pound medium shrimp, shelled and deveined
3/4 cup walnut tarator dressing (page 305)
4 cups coarsely chopped romaine
1 cup chopped fresh flat-leaf parsley leaves
1/2 cup fresh mint leaves
1 English cucumber, peeled, seeded, and sliced or diced
1/2 cup walnuts, toasted and chopped, for garnish (optional)
1/4 pound feta cheese, crumbled, for garnish (optional)

In a large sauté pan, cook the shrimp in simmering salted water to cover until they turn pink, about 3 minutes. Drain. Toss them with 1/4 cup of the dressing.

In a salad bowl, combine the lettuce, herbs, and cucumber and toss with the remaining dressing. Place the greens on 4 salad plates. Top with the shrimp and garnish with the walnuts and crumbled feta if desired. Serve at room temperature.

ALTERNATE DRESSINGS:
lemon mustard cream dressing (page 308),
tarragon mustard cream dressing (page 310),
lemon mayonnaise dressing (page 316).

crab salad with walnuts and lemon mayonnaise dressing

THE CRUNCHY WALNUTS and the addition of toasted walnut oil to the mayonnaise contribute depth of flavor and play up the sweetness of the crab. You can serve this simply, on a bed of lettuce, or you can make it a composed salad with cooked potatoes, asparagus, or green beans, all drizzled with some of the thinned mayonnaise.

1 cup basic mayonnaise dressing thinned with 1/4 cup walnut oil, lemon juice, and water (page 315)
1 teaspoon finely pureed garlic
2 tablespoons freshly grated lemon zest
1 cup walnuts, toasted and finely chopped
Sea salt and freshly ground black pepper
2 cucumbers, seeded and cut in 1/2-inch dice (about 3 cups)
1 pound crabmeat, picked clean
1 tablespoon walnut oil
1 tablespoon fresh lemon juice
Lettuce or watercress
Chopped fresh flat-leaf parsley or dill, for garnish

Place the mayonnaise dressing in a small bowl and add the garlic, lemon zest, and 1/2 cup chopped walnuts. Mix and add salt and pepper to taste.

In a large bowl, combine the cucumbers and crabmeat with the walnut mayonnaise dressing.

In another bowl, combine the walnut oil and lemon juice and toss the lettuce or watercress with this light dressing. Distribute among 4 salad plates. Top with the crab and cucumber mixture. Sprinkle the crab with the remaining 1/2 cup walnuts and with chopped parsley or dill. Serve immediately.

VARIATION:

If you wish to make a composed salad, add 16 blanched asparagus spears and 8 cooked new potatoes, sliced or quartered. Dress the crab with half the mayonnaise, omit the cucumbers, and drizzle the vegetables with the remaining mayonnaise thinned with water.

ALTERNATE DRESSING:
walnut cream dressing (page 312).

NOTE: *If the cucumbers are bitter, peel them. English or Japanese cucumbers can remain unpeeled.*

tuna, roasted pepper, and avocado salad

I AM A COOKBOOK ADDICT and have a quite a large library. One day while browsing through some Moroccan cookbooks, I came across a recipe for a dish of tuna and roasted peppers. It sounded right up my alley, so I prepared it as directed. It was very good, but the next time I made it, I added avocado to make the dish more substantial and to add another texture, creaminess.

You have three options for the tuna in this salad. You can use tuna confit (see page 226), which can be made days ahead and stored in the refrigerator. Or you can cook fresh tuna or use olive-oil-packed tuna from a can or jar.

12 ounces tuna fillet, tuna confit (see page 226), or canned tuna
Olive oil
Sea salt and freshly ground black pepper
2 large red or yellow bell peppers
8 cups loosely packed chicory or other bitter greens (about 1/3 pound)
2 ripe avocados, cut into chunks
1 cup toasted cumin citrus dressing (page 301)
24 Moroccan or other oil-cured olives, for garnish

If you are using fresh tuna, preheat the broiler. Cut the tuna into 1-inch-thick slices. Brush lightly with olive oil, sprinkle with salt and pepper, and broil to medium rare or medium, about 4 minutes per side.

Set the tuna aside and cover it. You may refrigerate it and bring it to room temperature when ready to serve, or grill just before serving time if you want it a bit warm.

If you are using tuna confit, bring to room temperature when ready to serve.

Broil, grill, or flame-char the peppers until blackened on all sides. Place in a plastic container or paper bag, close, and let steam for about 15 minutes. When the peppers are cool enough to handle, peel them, remove the seeds, and slice into 1/2-inch strips.

Break the tuna into chunks. In a large bowl, toss the greens, tuna, peppers, and avocados with the toasted cumin dressing. Sprinkle the salad with olives and serve.

ALTERNATE DRESSINGS:
preserved lemon dressing (page 299),
charmoula citrus dressing (page 326).

MAKING
TUNA CONFIT

Heat the oven to 250 degrees F.

Cut a 2-pound piece of tuna fillet into 2-inch-thick pieces (I recommend albacore rather than yellowfin or ahi). Season with salt and pepper to taste and place the tuna in a Pyrex or other baking dish. Add 8 crushed black peppercorns, 3 bay leaves, 2 smashed garlic cloves, 1 teaspoon fennel seed, and 1 thinly sliced lemon to the dish and cover all with extra-virgin olive oil. Cover the dish with foil and bake for 45 to 60 minutes. The tuna is done when it is opaque and firm. Remove from the oven and cool completely. Pack the tuna into a glass jar or plastic container and add the strained juices from the baking dish and fresh olive oil to cover. Cover tightly and refrigerate. This will keep for about 1 week. Bring to room temperature before serving.

Instead of baking, you can cook the tuna on the stovetop over very low heat until cooked through, about 40 minutes. Store as directed.

salade niçoise

OVER THE YEARS, THIS CLASSIC PROVENÇAL composed salad has evolved quite a bit. It began as a vegetable salad, but gradually anchovies and tuna worked their way into the mix. Salade Niçoise is an ample first course and can be expanded to serve as a complete meal, depending on portion size and the amount of tuna you use. The tuna is usually canned white meat tuna packed in good olive oil. Purists say to use either anchovy or tuna, either artichokes or fava beans, but with such wonderful ingredients, who needs to be pure? While cooked potatoes and green beans are not "authentic," they are excellent additions as well.

6 ripe tomatoes
Sea salt
1 cucumber
6 small artichokes (or 12 tiny ones), cooked
3 hard-boiled eggs, cooked for 9 minutes
2 small green peppers, seeded
2 small bulbs fennel, trimmed and cored (optional)
12 ounces canned oil-packed tuna or tuna confit (see page 226)
1/2 pound fresh fava or lima beans, cooked briefly
About 1 cup anchovy garlic vinaigrette (page 286)
12 fresh basil leaves cut into fine strips, for garnish
1/4 cup oil-cured black olives, for garnish

Quarter the tomatoes and salt them. Peel and slice the cucumber.

Cut the artichokes and eggs into quarters. Slice the peppers and the fennel, if using.

Break up the tuna into large flakes. Arrange all the vegetables and the eggs attractively on 6 plates and distribute the tuna on top. Pour the vinaigrette over the salads and garnish with basil and olives. Serve immediately.

ALTERNATE DRESSINGS:
garlic vinaigrette (page 269),
tapenade vinaigrette (page 322),
caper and garlic citrus dressing (page 291).

(continued on next page)

salade niçoise sandwich
PAN BAGNAT

PAN BAGNAT MEANS "wet bread" in French.

Take the chopped ingredients of a salade Niçoise and place them in a slightly hollowed-out baguette, then allow the bread to marinate for hours until it has absorbed all the vinaigrette. To serve, cut a round loaf or baguette in half and scoop out some of the white interior. Rub the inside of the loaf with a cut clove of garlic, sprinkle with a little vinaigrette, put a serving of well-dressed salade Niçoise into the bread, and press the two halves of the bread together. Wrap well in foil or plastic wrap and refrigerate for at least 1 hour. Serve at room temperature.

fried mussels with tarator sauce

MIDYE TAVASI

FRIED MUSSELS ARE A POPULAR street food in Turkey and a meze found in most restaurants specializing in small plates. Most recipes ask you to pry open the mussels before cooking to remove the meat. However, I think it's easier to steam the mussels for a few seconds until they crack open, then remove the mussels and cut away any beards that may remain. Allow 4 to 6 mussels per person, as these are rather rich. Since Turkey is renowned for its spectacular hazelnuts, I prefer to use them rather than walnuts in the tahini-based tarator sauce.

36 to 40 mussels
3 1/2 cups water
2 cups flour
1 teaspoon sea salt
Freshly ground black pepper
2 eggs
Canola oil or vegetable oil for deep frying
1 cup hazelnut tarator dressing (page 305)

Soak 12 bamboo skewers in water for 30 minutes.

Scrub the mussels with a brush and wash in a few changes of water. Pull off the beards. Discard any broken or open mussels, because they are dead. (Sometimes live mussels are open, but when you tap them on the countertop they will close.)

Place the mussels in a large sauté pan with 2 cups salted water over high heat, cover the pan, and steam just until they open, about 1 minute. Remove the mussels with a slotted spoon. (You can save the mussel broth for another use.) Pull off any beards that may remain.

Drain the skewers and thread 3 to 4 mussels on each one.

Heat 3 or 4 inches oil in a deep fryer or wok until it reaches 360 degrees F. Spread the flour in a shallow bowl and season it with the salt and a few grindings of pepper. In another bowl, whisk together the eggs and 1 1/2 cups water.

Dip each skewer in flour, then into the egg and water, and then in the flour again. Slip the skewers into the hot oil with tongs. Deep-fry in batches until golden and crisp, 2 or 3 minutes. Remove the skewers with tongs and drain well on paper towels. Serve the mussels hot, with a bowl of tarator dressing for dipping.

seafood, potatoes, and green beans
with pesto vinaigrette

YOU CAN SERVE THIS as a light supper or lunch, adding pieces of poached salmon, cooked tuna, shrimp, scallops, or lobster to the humble vegetables, which elevates this dish to greater culinary heights. It is worth the expense of the seafood. If you like, add cooked beets or cauliflower, even some wedges of tomato and quartered hard-boiled eggs.

1 1/2 pounds little new potatoes
Sea salt
1 pound small green beans, topped and tailed, cut in 2-inch lengths, or left whole if they are haricots verts
Three 1/4 pound lobsters, or or 1 1/2 pounds shrimp, shelled and deveined, or 1 1/2 pounds sea scallops, foot muscles removed, or 1 1/2 pounds boneless salmon or tuna fillets
White wine (optional)
Olive oil (optional)
Freshly squeezed lemon juice (optional)
About 1 1/2 cups pesto vinaigrette (page 320)
Lettuce leaves, for garnish (optional)
Tiny cherry tomatoes, for garnish (optional)

Put the potatoes in a large saucepan and cover with cold water. Bring to a boil, reduce the heat, add 1 teaspoon salt, and simmer until the potatoes are cooked through but still firm. Cooking time will vary according to the size of the potato. You might want to cook a few extra so you have one or two to test. When the potatoes are done, drain, rinse with cold water to stop the cooking, and cool at room temperature.

Bring a large saucepan of salted water to a boil. Drop in the green beans and cook for 2 to 4 minutes, or until tender-crisp. Drain and refresh in ice water. Dry them well.

If using lobsters, bring a large kettle of salted water to a boil. Drop in the lobsters, reduce the heat, and simmer for 8 to 10 minutes. Remove the lobsters from the kettle and plunge into a sink filled with ice water. When they are cool enough to handle, remove the meat from the shells and cut it into large bite-sized pieces. Place in a bowl and set aside, covered, in the refrigerator. Discard the shells.

If using shrimp, bring a small saucepan of salted water or a combination of white wine and water to a simmer. Drop in the cleaned shrimp, and when they turn pink, in 2 to 3 minutes, drain them. Serve them warm or chill until using.

If using scallops, poach them as you would the shrimp or, to maximize their sweetness, sauté them and serve them warm. In a large sauté pan, heat 3 tablespoons olive oil over high heat. Add the scallops and sauté, turning once, until golden on the outside and just opaque at the center, 4 to 6 minutes.

If using salmon, poach the fillets in wine and water, as for shrimp, but cook for 6 to 8 minutes. Salmon may also be slow-cooked in the oven. Heat the oven to 200 degrees F. Season the fish with salt and pepper to taste and drizzle liberally with olive oil and a few tablespoons lemon juice. Cover with parchment and cook for about 45 minutes for medium-rare, 50 to 55 minutes for well cooked. Serve warm or at room temperature.

Fresh fillets of tuna may be broiled or pan-seared in olive oil to your desired degree of doneness. Keep in mind that most Europeans eat their fish a bit more cooked that we do—unless they are serving *crudo* or carpaccio (see page 00).

To serve, cut the potatoes into 1/4-inch slices, or halves if small. Arrange the seafood, potatoes, and green beans on 6 salad plates and drizzle with pesto vinaigrette. Garnish with lettuce leaves or cherry tomatoes if you like. Serve warm or at room temperature.

ALTERNATE DRESSINGS:
romesco vinaigrette (page 325),
lemon cream dressing (page 308),
tarragon mustard cream dressing (page 310),
mustard shallot citrus dressing (page 292).

catalan salad of salt cod or tuna
with chicory and romesco vinaigrette XATO

PALE GREEN-AND-WHITE CHICORY, also known as curly endive or frisée, is the basis for a wonderful winter salad in Barcelona.

1/2 pound salt cod or 8 ounces cooked fresh or oil-packed canned tuna
3 heads chicory
1 1/2 cups romesco vinaigrette thinned to a creamy puree (page 325)
3 hard-boiled eggs, cooked for 9 minutes, halved or quartered, for garnish
1/2 cup oil-cured black olives, for garnish

If using salt cod, soak it in cold water for 1 to 2 days, changing the water at least 3 times. The soaking time will depend on the saltiness of the cod; thicker pieces take longer than thinner pieces.

Drain the salt cod and place it in a saucepan. Add water or equal parts water and milk to cover and bring slowly to a gentle simmer. Cook until the fish is tender, about 10 minutes. Drain and let cool slightly, then break the cod into 2-inch pieces, removing any bones, traces of skin, and discolored or tough parts. Flake the fish with your fingers.

If you are using fresh tuna, preheat the broiler. Cut the tuna into 1-inch-thick slices. Brush lightly with olive oil, sprinkle with salt and pepper, and broil to medium rare or medium, about 4 minutes per side.

Set the tuna aside and cover it. You may refrigerate it and bring it to room temperature when ready to serve, or grill just before serving time if you want it a bit warm.

Break up the heads of chicory and distribute among 6 salad plates. If using seared tuna, cut into slices. If using canned tuna, break it into bite-sized morsels. Place the fish on top of the greens, drizzle with the vinaigrette, and garnish with the eggs. Sprinkle olives on top and serve.

ALTERNATE DRESSING:
tomato vinaigrette (page 282).

facing page: catalan salad of seared tuna with chicory and romesco vinaigrette

mussel and potato salad
with saffron mayonnaise dressing

IN THE SOUTH OF FRANCE, sweet mussels are often combined with cooked potatoes in a creamy dressing. I love the slightly bitter edge that saffron adds to the dressing. If you want to echo the sweetness of the mussels, add a bit of chopped tarragon and omit the saffron.

2 pounds small new potatoes
4 quarts mussels
4 cups water
2 onions, chopped
4 cloves garlic, minced
1/2 cup chopped fresh flat-leaf parsley
1 cup saffron mayonnaise (page 316)
Freshly ground black pepper

In a large saucepan, cook the potatoes over medium-low heat in lightly salted water until cooked through but still firm, 12 to 15 minutes. Drain and refresh with cold water to stop the cooking. When the potatoes are cool enough to handle, cut them in halves or quarters and place them in a salad bowl.

Scrub and rinse the mussels and remove the beards. In a large saucepan or kettle, bring the water to a boil and add the onions, garlic, and parsley. Over high heat, reduce the liquid to 1 1/2 cups. Add the mussels and steam, covered, until they open, about 5 minutes. Discard any mussels that do not open. Transfer the opened mussels to a bowl, using a slotted spoon.

Remove the mussels from their shells and discard the shells. Strain and reserve the poaching liquid, which can be used to thin the dressing. Add the mussels to the potatoes.

Thin the saffron mayonnaise with 1/2 cup reserved poaching liquid. Toss the mussels and potatoes with the dressing and add pepper to taste. Serve warm.

ALTERNATE DRESSINGS:
tarragon mustard cream dressing (page 310),
tarragon mayonnaise dressing (page 316).

facing page: mussel and potato salad with saffron mayonnaise dressing

fish with tahini sauce

SAMAK BI TAHINI

THIS CLASSIC ARABIC FISH DISH is popular in Syria and Lebanon. The fish is baked, then coated with a tahini sauce and elaborately decorated with cucumbers, radishes, pine nuts, and pomegranate seeds. It is served at room temperature and makes a wonderful centerpiece for a meze buffet.

- 2 1/2 to 3 pounds whole fish, such as snapper or sea bass
- 3 tablespoons extra-virgin olive oil
- 2 tablespoons fresh lemon juice
- Sea salt and freshly ground black pepper
- 1 1/2 to 2 cups not-too-thin tahini dressing (page 303)
- 1/4 cup toasted pine nuts, for garnish
- 1/4 cup chopped fresh flat-leaf parsley, for garnish

Heat the oven to 400 degrees F.

Wash the fish and cut 3 or 4 slits on each side of the body. Combine the olive oil, lemon juice, and salt and pepper to taste and rub this mixture over the fish and into the slits.

Place the fish in an oiled baking pan and bake for 25 to 35 minutes or until cooked through, basting occasionally with the pan juices. Test with a fork to make sure the fish is done. With wide slotted spatulas, carefully lift it onto a serving platter, cover, and refrigerate.

When the fish is chilled, carefully peel away the skin and blot up any accumulated fish juices with paper towels. Cover the fish with the tahini dressing and garnish with the toasted pine nuts and parsley. Serve cold or at room temperature.

VARIATION:

Add 1/2 cup chopped fresh cilantro and 1/2 teaspoon cayenne to the tahini dressing when pureeing. Spread the dressing over the fish after removing the skin and bake 15 minutes. Serve hot or cold.

poultry and meat salads and small plates

IN MEDITERRANEAN countries, unlike in the United States, protein has not been at the center of the plate. Meat, poultry, and seafood traditionally have been served in small amounts as flavoring agents, partnered with larger portions of grains, beans, greens, and vegetables. This is, of course, the Mediterranean diet and a satisfying and healthy way to eat. Adding protein in small portions is an ideal way to enrich a salad or small plate and transform it into a complete meal. The cooked meat or poultry (or seafood, for that matter) can be tossed with the greens, beans, or grains or served alongside the other ingredients as part of a composed salad.

As you can tell, small plates and composed salads are some of my favorite meals. In fact, I plan for them. For example, when I sauté or broil chicken for dinner, I always cook an extra piece. When I roast a chicken, I set aside some to use in another dish. If I cook roast leg of lamb, roast pork, or steak for a family dinner, I prepare more than I need for just one meal. And in some instances I cook chicken, quail, duck, or veal just for a special salad.

Here are some suggestions to inspire you to make your own composed salads, which never go out of style and can be prepared in every season. These are just a few ideas for plates using protein. I like to think of the flavors on hand and what salad dressings will make them shine.

IN THE SUMMER, tomatoes make every dish special with their brilliant color and fragrance. I love a plate of cold roast chicken, sliced tomatoes, sliced fresh mozzarella, some baby green beans, and roasted new potatoes with a garlicky pesto vinaigrette. Or I might transport my palate to France with anchovy garlic vinaigrette or remoulade mayonnaise, or to the Middle East with tahini dressing.

IN SPRING, I combine local asparagus, baby new potatoes, or tiny multicolored beets with cooked chicken and drizzle the plate with lemon cream dressing, tarragon mustard cream dressing, or hazelnut vinaigrette. A slice of spring lamb, some small green beans, some cherry tomatoes, and a few potatoes might inspire me to use mint vinaigrette, tapenade vinaigrette, or charmoula vinaigrette.

IN THE FALL AND WINTER, when citrus fruits are at their best and Fuyu persimmons, blood oranges, buttery pears, and tart apples appear at the market, I pair a grilled quail or duck breast with greens and fruit in a pomegranate or orange balsamic dressing. Sliced roast pork served with a rice salad and basic citrus dressing is a satisfying meal at any time of year.

To show the versatility of salad dressings as marinades, this chapter offers a few recipes for chicken, pork loin, lamb chops, and assorted kebabs that are marinated in some of the dressings and then broiled or grilled. There are also recipes for roast pork, merguez, and kefta burgers, for sandwiches that do well with dressings as finishing sauces.

duck breast with pears, walnuts, and belgian endive

WHENEVER I'M IN ITALY, instead of dining in restaurants all the time, I love to have a meal in a regional wine bar. It's a great way to sample local food products: specialty breads, salumi, cheeses, and oils, and of course the local wines from small producers. One of my favorite wine shops in Rome is the Enoteca Costantini, just off the Piazza Cavour. It has a small signature restaurant called Il Simposio, where I first tasted this dish. Sliced duck breast was dressed with orange balsamic vinaigrette and surrounded by slivers of pear and tiny leaves of wild arugula, a well-balanced contrast of bitter greens, rich duck, and sweet fruit. The duck was served warm. As wild arugula is not always easy to come by, I decided to make this at home with Belgian endive and chicory, but you can also use a mixture of bitter greens, even baby spinach.

At first the only duck breasts I could find at my market (without having to buy the whole duck) were giant Muscovy duck breasts, each big enough to feed two people. But the butcher at the meat counter directed me to the freezer case, where I found boneless Peking duck breasts, each an ideal serving for one person. Both kinds of duck breast will work here. This dish requires last-minute attention, as it is best when the duck is served warm.

> 2 boneless Muscovy duck breast halves, about 1/2 to 3/4 pound each,
>   or 4 boneless Peking duck breasts, 4 to 5 ounces each
> Sea salt and freshly ground black pepper
> Pinch of ground cinnamon or cloves (optional)
> 4 tablespoons walnuts or hazelnuts, toasted and coarsely chopped
> 1/2 cup orange balsamic vinaigrette with nut oil (page 277)
> 2 or 3 heads Belgian endive, leaves separated and cut crosswise into
>   1-inch-wide pieces
> 1 head chicory, leaves separated
> 2 small Anjou or Comice pears, halved, cored, and sliced

Using a sharp knife, score the skin of the duck breasts in a crosshatch pattern, but do not cut into the meat. Rub the breasts with salt and pepper and a pinch of cinnamon, if you like. Let stand at room temperature for about 30 minutes.

Heat the oven to 350 degrees F.

Place a large ovenproof sauté pan over medium heat. When it is hot, add the duck breasts, skin side down, and cook until the breasts render their fat, 8 to 10 minutes. Drain off the fat and slip the pan into the oven.

(continued on page 241)

Roast the duck for about 8 minutes for medium-rare. (If you like, you can finish the breasts on the stovetop, reducing the heat to low and sautéing, turning once, for 8 to 10 minutes.) Transfer the duck to a cutting board and let rest for 5 minutes. When the duck is cool enough to handle, cut it on the diagonal into 1/4-inch thick slices.

In a small bowl, macerate the nuts in 1 tablespoon dressing.

In a bowl, combine the Belgian endive and chicory. Sprinkle with salt to taste and toss with 1/4 cup dressing. Arrange on 4 salad plates. Top with slices of duck and pear and drizzle with the remaining dressing. Sprinkle the nuts on top and serve warm.

ALTERNATE DRESSINGS:
sherry vinaigrette (page 270),
mixed citrus dressing II (page 293).

facing page: duck breast with pears,
walnuts, greens, and sherry vinaigrette

grilled quail
with pomegranate dressing and oranges

IN GREECE, I WAS SERVED a dish described as Byzantine quail. It was quite similar to this Renaissance-inspired recipe for quail from the Veneto. They both hark back to the time when pomegranate was a common marinade and flavoring agent. During the fall and winter, I like to garnish the dish with colorful orange segments and a sprinkling of ruby-red fresh pomegranate seeds. Serve the quail atop a bed of bitter greens or wilted spinach with pine nuts and you have a very elegant and dramatic plate.

> 4 boneless quail (about 6 ounces each)
> 1 cup pomegranate dressing from concentrate (page 298)
> 1/2 cup fresh orange juice
> 2 tablespoons freshly grated orange zest
> 3 tablespoons honey
> Sea salt
> 2 large navel oranges or 4 blood oranges
> 2 handfuls of arugula or watercress
> 2 small heads radicchio, leaves separated and torn if large
> 1/2 cup pomegranate seeds

Place the quail side by side in a nonreactive container. Combine the pomegranate dressing with the orange juice and zest and the honey and salt to taste.

Pour half the mixture over the birds, toss to coat, and marinate, covered, for 6 to 8 hours, or overnight in the refrigerator.

Working with 1 orange at a time, cut a thin slice off the top and bottom to reveal the flesh. Stand the orange upright and remove the peel in wide strips, cutting downward and following the contour of the fruit. Holding the orange over a bowl, cut along both sides of each segment, releasing the segments from the membrane and allowing them to drop into the bowl. Using the knife tip, pry out any seeds. Set the orange segments aside. If you are using blood oranges, which are small and difficult to segment, you may want to cut them into slices and push out the seeds with a toothpick or paring knife. Set aside.

Preheat the broiler or gas grill to high or make a charcoal fire. Bring the quail to room temperature and remove them from the marinade. Grill or broil the quail for 4 minutes on each side, or until medium-rare. Set aside.

Place the bitter greens in a large bowl and toss with most of the remaining dressing and the orange segments. Arrange the salad on 4 salad plates. Place a quail on each serving and drizzle with the last of the dressing. Sprinkle with pomegranate seeds. Serve warm.

turkish chicken salad
with walnut tahini dressing

CHICKEN SALAD WITH WALNUT SAUCE, known as Circassian chicken, is one of the glories of Turkish and Georgian cuisine. Because this dish is so rich, it is usually served as a meze or small plate, but you can increase the portions and serve it as a main course for lunch or supper. Some versions of this recipe are spicy with hot pepper; others are mild, with just a drizzle of paprika-flavored oil. You can prepare this with a whole chicken or just chicken breasts.

- 3 pounds chicken, parts or breasts
- 4 cups water, or as needed
- 1 onion, chopped
- 1 carrot, peeled and cut into chunks
- About 1 1/2 cups walnut tarator dressing (page 305)
- 2 bunches watercress or 2 hearts of romaine, cut crosswise into 1-inch pieces
- About 2 cups peeled, seeded, and sliced cucumbers
- 2 teaspoons sweet Hungarian paprika
- 2 tablespoons toasted walnut oil
- Pinch of cayenne or 2 generous pinches of Aleppo pepper (optional)
- 2 tablespoons chopped fresh flat-leaf parsley or fresh dill, for garnish

Rinse the chicken and pat it dry. Put it in a large saucepan with the water, onion, and carrot. (You may add a bay leaf, some thyme, and a few cloves if you like.) Gradually bring the water to a boil over medium-high heat, then reduce the heat to low and simmer gently until the chicken is tender, 20 to 25 minutes. Remove the chicken from the pot and set it aside. Strain the broth and reserve for another use.

When the chicken is cool enough to handle, remove the meat from the bones and shred it with your fingers. Place in a bowl and toss with enough dressing to moisten, about 1 cup.

Place the watercress or romaine and cucumbers in a salad bowl. Toss with enough dressing to coat. Transfer the dressed greens to a platter and top with the chicken.

In a small sauté pan, warm the paprika in the walnut oil over medium heat. You may add the cayenne or Aleppo pepper if you want the oil a bit hot. When the oil bubbles, remove from the heat and drizzle over the salad. Sprinkle the parsley or dill on top and serve warm.

ALTERNATE DRESSINGS:
Omit the paprika-and-walnut-oil garnish and use **basic mayonnaise dressing** (page 315), **tarragon mayonnaise dressing** (page 316), **tarragon mustard cream dressing** (page 310), or **walnut cream dressing** (page 312).

chicken and radicchio salad agrodolce
with warm balsamic vinaigrette

WHEN YOU SEE THE TERM *AGRODOLCE* on an Italian menu, you know that sweet-and-sour is the flavor theme and that the classic combination of pine nuts and raisins is likely to be included in the dish. Sweet-and-sour dishes are of Arabic origin and were brought to Spain in the eighth century by the Moors, who stayed for over seven hundred years. After the Spanish Inquisition, when the Jews and Moorish Arabs were expelled from Spain and Portugal, these dishes migrated to Italy. So I was not surprised to find a delicious dish of this genre at La Rosetta, a Roman seafood restaurant near the Pantheon. There I was served a salad of tiny, tiny calamari and radicchio, with sweet raisins and pine nuts mixed in. I decided to experiment with this salad. I remembered that many *agrodolce* dishes originally were prepared with meat or poultry, so I decided to try this with cooked chicken.

Sweet flavors dominate here. The sweet wine used for plumping the raisins is accentuated by the sweetness of the balsamic vinegar. However, the vinaigrette needs the depth of flavor from a bit of sherry vinegar so it isn't too wimpy to stand up to the bitter radicchio. This salad also would be delicious with quail, and, if you wanted seafood, you could try it with shrimp, scallops, or baby squid. If you decide to make it with leftover roast chicken or turkey, cut the meat into 1/2-inch-wide strips about 1 1/2 inches long and warm them gently in the vinaigrette along with the pine nuts and raisins for just a minute or two.

> 3 large heads Treviso radicchio, cut in half and sliced into 1-inch-wide
>   strips
> Sea salt
> 2 to 3 tablespoons olive oil
> 2 boneless chicken breasts (4 halves) or 4 small boneless chicken thighs,
>   cut into 1/2-inch-wide strips
> About 1 cup orange balsamic vinaigrette (page 277)
> 1/4 cup toasted pine nuts
> 1/4 cup golden raisins plumped in sherry or marsala

Place the radicchio in a large bowl and sprinkle lightly with salt.

Heat the olive oil in a large sauté pan. Add the chicken strips and sauté over medium heat, turning from time to time, until the chicken is almost completely cooked, about 10 minutes. Add 1/2 cup vinaigrette to the pan along with the pine nuts and raisins and continue to sauté until the chicken is cooked through, another 2 to 3 minutes.

Add the chicken mixture to the greens and mix well. Serve at once.

ALTERNATE DRESSING:
sherry vinaigrette (page 270).

facing page: chicken and radicchio salad
agrodolce with warm balsamic vinaigrette

chicken livers, mushrooms, and greens with sherry vinaigrette

I HAVE A WEAKNESS FOR sautéed chicken livers. I usually add them to pasta or risotto, Italian style. French cooks, however, love to combine them with greens for a voluptuous wilted salad. So here I can indulge my passion for chicken livers in another way.

4 large handfuls of arugula or baby spinach (about 1/3 pound), chilled
Sea salt
4 tablespoons extra-virgin olive oil, plus more if needed
1 pound chicken livers, trimmed of connective tissue and any discolored spots
Freshly ground black pepper
2 shallots, minced
1/2 pound flavorful mushrooms, such as chanterelles or cremini, sliced 1/4-inch thick
About 1/2 cup sherry vinaigrette (page 270)

Place the greens in a large bowl and sprinkle lightly with salt.

In a large sauté pan, heat 2 tablespoons olive oil over high heat and quickly sauté the chicken livers, turning them with tongs a few times. Add a bit more oil if they start to stick. Sprinkle with salt and a few grindings of pepper. You want them to be nice and crusty on the outside but with the centers still quite pink, about 5 minutes total. Slide them onto a plate and cover to keep warm.

Add the remaining 2 tablespoons olive oil to the pan. Add the shallots and sauté for about 2 minutes. Add the mushrooms and sauté over medium heat, adding a bit more oil if the mushrooms begin to stick or scorch. When the mushrooms are wilted, about 3 minutes, season with salt and pepper to taste and slide the mushrooms and shallots onto the plate with the livers.

Quickly deglaze the pan with most of the dressing and toss with the salad greens. Distribute the slightly wilted greens among 4 salad plates. Top with the warm mushrooms, shallots, and livers, drizzle with the remaining dressing, and add pepper to taste. Serve immediately.

ALTERNATE DRESSINGS:
balsamic vinaigrette (page 276),
or omit the shallots and use mustard shallot vinaigrette (page 271).

veal with tuna mayonnaise
VITELLO TONNATO

VEAL AND TUNA MAY SOUND LIKE an odd couple, but braised veal
with a creamy tuna sauce is a classic antipasto dish in Piedmont. The veal
is mild and tender and a lovely foil for the rich tuna mayonnaise. This same
voluptuous sauce may be spooned over slices of grilled eggplant or zucchini
or on cooked chicken breasts. You could even spread it on slices of seared
rare tuna for a double-tuna jolt. For a fuller meal, extend this plate by adding
boiled potatoes and blanched green beans.

3 tablespoons unsalted butter

1 tablespoon olive oil, plus more if needed

One 3-pound boneless leg of veal, rolled and tied

Sea salt and freshly ground black pepper

1 large yellow onion, finely diced

3 carrots, peeled and finely diced

3 celery stalks, finely diced

3 to 4 cups dry white wine

3 to 4 cups chicken or veal stock

2 cups tuna mayonnaise (page 316)

Salt-packed capers, rinsed, for garnish

Chopped fresh flat-leaf parsley, for garnish

In a large Dutch oven, melt the butter with the olive oil over medium-high
heat. Season the veal with salt and pepper and brown it well on all sides,
8 to 10 minutes. Remove the veal from the pot and set aside.

If the butter has burned, pour it out, wipe out the pot, return the pot to
medium heat, and add 3 tablespoons olive oil. Add the onion, carrots, and
celery and sauté until pale gold, about 15 minutes. Return the veal to the
pot and add equal amounts of wine and stock almost to cover the roast.
(The amount of wine and stock you will need depends on the dimensions
of your Dutch oven.) Gradually bring the liquid to a gentle boil, reduce the
heat to low, cover, and simmer until cooked through, 1 1/2 hours or a little
longer. (If you like, you can braise the leg in a 350-degree F oven for about
the same amount of time.)

Remove the veal from the pot and place it on a platter. Let cool, cover, and
refrigerate until well chilled, at least 8 hours or up to 2 days. Strain the
cooking liquid through a fine-mesh sieve and reserve.

(continued on next page)

If the tuna mayonnaise is very thick, thin with a little of the liquid reserved from cooking the veal. (The sauce can be made a day in advance, covered, and refrigerated; bring to room temperature before serving. The veal stock is a plus for your larder and should be saved for another use.)

To serve, place the veal on a cutting board and snip and remove the strings. Cut crosswise into slices about 1/4-inch thick. Arrange the veal on a platter or on individual plates and spread the tuna sauce on top to cover completely. Sprinkle with the capers and parsley and serve immediately.

leg of lamb with tapenade

I LIKE TAPENADE enough to have it do double duty. Here a boneless leg of lamb is spread with tapenade, rolled, tied, and roasted. It is, of course, delicious when served warm. When it is cold, slice it and serve it as part of a composed salad with potatoes, green beans, and cherry tomatoes drizzled with tapenade vinaigrette.

> 1 1/2 cups tapenade (page 322), plus more if needed
> 2 tablespoons freshly grated orange or lemon zest
> One 3-pound boneless leg of lamb
> Slivered garlic (optional)
> 18 to 24 small new potatoes
> Sea salt
> 3/4 pound small, slender green beans, trimmed
> Tiny cherry tomatoes

Combine 1/2 cup tapenade with the citrus zest and spread it all over the inside of the lamb. Roll the lamb and tie it at discreet intervals. You may want to cut a few slits in the leg and insert slivers of garlic.

Heat the oven to 400 degrees F.

Place the leg of lamb in a roasting pan and roast for 45 to 60 minutes for rare. Allow the meat to rest for about 10 minutes before slicing. Enjoy some of it warm and save half for the salad.

In a large saucepan, combine the potatoes with water to cover, add a little salt, and bring to a boil over high heat. Reduce the heat to medium and simmer until the potatoes are cooked through but still firm. The cooking time will vary with the size of the potatoes; very small ones will cook in about 15 minutes, and larger ones can take 20 minutes or longer. When done, drain well, rinse with cold water to stop the cooking, drain again, and let cool to room temperature. Cut them in half.

Meanwhile, bring a second saucepan filled with water to a boil over high heat. Lightly salt the water and then add the green beans and cook until tender-crisp, 2 to 3 minutes. Drain and refresh in a bowl filled with ice water. When cold, drain again and pat dry.

Thin the remaining 1 cup tapenade with oil and vinegar as directed on page 323.

Cut the lamb into 1/4-inch-thick slices and place on a platter. Surround with the potatoes, cut in half, the green beans, and the cherry tomatoes. Spoon the tapenade vinaigrette over all and serve.

ALTERNATE DRESSINGS:
charmoula vinaigrette (page 326),
oregano garlic vinaigrette (page 284),
mint vinaigrette (page 280).

grilled chicken in
hot pepper citrus marinade

HOT PEPPERS AND CITRUS are a lively marinade for broiled birds. You can use half broilers, quail, or baby chickens, also known as poussins. They will emerge from the grill smoky, spicy, and aromatic. The birds can marinate for 8 hours or a full day.

> **About 2 cups hot pepper citrus dressing (page 295)**
> **Freshly grated zest of 3 large oranges or 4 tangerines**
> **6 gloves garlic, smashed**
> **Six 1-pound poussins, backbones removed, butterflied, or 6 half**
> **   broilers, or 12 quail**
> **Sea salt**

In a saucepan, warm the dressing over low heat and add the orange or tangerine zest and the garlic. Remove from the heat and let steep for 10 minutes.

Arrange the birds in a large container or a Pyrex baking dish.

When the marinade has cooled completely, pour it over the birds. Cover and refrigerate overnight or for 24 hours. Bring to room temperature before broiling or grilling.

Make a charcoal fire or preheat the broiler or gas grill. Remove the birds from the marinade, sprinkle with salt, and cook for 4 to 5 minutes on each side. Serve warm or at room temperature.

ALTERNATE DRESSING:
oregano garlic vinaigrette (page 284).

chicken kebabs
with oregano garlic vinaigrette marinade

serves 6

ALTHOUGH MOST RECIPES for chicken kebabs specify boneless, skinless, cubed chicken breasts, breasts are easily overcooked and can toughen on the grill. I prefer to use boned chicken thighs with the skin on. They remain moist and juicy throughout the broiling or grilling process, and the skin retains a wonderful flavor of the marinade. It is best to marinate the chicken for at least 6 hours and preferably overnight in the refrigerator. This recipe is an adaptation of *jujeh kababe* and was given to me by an Iranian friend, but I have seen other versions of this dish in cookbooks from the Caucasus. Some use saffron instead of paprika; others use no herbs at all. If you like the smokiness of Spanish pimentón, by all means use it. Serve with rice pilaf or atop a rice salad.

18 small boneless chicken thighs
1 large onion, cut in chunks (about 1 1/2 cups)
2 cups oregano garlic vinaigrette (page 284)
1 tablespoon sweet paprika or pimentón dulce
Sea salt and freshly ground black pepper

Place the chicken thighs in a nonreactive container.

Put the onion, dressing, and paprika in a blender or food processor. Puree until the ingredients are well mixed. Pour the marinade over the chicken and refrigerate overnight. Bring the chicken to room temperature before broiling or grilling.

Preheat the broiler or gas grill or make a charcoal fire. Soak the wooden skewers in water for 30 minutes.

Remove the chicken from the marinade and thread on skewers, 3 thighs per person. Sprinkle with salt and pepper to taste. Broil or grill for about 4 minutes on each side, or until the juices run clear and the chicken is cooked through. Serve immediately.

roast pork in oregano garlic vinaigrette

NOW THAT IT HAS BECOME the "other white meat," most pork does not have a great deal of fat or flavor, just like most of our chickens. That is why chefs brine pork and chicken or put them in savory marinades. These marinated pork tenderloins may be served hot as a main course, but they can be served at room temperature paired with a rice salad with strips of grilled eggplant and peppers, or paired with *bazergan* (see photo), a Syrian wheat salad with walnuts and peanuts. The pork is also great sliced for sandwiches when the bread is spread with romesco mayonnaise (page 324).

> 2 pounds pork tenderloin, well trimmed, or one 2-pound boneless pork loin
> 2 tablespoons pimentón de la Vera or sweet paprika
> 1 1/2 tablespoons ground cumin, toasted
> 1/2 cup oregano garlic vinaigrette (page 284)
> Sea salt and freshly ground black pepper

Put the trimmed pork tenderloins in a shallow nonreactive container. Whisk the pimentón and cumin into the dressing. Pour this marinade over the meat and rub it in well. Refrigerate overnight or for as long as 3 days. Bring to room temperature before broiling or grilling.

Preheat the broiler or gas grill or make a charcoal fire. Sprinkle the meat lightly with salt and pepper. Broil or grill until cooked through, about 10 minutes in all, turning the meat occasionally. (Ideally the pork should be cooked on a grill, but you can sear the tenderloins on a stovetop griddle over high heat, turning them to color the outside evenly. Transfer them to a pan and roast in a preheated 350-degree F oven for about 20 minutes.)

Let the meat rest on a cutting board for 10 minutes, then slice. Serve with *bazergan* (page 171) with pomegranate citrus dressing, or Spanish rice salad (page 174) dressed with oregano garlic vinaigrette or citrus dressing, or use in sandwiches with romesco mayonnaise, grilled peppers, and some lettuce.

NOTE: *You can use this marinade on pork kebabs as well as tenderloin.*

ALTERNATE MARINADE:
toasted cumin citrus dressing (page 301).

facing page: roast pork in oregano garlic vinaigrette, accompanied by syrian wheat salad (page 171) with pomegranate citrus dressing (page 297)

lamb kebabs
with charmoula citrus dressing

THIS VERSATILE MARINADE IS also good on a butterflied leg of lamb and lamb chops. Serve with couscous or couscous salad (page 176).

**2 pounds leg of lamb, trimmed of excess fat and sinews, cut into
    1 1/2- to 2-inch pieces**
1 small onion, roughly chopped
1 cup charmoula citrus dressing made with lemon juice (page 326)
Olive oil
Sea salt and freshly ground black pepper
Lemon wedges, for garnish

Put the lamb in a nonreactive container. Combine the onion and charmoula citrus dressing in a blender and puree. Pour this mixture over the meat and toss well to cover. Marinate overnight in the refrigerator or at room temperature for a few hours, or both. Bring to room temperature before broiling or grilling. Preheat a broiler or a gas grill or make a charcoal fire. Thread the meat on 4 metal skewers. Brush with olive oil and sprinkle with salt and pepper. Broil or grill the meat to the desired degree of doneness, turning once, 8 to 10 minutes for medium rare. Serve immediately with lemon wedges.

VARIATION:
Marinate the lamb in **oregano garlic vinaigrette** (page 284) and serve with **yogurt dressing** (page 306) on the side.

ALTERNATE MARINADES:
preserved lemon dressing (page 299),
harissa dressing (page 329).

facing page: lamb kebabs with charmoula citrus dressing, accompanied by couscous salad with almonds, raisins, and saffron onions (page 176)

middle eastern hamburger
KEFTA

HERE IS TAHINI DRESSING at work in a sandwich format. To my palate, a kefta burger tastes much better than a regular burger, but then, I'm a Mediterranean gal.

FOR THE KEFTA
2 pounds ground beef
1 medium onion, grated (about 3/4 cup)
1/3 cup chopped fresh flat-leaf parsley
2 teaspoons ground cumin, toasted
1 teaspoon sea salt
1/2 teaspoon freshly ground black pepper

6 pita breads
3/4 to 1 cup chopped ripe tomatoes
3/4 to 1 cup chopped peeled cucumbers
1 cup tahini dressing (page 303)

Combine all of the ingredients for the kefta and knead together with your hands. Then form into two small oval patties per person, or twelve 4-ounce keftas.

Preheat a broiler or gas grill or make a charcoal fire. Broil or grill the keftas, turning once, until done, about 6 minutes total. Or fry them in a cast-iron skillet, turning once.

To serve, warm the pita breads in a microwave or conventional oven. Cut the breads in half crosswise. In the bottom of each half, put about 2 tablespoons each of chopped tomatoes and cucumbers and some of the tahini dressing. Then slip in the kefta. You may want to spoon a little more tahini over the meat. Serve immediately.

moroccan lamb sausage
MERGUEZ

THESE SPICY SAUSAGES NEED to have a certain amount of fat if they are to grill well and taste like the real thing. Serve with strips of grilled or sautéed bell pepper and onion, on a soft roll spread with either harissa mayonnaise (page 329) or charmoula mayonnaise (page 326).

2 pounds ground lamb, at least one-third fat
2 tablespoons chopped fresh cilantro
2 tablespoons chopped fresh flat-leaf parsley
2 tablespoons water
2 tablespoons sweet paprika
1 1/2 tablespoons minced garlic
1 1/2 teaspoons ground cumin, toasted
1 1/2 teaspoons ground coriander
1 1/4 teaspoons ground cinnamon
1 1/4 teaspoons sea salt
3/4 teaspoon cayenne, or more to taste
1/2 teaspoon freshly ground black pepper

In a large bowl, mix all the ingredients well with your hands. Fry up a small sample in a skillet over medium-high heat and adjust the seasoning to taste. Then form the mixture into long lozenge shapes that are about 3 inches long, slightly fatter in the middle.

To grill, thread the merguez onto metal skewers, alternating them with pieces of onion and pepper. Grill over high heat, turning occasionally, until the meat is cooked and the vegetables have softened, about 4 minutes on each side. You also may fry the merguez on a griddle like burgers. Serve immediately.

MEDITERRANEAN VINAIGRETTES, SALAD DRESSINGS, AND SAUCES

2

iN THE MEDITERRANEAN REGION, THERE ARE FOUR GENERAL categories of salad dressings. First are the **vinaigrettes**, which, as their name suggests, are made with oil and vinegar or a combination of oil, vinegar, and citrus juice. Next are the **citrus-based dressings**, prepared with oil and citrus- or fruit-based juice. These tend to be light and bright. Then there are the **creamy dressings**, made with cream, cheese, yogurt, mayonnaise, or tahini. These tend to be richer and have a mouth-coating effect. I have added another category, **sauce-based dressings**, created from classic Mediterranean sauces or condiments such as pesto, tapenade, romesco, charmoula, and harissa that have been thinned with oil and vinegar or lemon juice. Here we'll examine all of these in depth and then look at ways to use them.

matchmaking, oil-and-vinegar style

WHENEVER I TEACH A COOKING class, someone invariably asks, "What's your favorite olive oil?" or "What's the best vinegar?" There's no easy answer. Olive oils vary in intensity and flavor, from quite green and peppery to golden and fruity. Some taste of grass, others of almonds. Each of these oils calls for a different kind of acid to truly sing. Achieving balance between the particular oil and the selected vinegar or citrus juice and the designated salad ingredients takes practice in tasting, and it is the goal and the art of salad preparation. I am not being evasive when I reply, "It depends on the dish and its components."

I may respond with a question of my own. Is there a taste memory you are trying to match? Does this recipe have a country of origin? Are you cooking a Spanish recipe? For maximum Spanish flavor, I'd use Spanish extra-virgin olive oil and aged sherry vinegar, the lighter Cava vinegar, or Spanish wine vinegar.

Is your recipe Italian in inspiration? Then why not try an Italian olive oil from one of the regions closest to the origin of your salad concept and then find a wine vinegar to match? Traveling at table to the South of France? Seek fruity, golden Provençal oil; you then have the option of using French red or white wine vinegar. Some Greek olive oils have a distinctive aroma and viscosity that is unique to the Peloponnese. Tunisian oils are light and golden. Moroccan oils are deep and intense. Olives are cultivated all over the Mediterranean, in California, even in New Zealand. Each country and each kind of olive produces distinctive oil. To borrow a term from the wine guys, terroir can be a consideration.

In other words, I don't have set formulas and I don't play favorites. I like many different olive oils and have quite an assortment tucked away in my cool, dark pantry. Which oil I choose for a dish is based in part on my interest in culinary geography and on the choice of ingredients. However, if location is of no major consequence and you are not as picky or esoteric as I am, please use whatever oil you have in your pantry, an oil whose flavors you have experienced. If you understand your salad ingredients and their flavor profiles, you'll know whether you should reach for an assertive oil or a milder one.

Of course, olive oil is not the only oil used in salad dressings. Consider slightly nutty grapeseed oil or sunflower oil, which is very mild and pale. Toasted nut oils such as walnut and hazelnut make for a very rich dressing.

Selecting oils may be easier than finding vinegars you like that are not so harsh as to upset the balance of a dish. Some are quite bitter and tannic. Others are mellow and mild. These characteristics affect the overall balance of the vinaigrette. Champagne and Cava vinegars tend to be on the mild side. White wine vinegars are more neutral and less assertive than those made from red wine. They combine well with milder-tasting greens. Other salad-friendly vinegars have less than 6 percent acidity and are called "drinking vinegars." They are somewhat sweet rather than tart. These include Minus 8 (a Canadian ice-wine vinegar), fruit-based vinegars,

muscatel vinegars from Spain, and balsamic vinegars. You must decide whether your ingredients will harmonize with a sweet vinegar or need a stronger note of acidity to bring them into play.

Let's consider the overly popular balsamic vinegar. If we are talking about the real deal, *aceto balsamico tradizionale*, rest assured that you will not be using it by the half cupful. It is too intense, too concentrated, and too costly. Authentic balsamic vinegar is used sparingly, as a condiment. What is sold in the supermarket as balsamic vinegar is for the most part white wine vinegar sweetened with caramel. Some of these so-called balsamics are now infused with fruit essences, making them even sweeter. This flavor profile dovetails with the American predilection for sweetness. No wonder these vinegars are such a hit! But will they work with your dish?

Fruit vinegars also run on the sweet side, so they need to be used with discretion and paired with appropriate ingredients. Taste before you use them, as you may find that they should be cut with citrus juice or call for a nut oil to balance their sweetness. Fig, raspberry, red currant, pear, cherry, and pomegranate vinegars are now on supermarket shelves, and conceptually they are seductive, but sweetness is not always the answer and may be too much for your dish. One of the worst salads I ever tasted was a combination of bitter greens, raw onions, tart apples and strawberries, and salty blue cheese drowned in raspberry vinaigrette. It was almost inedible.

It is in the area of red wine vinegars that there is the greatest range of quality. Some burn your throat and are simply too tannic to tame and too harsh for most salad dressings. I look for red wine vinegar that still has a hint of the wine, not just the flavor of the wooden cask it was aged in. I prefer red wine vinegars made from specific wines like Cabernet, Chianti, and Barolo.

If you are looking for a vinegar that is never bitter and is subtly sweet, not adulterated and syrupy, you might want to try sherry vinegar. Some of these vinegars have an undertone of almonds and a hint of the wood aging barrel. They are light in texture. Sometimes I add a bit of sherry wine to accent the wine notes in the vinegar.

Not all dressings, however, call for vinegar. Citrus, such as lemon juice or a combination of lemon and orange juice, may be a better choice. Lemons vary quite a bit in their sourness: some are sweet-tart, others bitter-tart. For some salads you may find lemon juice too sharp, so you might add a spoonful of sugar or honey for balance. On the other hand, sometimes a citrus dressing is not tart enough for the salad components to show well, so you need to add a little vinegar. You can determine the proper acidity only by tasting.

Many cookbooks suggest using four parts oil to one part vinegar for a basic vinaigrette. Others say three to one. But this is not an all-purpose magic formula. One size does not fit all. It depends on what is in your salad and what you like. If the olive oil is too strong for the salad ingredients, the dish will be out of balance. Some peppery green olive oils overpower the sweetness of fruits or cream-based dressings. Certain vinegars are so sharp they bury the taste of delicate greens or make a cheese taste bitter. The choice of acid in the dressing is also important for flavor harmony. It might be citrus juice, a mixture of lemon juice and vinegar, or just vinegar. The vinegar might be sweet or nutty as well as sharp. The choice of acid should complement the salad it is going to adorn. With such taste variability in oils and vinegars or citrus juices, a rigid formula of three to one or four to one goes out the window.

how much dressing do you need?

JUST AS I CAN'T SPECIFY a hard-and-fast ratio of oil to acid, I can't tell you exactly how much dressing you'll need for a particular salad, because of variables like component size, absorption, and of course personal taste. But I can give you some general advice.

I was dining out with my grand-daughter, who has just come to really enjoy salad. She ordered one with pears, fennel, and hazelnuts with a Gorgonzola dressing. How is it? I asked. She said, "It has way too much dressing. It needs more greens." So how much is enough? With leafy salads you need *just enough to coat the ingredients lightly*.

I find it ironic that diners on a diet who ask for the dressing on the side end up using twice as much dressing as they would if they'd let the kitchen staff dress the salad. When dressing is served on the side, in a ramekin or even a small cream pitcher, you can either keep anointing the top ingredients as you work your way through the salad, or risk drowning your salad in too much dressing in order to moisten the bottom. When a salad is tossed, you can add just enough dressing to coat all the ingredients lightly, not just the ones on top. This holds true not just for leafy salads but also for cooked vegetable salads, grain salads, bean salads, even egg, poultry, or seafood salads.

storing dressing

LEFTOVER DRESSING IS EASY to keep. Most salad dressings can be stored in jars in the refrigerator. Just remember to bring them to room temperature before using them, so the oil has a chance to return to its normal clear, liquid state.

Most vinaigrettes keep well for up to a week. Before you use them, taste and readjust the salt and acid components, as they may have faded.

Dressings with chopped shallots will keep for only a day or so before the shallots start to taste gassy.

Dressings with orange juice as the predominant ingredient will not last more than a day at best. Lemon juice is hardier than orange juice, and citrus dressings based on lemon juice will hold for up to three days. Taste before using and refresh if necessary. They will need salt and maybe a pinch of sugar if the lemon has turned bitter.

Dressings with herbs like basil, tarragon, and mint will taste all right after a few days, but the herbs will fade and lose color. To prevent this, assemble the dressing ahead of time and add fresh herbs just before you serve it. If you've made mint vinaigrette, the flavor of the infusion will hold, but you will want to add more fresh mint to brighten the dressing and add to its visual appeal at serving time.

Mayonnaise dressings will keep for up to a week but may thicken and need readjustment.

Creamy dressings based on yogurt will keep well for a week.

Cheese- and tahini-based dressings will keep for three or four days, but they will thicken and will need to be thinned with water or citrus juice before use.

Cream-based dressings will not hold for more than a day. They tend to break down.

Sauces such as pesto, tapenade, romesco, and harissa have a very long life in the refrigerator—months! They should be stored as condiments and thinned into dressings as you need them.

Charmoula dressing can be made ahead of time, but if possible, add the chopped parsley and cilantro at serving time. If you have any left over with herbs, it will taste good for up to three days, but it will look pretty funky.

vinaigrettes

A SALAD DRESSING COMPOSED of oil and vinegar is called a vinaigrette. While some say that the ideal ratio is three parts oil to one part vinegar, proportions really should vary according to the salad components and your personal palate predilections. I, for one, prefer a higher degree of acidity in my salads. I have what my friend the late Barbara Tropp would call a "tart mouth" (she was referring to salads at the time).

The technique for assembling vinaigrettes is simple. A wire whisk and a bowl are really all you need. Some cooks prefer to put the dressing ingredients in a small jar and shake it. Others emulsify the dressing by whirring it in a blender or beating it with an electric wand or immersion blender. Emulsification is not necessary, but it does hold the dressing in suspension a while longer than is the case with one that is simply whisked together.

Herbs, mustard, shallots, and garlic may be added to vinaigrette, and then the balance game becomes a bit more complex. It's important to remember, however, that everything in the salad must be in harmony with the dressing.

classic vinaigrettes

THESE ARE THE CLASSIC DRESSINGS used in France, Italy, and Spain and occasionally in Greece and Turkey. They pair well with leafy and chopped salads, bean salads, and bread and grain salads and are a good dressing for oily fish such as sardines, anchovies, mackerel, and salt cod. They can be used with discretion on full-flavored cooked vegetables too. Please keep in mind that green vegetables like broccoli, asparagus, and green beans must be dressed at the last minute so they do not lose color.

basic vinaigrette

makes about 1 cup

3 to 4 tablespoons red wine vinegar, or white or Champagne vinegar
Sea salt and freshly ground black pepper
2/3 cup extra-virgin olive oil

OPTIONAL ADDITIONS
1 clove garlic, crushed
2 tablespoons chopped fresh basil, tarragon, mint, chervil, or flat-leaf parsley
1 tablespoon Dijon mustard

When making vinaigrette, always start with vinegar and salt, or vinegar, mustard, and salt, in the mixing bowl and then whisk in the oil. Add the herbs last.

Taste and then reseason to taste with salt and pepper. Test by dipping a leaf into the dressing to check the acid and salt balance.

basic vinaigrette variation

makes 1 1/2 cups

FOR THOSE WHO FIND extra-virgin olive oil too intense.

4 or 5 tablespoons wine vinegar
1 tablespoon good balsamic vinegar or sherry vinegar
Sea salt and freshly ground black pepper
1/3 cup fruity extra-virgin olive oil
2/3 cup pure olive oil

Whisk all the ingredients together in a small bowl.

garlic vinaigrette

5 tablespoons red wine vinegar
2 teaspoons finely minced garlic
Sea salt and freshly ground black pepper
1/3 cup fruity olive oil
2/3 cup mild olive oil

makes
1 1/4 cups

Whisk all the ingredients together in a small bowl.

THESE DRESSINGS GO WITH THE FOLLOWING RECIPES:

green salad with croutons and gruyère cheese, page 37

insalata capricciosa, page 38

green salad with lardons, mushrooms, and chopped egg, page 41

turkish chopped salad, page 73

chopped summer salad from jaen, page 75

chopped eggplant with preserved lemon, page 85

roasted peppers and onions, page 96

zucchini with mint and vinegar, page 99

poached leeks, page 127

cracked wheat salad with garden vegetables, page 167

wheat salad with vegetables, page 169

paella rice salad, page 173

pasta salad, page 181

tuscan bread salad, page 182

white bean salad, page 191

cannellini beans, page 193

tunisian-inspired chickpea salad with peppers and capers, page 195

lentil salad, page 199

marinated anchovies, page 211

marinated fish, page 212

catalan salt cod and pepper salad, page 213

salade niçoise, page 227

leafy salads

chopped salads

bean salads

bread salads

oily fish such as sardines, anchovies, and mackerel

salt cod salads

sherry vinaigrette

makes
3/4 cup

1/4 cup sherry vinegar
1 clove garlic, minced (optional)
Sea salt and freshly ground black pepper
1/2 cup extra-virgin olive oil, plus more to taste

Whisk all the ingredients together in a small bowl.

THIS DRESSING GOES WITH THE FOLLOWING RECIPES:

green salad with croutons and gruyère cheese, page 37

insalata capricciosa, page 38

green salad with sautéed mushrooms, page 39

green salad with lardons, mushrooms, and chopped egg, page 41

andalusian green salad with eggs and ham, page 43

arugula, mushroom, gruyère, and prosciutto salad, page 54

grilled radicchio salad with beets and oranges, page 60

chopped summer salad from jaen, page 75

sweet-and-sour winter squash, page 103

fresh fava bean salad, page 143

tunisian-inspired chickpea salad with peppers and capers, page 195

lentil salad, page 199

catalan salt cod and pepper salad, page 213

duck breast with pears, walnut, and belgian endive, page 239

chicken and radicchio salad *agrodolce*, page 245

chicken livers, mushrooms, and greens, page 246

leafy salads

mustard vinaigrette

BECAUSE MUSTARD POWDER is quite bitter, vinegar by itself would be too strong for this dressing. Lemon juice is added to temper the sharpness.

1 teaspoon dry mustard powder
2 tablespoons red wine vinegar
1 to 2 tablespoons prepared Dijon mustard
3 tablespoons fresh lemon juice
3/4 cup mild and fruity olive oil
Sea salt and freshly ground black pepper

makes
1 cup plus
2 tablespoons

Make a paste of the dry mustard and vinegar. Add the Dijon mustard, lemon juice, and olive oil and whisk together. Season to taste with salt and pepper.

mustard shallot vinaigrette

2 tablespoons Dijon mustard
2 tablespoons red wine vinegar
1/2 cup mild olive oil
4 tablespoons finely minced shallots
Sea salt and freshly ground black pepper

makes about
3/4 cup

Whisk the mustard and vinegar in a bowl. Beat in the oil, fold in the shallots, and season to taste with salt and pepper.

THESE DRESSINGS GO WITH THE FOLLOWING RECIPES:

green salad with croutons and gruyère cheese, page 37
green salad with sautéed mushrooms, page 39
green salad with cucumbers and walnuts, page 42
poached leeks, page 127
grilled leeks and asparagus, page 129
steamed asparagus, page 131
green and white asparagus, page 133
chicken livers, mushrooms, and greens, page 246

green salads
beet salads
potato salads
oily fish

hot pepper vinaigrette

THIS IS ONE TO SURPRISE YOUR PALATE and enliven your ingredients, especially salads with broccoli, cauliflower, artichokes, potatoes, strongly flavored fish, and hard-boiled eggs. Pepper flakes vary wildly in degree of hotness, and so do people's capacity to take the heat. Some hot pepper dressings use lemon juice instead of vinegar; they are more often used on fruit and seafood salads.

**makes
1 1/4 cups**

> 1 cup extra-virgin olive oil
> 1 1/2 to 2 tablespoons crushed red pepper flakes
> 1/4 cup red wine vinegar
> 1 teaspoon finely minced garlic
> Sea salt and freshly ground black pepper

Heat the olive oil in a small saucepan over medium heat until quite hot but not boiling. Drop in a pepper flake; if the flake skips on top of the oil and doesn't burn or sink, add the rest of the pepper flakes and remove the pan from the heat. Let the pepper flakes steep in the oil about 30 minutes, then strain and let cool. This is called *olio santo*, or hot pepper oil.

Whisk the hot pepper oil and vinegar together in a mixing bowl. Whisk in the garlic and season to taste with salt and pepper. You may need to add a little more olive oil if the hot oil is too hot. Or you may want a bit more vinegar.

THIS DRESSING GOES WITH THE FOLLOWING RECIPES:

turkish chopped salad, page 73

tunisian cauliflower, artichoke, and potato salad, page 136

broccoli, olive, and ricotta salata, page 139

broccoli and potato salad, page 140

cracked wheat salad with garden vegetables, page 167

tunisian-inspired chickpea salad with peppers and capers, page 195

chickpeas with squid and chorizo, page 197

bean salads

rice salads

seafood and tuna salads

nut oil vinaigrettes

NUT OILS ARE FRAGILE AND turn rancid easily, so once you've opened the containers, store them in the refrigerator. Just bring to room temperature before assembling the dressings. Look for nut oils that are made from roasted nuts. They are usually brown-gold in color. Some come in bottles, others in cans (which keep out the light, slowing rancidity, but then you can't see whether the oil is dark and toasted). Many are imported from France. Avoid mass-produced nut oils that are pale and clear, as they have virtually no nut flavor.

walnut vinaigrette

WALNUT VINAIGRETTE IS EXCELLENT on beets and leeks as well as on greens and endive.

2 to 3 tablespoons vinegar (sherry or wine, or sherry or wine and balsamic)
Sea salt and freshly ground black pepper
1/2 cup toasted walnut oil
2 tablespoon extra-virgin olive oil

makes about 3/4 cup

Whisk all the ingredients together in a small bowl.

hazelnut vinaigrette

2 tablespoons balsamic vinegar
1 tablespoon sherry vinegar
Sea salt and freshly ground black pepper
1/2 cup hazelnut oil
2 tablespoons extra-virgin olive oil

makes about 3/4 cup

Whisk all the ingredients together in a small bowl.

THESE DRESSINGS GO WITH THE FOLLOWING RECIPES:

green salad with sautéed mushrooms, page 39
green salad with cucumbers and walnuts, page 42
romaine, gorgonzola, and walnut salad, page 45
spinach salad with mushrooms and walnuts, page 52
belgian endive, fennel, mushroom, and walnut salad, page 53
belgian endive with apples and hazelnuts, page 57

(continued on next page)

balsamic vinegar

FOR GENERATIONS *ACETO BALSAMICO tradizionale* was produced in small quantities in the town of Modena in Emilia-Romagna, and it was not exported, even to other regions of Italy. But in the late 1980s, a flood of industrial balsamic imposters washed up on our shores. Most of this so-called balsamic vinegar is harsh wine vinegar sweetened with sugar and colored with caramel. Americans have always liked sweetened salad dressings—most of our commercial dressings contain sugar—so these industrial balsamic vinegars appealed to our national sweet tooth. They have been a raging success, enthusiastically embraced by the dining public. Some restaurants, under the delusion that it is a very Italian thing to do, pour puddles of olive oil with a few drops of this fake balsamic vinegar into saucers as an accompaniment for bread. Italians are nonplussed.

Aceto balsamico tradizionale is not a wine-based vinegar but is made from the reduced juice of Trebbiano grapes, called grape must, carefully aged in a series of wooden casks. Different woods—cherry, juniper, oak, chestnut, and mulberry—impart complex flavors to the vinegar. Artisanal *aceto balsamico* is costly because it is produced in small batches with great care and it takes a long time to mature. Unlike commercial balsamic vinegars, true *aceto balsamico* will not have an age listed on the bottle. Age may be discreetly indicated by the color of the label: red, white, silver, or gold. True artisanal balsamic vinegar is used sparingly as a condiment, added by drops over a veal chop, berries, or a wedge of Parmesan cheese. Occasionally a few spoonfuls are added to a salad along with extra-virgin olive oil, but never in the amounts specified in most American salad dressing recipes.

To stay active in the marketplace, a few genuine artisanal balsamic producers have learned how to make a less costly alternative to this treasured elixir. However, they do not label these as authentic balsamic vinegar but call them *salse* or *condimenti*, sauces or condiments. The best of these are made by Cavalli and Vecchia Dispensa. Their condiments are made just with grape must, with no added vinegar. Other companies combine traditional grape must with some mild vinegar. These are the balsamic vinegars from Giusti, Elsa, and Leonardi. Before you buy balsamic vinegar, read the label. It should include the words *grape must* or *grape must* and *vinegar.* No sugar; no caramel or other coloring agents.

Because some citrus dressings are too sweet or too light in acidity, adding a few drops of artisan-made balsamic vinegar will deepen the flavor. Citrus balsamic vinaigrettes can be intensified by adding a bit of nutty sherry vinegar. Olive oil or the more robust nut oils work well with this combination.

basic balsamic vinaigrette

3 or 4 tablespoons artisan-produced balsamic vinegar or condiment
Sea salt and freshly ground black pepper
3/4 cup fruity extra-virgin olive oil or a combination of 1/2 cup pure olive
    oil and 1/4 cup extra-virgin olive oil

Whisk all the ingredients together in a small bowl.

THIS DRESSING GOES WITH THE FOLLOWING RECIPES:

green salad with sautéed mushrooms, page 39

green salad with lardons, mushrooms, and chopped egg, page 41

arugula, mushroom, gruyère, and prosciutto salad, page 54

grilled radicchio salad with beets and oranges, page 60

sweet-and-sour winter squash, page 103

chicken and radicchio salad *agrodolce*, page 245

chicken livers, mushrooms, and greens, page 246

leafy green salads

orange balsamic vinaigrette

2 tablespoons artisan-produced balsamic vinegar or condiment
2 tablespoons sherry vinegar
1/4 cup fresh orange juice
2 tablespoons freshly grated orange zest
Sea salt and freshly ground black pepper
2/3 cup pure or mild and fruity extra-virgin olive oil

makes
1 1/3 cups

Whisk all the ingredients together in a small bowl.

orange balsamic vinaigrette with nut oil

2 tablespoons artisan-produced balsamic vinegar or condiment
2 tablespoons sherry vinegar
1/3 cup fresh orange juice
2 tablespoons freshly grated orange zest
Sea salt
1/3 cup toasted hazelnut oil
2/3 cup extra-virgin olive oil

makes
1 1/2 cups

Whisk all the ingredients together in a small bowl.

THESE DRESSINGS GO WITH THE FOLLOWING RECIPES:

belgian endive, radicchio, and orange salad, page 59

grilled radicchio salad with beets and oranges, page 60

roasted winter squash with bitter greens, page 105

steamed asparagus, page 131

peach and tomato salad, page 153

figs, almonds, greens, and cabrales cheese, page 155

duck breast with pears, walnuts, and belgian endive, page 239

leafy green salads

part citrus and part vinegar dressings

catalan vinaigrette

WHEN I TAUGHT MY FIRST CLASS on Mediterranean salad dressings at the Culinary Institute of America in St. Helena, California, Catalan vinaigrette was a runaway favorite. This Spanish-inspired dressing has sweetness from orange juice and zest, salt from capers and anchovies, nuttiness from toasted almonds and mildly acidic sherry vinegar. It lends itself to a variety of leafy salads and cooked vegetables such as asparagus, artichokes, mushrooms, and potatoes, and will work on salads with citrus fruits and avocado. It is also a great finishing sauce spooned on cooked fish such as salmon or sole and on sautéed or broiled chicken or quail.

**makes
1 3/4 cups**

1/4 cup sherry vinegar
1/4 cup fresh orange juice, plus more to taste
3/4 cup sliced almonds, toasted and coarsely chopped
2 tablespoons capers, rinsed and medium finely chopped
2 tablespoons freshly grated orange zest
1 tablespoon pureed or finely chopped anchovies
Sea salt and freshly ground black pepper
1 cup fruity extra-virgin olive oil

Whisk together all the ingredients in a bowl. As this dressing is a bit chunky, you may want to thin it with more oil if necessary to achieve a spoonable consistency.

THIS DRESSING GOES WITH THE FOLLOWING RECIPES:

spinach salad with potatoes and oranges, page 49

belgian endive, radicchio, and orange salad, page 59

grilled radicchio salad with beets and oranges, page 60

roasted pepper and celery salad, page 97

sweet-and-sour winter squash, page 103

moroccan artichoke and orange salad, page 110

steamed asparagus, page 131

green and white asparagus, page 133

peach and tomato salad, page 153

spanish orange and fennel salad, page 154

grapefruit and avocado salad with leafy greens, page 161

warm scallop, orange, and fennel salad, page 216

warm salad of scallops and mushrooms, page 218

shrimp and artichokes, page 219

artichoke salads

avocado salads

beet salads

carrot salads

mushroom salads

cooked fish

mint vinaigrette

POPULAR IN Italy, Greece, Turkey, the Arab nations, and Morocco, this is an exceptionally versatile vinaigrette. It uses both lemon juice and wine vinegar for balance. Making an infusion intensifies the mint flavor. Strong green extra-virgin olive oils may prove too intense for this dressing, so look for golden, fruity olive oil. I love to serve this dressing on spinach salads and salads with carrots, beets, and citrus fruits. Mint vinaigrette also brightens asparagus, potatoes, bean salads, grain salads, and seafood salads. It even makes a wonderful sauce spooned over cooked fish. Added to mayonnaise, it is an excellent spread for chicken and lamb sandwiches with cucumber and watercress.

makes
1 1/2 cups

INFUSION
1/4 cup fresh lemon juice
1/4 cup chopped fresh mint

1/4 cup red wine vinegar
2 tablespoons fresh lemon juice
1/2 cup tightly packed chopped fresh mint
1 teaspoon honey
1/2 teaspoon sea salt
1 1/4 cups mild and fruity olive oil

To make the infusion, combine the lemon juice and chopped mint in a small saucepan. Bring to a boil and remove from the heat. Let steep for about 10 minutes. Strain into a mixing bowl, pressing the leaves against the strainer to extract all of the liquid. There will be about 1/4 cup. It will not be green because of the lemon juice.

To make the dressing, add the remaining ingredients and whisk together.

THE CIGAR METHOD FOR CUTTING MINT AND BASIL

I like to have my prep done ahead of time. That means chopping herbs too. When you chop parsley or dill, they can sit for a while at room temperature or in a container in the refrigerator and hold their color. But mint and basil are delicate and bruise easily. They darken when left to sit, even under refrigeration. To preserve their color, stack the leaves, roll them into a cigar, and cut crosswise into thin strips. For a garnish on salads or any dish where you want to see splashes of green, use the cigar method.

When any green herb is mixed with lemon juice or vinegar, it will fade and lose color. To be sure you have that accent note of green, add the herbs at the last minute.

THIS DRESSING GOES WITH THE FOLLOWING RECIPES:

spinach salad à la grecque, page 48

spinach salad with potatoes and oranges, page 49

arugula and fennel salad with baked goat cheese, page 55

belgian endive, radicchio, and orange salad, page 59

turkish chopped salad, page 73

grilled eggplant, page 80

zucchini with mint and vinegar, page 99

sweet-and-sour winter squash, page 103

tunisian squash puree, page 106

moroccan carrot salad with cumin, page 117

beets, oranges, and greens, page 121

fresh fava bean salad, page 143

melon, cucumber, watercress, and goat cheese salad, page 150

orange, onion, and olive salad, page 151

peach and tomato salad, page 153

spanish orange and fennel salad, page 154

figs, almonds, greens, and cabrales cheese, page 155

figs, greens, and prosciutto, page 157

persian pomegranate and cucumber salad, page 158

grapefruit and avocado salad with leafy greens, page 161

lebanese bulgur wheat salad, page 168

wheat salad with vegetables, page 169

syrian wheat salad, page 171

couscous salad with grilled shrimp, page 175

couscous salad with almonds, raisins, and saffron onions, page 176

fattoush, page 184

gazpacho bread salad, page 188

lentil salad, page 199

leg of lamb, page 249

artichoke salads

asparagus salads

beet salads

carrot salads

orange and radish salads

potato salads

rice salads

good spooned on grilled seafood

can be added to mayonnaise or aioli for sandwiches (chicken, fish, lamb)

flavored vinaigrettes

tomato vinaigrette

WITH THIS VINAIGRETTE WE TRAVEL to Spain: cumin, sherry vinegar, and pimentón (Spanish smoked paprika) provide the taste of *terroir*. Tomatoes add body and acid, and garlic provides a deep flavor note. Use a Spanish olive oil and you'll have the whole package.

makes about 2 cups

- 1 pound ripe tomatoes (3 to 4 medium), peeled, seeded, and coarsely chopped
- 3 cloves garlic, minced
- 1 tablespoon pimentón dulce
- 1 1/2 teaspoons ground cumin
- 1 teaspoon sea salt
- 1/2 cup extra-virgin olive oil
- 4 to 6 tablespoons sherry vinegar

Combine the tomatoes, garlic, pimentón, cumin, and salt in a food processor or blender and pulse to puree. With the motor running slowly, add the vinegar and then the olive oil. If the tomatoes are too mild in flavor, add 1 or 2 tablespoons tomato paste to the dressing.

THIS DRESSING GOES WITH THE FOLLOWING RECIPES:

andalusian green salad with eggs and ham, page 43

spinach salad with potatoes and oranges, page 49

roasted pepper and celery salad, page 97

zucchini and eggplant, page 100

poached leeks, page 127

tuscan bread salad, page 182

gazpacho bread salad, page 188

tunisian-inspired chickpea salad with peppers and capers, page 195

chickpeas with squid and chorizo, page 197

salt cod–stuffed peppers basque style, page 222

catalan salad of salt cod or tuna with chicory, page 233

bean salads

bread salads

potato salads

rice and grain salads

seafood and avocado salads

sun-dried tomato vinaigrette

I'M DEPRESSED WHEN I SEE tomatoes on a menu in the dead of winter. Yes, we love them, but we cannot succumb to serving those tasteless, hard pink orbs. When tomatoes are out of season, this vinaigrette is a way to get their flavor into a salad without resorting to poor quality produce. For this dressing, I use only oil-packed sun-dried tomatoes, not the dried tomatoes that require reconstitution in water. The water leaches most of the flavor out of them. Olive-oil-packed sun-dried tomatoes are intense and fruity in flavor. When they first entered our markets and recipe lists, they were overused and abused. I reached sun-dried tomato fatigue and avoided them for a few years. But I have come to enjoy them again, used appropriately and with discretion.

1/2 cup extra-virgin oil
1/4 cup sun-dried-tomato-infused oil
3 tablespoons red wine vinegar
2 tablespoons chopped sun-dried tomatoes
Sea salt and freshly ground black pepper

makes about 1 cup

Sun-dried-tomato-infused oil is the oil in which the tomatoes are packed. If you do not have enough for this recipe, warm extra-virgin olive oil in a small saucepan over low heat. Add 2 tablespoons chopped sun-dried tomatoes, remove from the heat, and allow to steep for a few hours.

To make the dressing, whisk all the ingredients together in a bowl.

THIS DRESSING GOES WITH THE FOLLOWING RECIPES:

arugula and fennel salad with baked goat cheese, page 55

zucchini and eggplant, page 100

broccoli, olive, and ricotta salata, page 139

broccoli and potato salad, page 140

cannellini beans, page 193

bitter greens

green bean salads

rice salads

pasta salads

seafood salads

chicken salads

oregano garlic vinaigrette

WIDELY USED IN Greece, Italy, and Spain, this vinaigrette is delicious as a marinade for grilled vegetables, tossed in potato, rice, or bean salads, or spooned onto cherry tomatoes, regular tomatoes, mozzarella bocconcini, and cooked cauliflower and broccoli. It enhances salads where tuna, seafood, and hard-boiled eggs play a prominent role. It is also excellent as a marinade for lamb, chicken, and fish and may be drizzled on cooked chicken, fish, and lamb as a finishing sauce. In Sicily, it's known as *salmoriglio* or salmorigano sauce. And it's one of my favorite dressings.

**makes
1 3/4 cups**

3 tablespoons dried oregano
1/2 cup red wine vinegar
2 to 3 cloves garlic, very finely minced
Sea salt and freshly ground black pepper
1 1/4 cups mild and fruity olive oil

Rub the oregano in your hands to warm it and release its oils. Toast it in a dry skillet over low heat for a minute or two.

Whisk all the ingredients together in a bowl. If you have time, warm the dressing over low heat for a few minutes to intensify the flavors.

THIS DRESSING GOES WITH THE FOLLOWING RECIPES:

spinach salad à la grecque, page 48

spinach and chicory salad with cauliflower and artichokes, page 50

greek country salad, page 77

slow-roasted eggplant, page 81

chopped eggplant with preserved lemon, page 85

cheese-stuffed eggplant rolls, page 89

spanish salad of grilled eggplant, onions, and peppers, page 90

paella rice salad, page 173

pasta salad, page 181

tuscan bread salad, page 182

gazpacho bread salad, page 188

white bean salad, page 191

cannellini beans, page 193

tunisian-inspired chickpea salad with peppers and capers, page 195

chickpeas with squid and chorizo, page 197

lentil salad, page 199

bean puree, page 201

grilled squid stuffed with rice and shrimp, page 220

leg of lamb, page 249

grilled chicken, page 250

chicken kebabs, page 251

roast pork, page 253

marinade for chicken, pork tenderloins, lamb kebabs and chops, fish and seafood

finishing sauce for cooked tuna, swordfish

can be added to mayonnaise for sandwich spread—cooked chicken, turkey, fish

sandwich with white bean puree, salami, roasted peppers, and arugula

anchovy garlic vinaigrette

IT IS AMAZING HOW MANY people say they hate anchovies but love this dressing. I think it's because they can't see them! This lively dressing is used quite often in France and Italy and sometimes in Spain. If you have a can of salt-packed anchovies in the fridge, rinse them well under a thin stream of cold water and remove the bones. Puree the fillets with a bit of olive oil. You may also use anchovies packed in extra-virgin olive oil. The olive oil for this dressing should be mild and fruity, such as a golden-hued Provençal or Ligurian oil. This vinaigrette is excellent on bitter greens, roasted peppers, potatoes, and cooked seafood, especially tuna, swordfish, and mackerel. You can drizzle some on hard-boiled eggs, green beans, broccoli, and cauliflower. And it is ideal for a classic salade Niçoise (page 227).

makes about 1 1/2 cups

3 tablespoons finely minced anchovies
1 tablespoon finely minced garlic
1 cup fruity extra-virgin olive oil
1/3 cup red wine vinegar
Freshly ground black pepper

Combine the anchovies and garlic in a small saucepan with a bit of olive oil and warm slightly over low heat. Remove the pan from the heat and whisk in the rest of the olive oil and the vinegar. Season to taste with black pepper.

THIS DRESSING GOES WITH THE FOLLOWING RECIPES:

spinach and chicory salad with cauliflower and artichokes, page 50

puntarelle e peperoni, page 64

moroccan pepper and tomato salad, page 92

tunisian roasted pepper salad, page 95

roasted peppers and onions, page 96

roasted pepper and celery salad, page 97

roasted peppers filled with herbed goat cheese, page 98

winter squash with ricotta salata, page 104

tunisian cauliflower, artichoke, and potato salad, page 136

broccoli, olive, and ricotta salata, page 139

broccoli and potato salad, page 140

salade niçoise, page 227

tomato salads

egg salad, deviled eggs

potato salads

marinade for lamb

drizzle on cooked fish

**can be added to mayonnaise for sandwich spread for tuna salad, egg salad, sliced
 tomato**

citrus dressings or citronettes

FOR THE SAKE OF SIMPLICITY, citrus dressings are often called vinaigrettes, in cookbooks and on restaurant menus, even though they don't contain a drop of vinegar. A citronette is a salad dressing made with only oil and citrus juices. While I don't find the name strange, to some linguistically sensitive types *citronette* sounds a bit like a bug spray, so for the sake of verbal aesthetics, these can be called citrus dressings.

In most Middle Eastern and North African countries, olive oil and lemon juice are used to dress both raw and cooked vegetable salads as well as a few leafy green salads. Because these are not primarily wine-drinking nations, wine vinegar is not a standard pantry item. Grapes are cultivated in these countries, though, so *verjus*, or sour grape juice, tart pomegranate juice, and pomegranate molasses have been used in dressings. Over time, however, lemon juice has become the most popular acid in salad preparations.

Citrus dressings are the ideal condiments for salads with fruit and avocado. They are also a good choice for seafood salads, as their mild acidity does not overpower delicate fish and shellfish. Raw fish dishes such as carpaccio, *crudo*, and tartare work especially well with citrus dressings rather than a dressing with a sharper vinegar base. For salads with strong cheese components, I opt for citrus, because wine vinegar can bring out a weird bitterness in the cheese.

When dressing salads, especially those featuring fruit, pay attention to the lemon juice. Some lemons are tart and sweet, others tart and bitter. If you find the lemon juice too sharp, you can accent the sweet components in your salad by choosing sweeter, more perfumed Meyer lemon juice or mild orange juice, or by adding a spoonful of sugar, honey, or *saba* (reduced grape must) to the dressing for balance.

Of course, sometimes a citrus dressing is not tart enough to complement the salad ingredients well. Taste the dressing to be sure the acidity is correct. If you are making a leafy salad, dip a leaf into the dressing. If it is a vegetable or grain salad, dress it and take a bite; stir in a drop or two of vinegar for added punch if the citrus dressing is not tart enough to balance all of the flavors.

There has been a time-honored taboo against serving wine with salad for fear that the vinaigrette could overwhelm the wine. Here's where a dressing made with oil and the juice of lemons or grapefruits, the sweeter limes, Clementines, oranges, or Meyer lemons will shine. *Verjus*, pomegranate juice or molasses, or even some of the wine itself can act as the acid component in the dressing, so wine lovers can have wine with the salad course and not worry.

The technique for assembling citrus dressings is really simple. A wire whisk and a bowl are all you need. Some cooks like to put the dressing ingredients in a small jar and shake it. Others emulsify the dressing by whirring it in a blender or beating it with an electric wand or immersion blender. Emulsification is not necessary but will hold the dressing in suspension a while longer than is the case with one that is simply whisked together.

CLASSIC CITRUS DRESSINGS

THREE MIXED CITRUS DRESSINGS

TWO CITRUS DRESSINGS WITH HEAT

OTHER CITRUS DRESSINGS

VERJUS

Before lemons arrived in Europe from China, the major culinary souring agent was **verjus** or **agresto** (its name in Spain and Italy). It is made from juice pressed from sour grapes and was used in many of the classic egg and lemon sauces and mayonnaises. It can also be added to a citronette for an extra note of acidity. You can find bottled **verjus** in the vinegar section of our markets. A premium brand used by chefs is Noble Sour T, made from Traminer grapes, and Noble Sour PX, made from Pedro Jimenez grapes. Other brands are made by Fusion, Minus 8, Navarro Vineyards, and Wolffer Estate Vineyards. Products labeled **vincotto** or **saba** are made from **verjus** that has been cooked and reduced, making it sweeter and more intense.

classic citrus dressings

CITRUS DRESSINGS ARE POPULAR all over the Mediterranean but especially in the Middle East and North Africa. They are used to dress leafy and chopped salads, cooked vegetables such as beets, fennel, favas, and artichokes, and bean and grain salads. Citrus dressings are particularly good on fruit salads, salads with strong cheese components, and salads that are served with wine. They are ideal for seafood salads and raw fish dishes and may be spooned liberally over cooked fish and seafood as a finishing sauce.

basic citrus dressing

IN GREECE, THE SIMPLE MIXTURE of olive oil and lemon juice is called *ladolemono*.

makes 3/4 cup

1/2 cup mild and fruity extra-virgin olive oil
4 tablespoons fresh lemon juice
Sea salt and freshly ground black pepper

Whisk all the ingredients together in a bowl.

VARIATION:

For garlic citrus dressing, add 2 teaspoons minced garlic.

THIS DRESSING GOES WITH THE FOLLOWING RECIPES:

italian parsley salad with walnuts and pecorino, page 61

cooked wild greens, page 67

greek country salad, page 77

artichoke and fennel salad, page 107

moroccan artichoke and orange salad, page 110

beets, oranges, and greens, page 121

lebanese bulgur wheat salad, page 168

couscous salad with grilled shrimp, page 175

couscous salad with almonds, raisins, and saffron onions, page 176

fattoush, page 184

scallop carpaccio, page 209

tuna tartare, page 210

beet salads

carrot salads

caper and garlic citrus dressing

THIS IS ONE OF MY FAVORITE DRESSINGS for *crudo*, fish carpaccio, grilled squid, tuna salads, and bean salads embellished with seafood.

4 tablespoons salt-packed capers, rinsed and coarsely chopped
1/4 cup fresh lemon juice
1 to 2 teaspoons finely minced garlic
3/4 cup extra-virgin olive oil, plus more if needed
Freshly ground black pepper
Sea salt, if needed

**makes about
1 cup**

Combine the capers, lemon juice, and garlic in a bowl and whisk in the olive oil. Add pepper and salt to taste (remember that capers are salty).

THIS DRESSING GOES WITH THE FOLLOWING RECIPES:

tunisian roasted pepper salad, page 95

artichoke and fennel salad, page 107

beets, oranges, and greens, page 121

poached leeks, page 127

fish carpaccio, page 207

tuna tartare, page 210

grilled squid stuffed with rice and shrimp, page 220

salade niçoise, page 227

mustard shallot citrus dressing

THIS DRESSING IS TART AND INTENSE, and is thus excellent on rich dishes such as shellfish or raw fish such as tuna. It is equally fine on starchy salads, such as those featuring white beans, and on radish or cucumber salads, which are assertive enough to stand up to it. It also works on simple leafy salads.

makes about 1 cup

3 tablespoons Dijon mustard
1/4 cup fresh lemon juice
1/2 cup extra-virgin olive oil
3 tablespoons finely minced shallots
Sea salt and freshly ground black pepper

Whisk together the mustard and lemon juice in a bowl, then whisk in the olive oil. Add the shallots, whisk again, and season to taste with salt and pepper.

THIS DRESSING GOES WITH THE FOLLOWING RECIPES:

fish carpaccio, page 207

tuna tartare, page 210

grilled squid stuffed with rice and shrimp, page 220

seafood, potatoes, and green beans, page 230

leafy greens

three mixed citrus dressings

TO PRESERVE THE SWEETNESS AND AROMA of orange juice, avoid an overly assertive olive oil as you don't want the oil to overpower the fruit. No bitter or peppery Tuscan oils here—mild and fruity oil from Liguria or Provence works best, but you can use a simple pure olive oil or grapeseed or sunflower oil. To concentrate the orange flavor, start with double the amount of juice and reduce it by half, or add freshly grated orange zest.

In the second dressing you have the option of adding just a bit of sherry or mellow aged sherry vinegar if you need to boost the acidity to balance the dressing with the salad ingredients.

The third dressing has a Moroccan or Middle Eastern feel because of the cinnamon and orange flower water.

mixed citrus dressing I

1/2 cup mild, fruity extra-virgin olive oil or pure olive oil
Freshly grated zest of 1 orange (about 1 tablespoon)
1/4 cup fresh blood orange juice or regular orange juice
2 tablespoons fresh lemon juice, plus more to taste
1/2 teaspoon sugar, if needed
1/2 teaspoon sea salt
Freshly ground black pepper

makes 1 scant cup

In a bowl, whisk together all of the ingredients. Dip a lettuce leaf into the dressing to see if it is tart enough, has enough salt, and is balanced. Add more lemon juice or sugar if needed.

mixed citrus dressing II

1 cup pure olive oil
1/4 cup fresh orange juice
2 tablespoons fresh lemon juice
Freshly grated zest of 2 oranges
2 tablespoons sherry or aged sherry vinegar
1 tablespoon sugar
1/2 teaspoon sea salt

makes 1 1/2 cups

In a bowl, whisk together all of the ingredients.

(continued on next page)

THESE DRESSINGS GO WITH THE FOLLOWING RECIPES:

moroccan artichoke and orange salad, page 110

sicilian artichokes, page 112

moroccan cooked carrot salad, page 113

moroccan carrot salad with cumin, page 117

beets, oranges, and greens, page 121

orange, onion, and olive salad, page 151

spanish orange and fennel salad, page 154

persimmon and pomegranate salad with butter lettuce, page 159

grapefruit and avocado salad with leafy greens, page 161

scallop carpaccio, page 209

smoked trout, carrots, and cucumbers, page 214

duck breast with pears, walnuts, and belgian endive, page 239

carrot salads

citrus cinnamon dressing

A LITTLE EXOTIC, this dressing can waft you to Morocco and the Middle East with ease. Orange, beet, carrot, and radish salads as well as couscous salads come to mind.

makes 3/4 cup

1/2 cup mild olive oil
3 tablespoons fresh orange juice
2 tablespoons fresh lemon juice
2 teaspoons freshly grated orange zest
1 teaspoon freshly grated lemon zest
1 tablespoon confectioners' sugar
1/2 teaspoon sea salt
1/2 teaspoon ground cinnamon
Orange flower water (optional)

Combine all the ingredients in a bowl with a whisk, then add orange flower water to taste if you like.

THIS DRESSING GOES WITH THE FOLLOWING RECIPES:

moroccan salad of raw grated carrots, page 115

beets, oranges, and greens, page 121

couscous salad with almonds, raisins, and saffron onions, page 176

two citrus dressings with heat

ONE GETS ITS HEAT from the addition of ample freshly ground black pepper, the other from an infusion of crushed red pepper flakes. The latter is considerably hotter. Both of these dressings work well with mild salads like potato, rice, couscous, and bean and on the more assertive vegetables, such as broccoli, cauliflower, and artichokes. Hot pepper citrus dressing also complements tuna and shellfish and creates a dynamic contrast with cool, sweet fruit salads.

citrus and black pepper dressing

1/2 cup extra-virgin olive oil
1/4 cup fresh orange juice
2 tablespoons fresh lemon juice
1 tablespoon coarsely ground black pepper
Sea salt

makes about 3/4 cup

Whisk the ingredients together in a small bowl.

THIS DRESSING GOES WITH THE FOLLOWING RECIPES:

peach and tomato salad, page 153
grapefruit and avocado salad with leafy greens, page 161
warm scallop, orange, and fennel salad, page 216

hot pepper citrus dressing

3/4 cup extra-virgin olive oil
1 tablespoon crushed red pepper flakes
1/4 cup fresh lemon juice
1 teaspoon finely minced garlic (optional)
Sea salt
Freshly ground black pepper (optional)

makes 1 cup

Warm the olive oil in a small saucepan over medium-high heat until quite hot but not boiling. Drop in a pepper flake; if the flake skips on top of the oil and doesn't burn or sink, add the rest of the pepper flakes and remove the pan from the heat. Let the pepper flakes steep in the oil about 30 minutes, then strain and let cool. In Italy this is called *olio santo,* or "holy oil."

(continued on next page)

Whisk the hot pepper oil and lemon juice together in a mixing bowl. Whisk in the garlic, if using, and season to taste with salt. You might even want a bit of black pepper. If the dressing is too hot for you, add a little more olive oil and maybe a touch more lemon juice.

(Another hot pepper dressing uses red wine vinegar instead of lemon juice and is more intense; see page 272).

THIS DRESSING GOES WITH THE FOLLOWING RECIPES:

tunisian squash puree, page 106

turkish-style artichokes and orange, page 109

moroccan artichoke and orange salad, page 110

tunisian carrot salad, page 116

broccoli and potato salad, page 140

orange, onion, and olive salad, page 151

peach and tomato salad, page 153

grapefruit and avocado salad with leafy greens, page 161

fish carpaccio, page 207

scallop carpaccio, page 209

tuna tartare, page 210

warm scallop, orange, and fennel salad, page 216

grilled squid stuffed with rice and shrimp, page 220

grilled chicken, page 250

carrot salads

other citrus dressings

pomegranate citrus dressing

BEFORE LEMONS CAME TO THE MIDDLE EAST from China, tart pomegranates were a source of acidity. Fabulous pomegranates are cultivated in California, but they are much sweeter than those from the Middle East. To get the amount of acidity traditionally produced by this spectacular fruit, we need either to reduce the juice by half or to use tart pomegranate concentrate. Salt is crucial to bring up the pomegranate flavor. Sometimes you'll want to add a few drops of sherry vinegar or balsamic vinegar for accent. That's literally a few drops, not more—you don't want to lose the pomegranate!

This recipe calls for bottled pomegranate juice, but you can juice the fruit yourself. It's messy—wear a plastic garbage bag over your clothes, because the pomegranates spray madly. Roll the pomegranates around in your hands to loosen the pulp and release the juice. Cut each one in half and place a half on the juicer. Back up a bit and squeeze.

If you do not want to use bottled juice and do not want to squeeze your own, you can use thick, tart pomegranate molasses, which you can find in stores selling Middle Eastern food (although my supermarket has just started to carry it, thank goodness). I recommend either Carlo or Cortas brand.

> 1 cup bottled or fresh pomegranate juice, reduced to 1/2 cup
> 1/4 cup mild olive oil
> 2 tablespoons fresh lemon juice, plus more to taste (or add a drop of
>   sherry vinegar)
> Sea salt

**makes
1 scant cup**

Whisk the pomegranate juice, olive oil, and lemon juice together in a small bowl and add salt to taste.

(continued on next page)

pomegranate dressing from concentrate

makes
about 1 cup

1/2 cup mild olive oil, plus more to taste
6 tablespoons pomegranate molasses
3 tablespoons fresh lemon juice
Sea salt

Whisk the olive oil, pomegranate molasses, and lemon juice together in a small bowl and add salt to taste.

pomegranate and nut oil dressing

makes
1/2 cup plus
2 tablespoons

4 tablespoons pomegranate molasses or 1/2 cup reduced pomegranate juice
2 tablespoons fresh lemon juice
2 tablespoons walnut oil or hazelnut oil
2 tablespoons olive oil or canola oil
Sea salt

Whisk the pomegranate molasses, lemon juice, nut oil, and olive oil together in a small bowl and add salt to taste.

THESE DRESSINGS GO WITH THE FOLLOWING RECIPES:

preserved lemon dressing

MOROCCAN PRESERVED LEMONS add pungency to a mildly spiced citrus dressing. Rinse the lemon of excess salt, discard the pulp, and either cut the peel into fine slivers or chop it. You can buy commercial preserved lemons, but they are very expensive, and it is easy to make your own (see page 300).

1/2 cup fresh lemon juice
1 teaspoon sweet paprika
1 teaspoon toasted cumin seed, ground
Pinch of cayenne
1 1/4 cups olive oil, plus more if needed
Peel of a preserved lemon, finely slivered or chopped
Sea salt and freshly ground black pepper

makes
1 3/4 cups

Whisk together the lemon juice, paprika, cumin, and cayenne in a mixing bowl until smooth.

Whisk in the olive oil and then stir in the lemon peel. Add salt and pepper to taste.

NOTE: *This dressing is also an ideal marinade for olives. Warm the olives in the dressing and let them sit for a few hours at room temperature.*

THIS DRESSING GOES WITH THE FOLLOWING RECIPES:

cooked wild greens, page 67

moroccan chopped salad, page 74

chopped eggplant with preserved lemon, page 85

spanish salad of grilled eggplant, onions, and peppers, page 90

moroccan pepper and tomato salad, page 92

moroccan green pepper salad, page 93

artichoke and fennel salad, page 107

cauliflower zahlouk, page 135

tunisian cauliflower, artichoke, and potato salad, page 136

israeli chopped salad with avocado, page 163

couscous salad with grilled shrimp, page 175

fish carpaccio, page 207

shrimp and artichokes, page 219

grilled squid stuffed with rice and shrimp, page 220

tuna, roasted pepper, and avocado salad, page 225

lamb kebabs, page 255

PRESERVED LEMONS

Preserved lemons are a staple of the Moroccan kitchen. The lemons need time to cure, so they must be prepared about a month before you want to use them. Keep a constant supply in your pantry and you'll probably find a way to use them in dishes that are not North African in inspiration.

To make 4 pints, start with 16 lemons (about 4 pounds), plus more if needed, and some kosher salt. Scrub 8 lemons with a brush, then place them in a nonreactive container, cover with cold water, and let soak for a few hours at room temperature. Drain the lemons and dry well. Cut them in quarters lengthwise with a sharp knife, but do not cut through the bottom of the lemons. Each cut lemon should be divided almost in quarters lengthwise, like a tulip.

Push a heaping tablespoonful of kosher salt into the center of each lemon. Place a heaping tablespoon of salt on the bottom of 4 sterilized pint jars and pack the salted lemons in tightly. Allow 4 lemons to a jar. (Small jars are best, because once opened, the lemons do not keep for as long as they do when sealed.)

Juice the remaining 8 lemons and pour the juice over the lemons in the jars. If there is not enough juice to cover them, squeeze a few more lemons. (You can add just enough boiling water to cover, but lemon juice is best.) Seal the jars.

Store the jars in a cool, dry place for 4 weeks, turning them occasionally in the first few days to distribute the salt. Do not be alarmed if a white film forms on the lemons; it will wash off. After opening the jars, store in the refrigerator. They will keep for 9 months to a year unopened.

To use the lemons, rinse them well under running water. Remove the pulp and discard. Cut the peel into thin slivers or fine dice.

You can also use an alternate brine: Prepare 4 lemons as directed and place in a sterilized pint jar. Dissolve 1/3 cup kosher salt in 1 cup boiling water. Bring to a boil. Cool to room temperature, then pour the brine over the lemons. Some cooks add whole peppercorns, cinnamon sticks, or other spices, but this is not necessary.

toasted cumin citrus dressing

THIS DRESSING, USED IN Spain, the Middle East, and North Africa, is intensely aromatic and works well with bland foods like avocado and grain and bean salads and with assertive ingredients like peppers and salt cod. It can be spooned over cooked carrots, eggplants, zucchini, and peppers or drizzled on grilled fish or shellfish.

2 tablespoons cumin seeds
1 cup mild, fruity olive oil
1/3 cup fresh lemon juice
2 cloves garlic, minced (optional)
Sea salt and freshly ground black pepper

**makes
1 1/3 cups**

Toast the cumin seeds in a small skillet over low heat, stirring occasionally, until fragrant; it will take just a minute or two. Grind the seads in a spice mill, then whisk together with the remaining ingredients, adding salt and pepper to taste.

THIS DRESSING GOES WITH THE FOLLOWING RECIPES:

moroccan green pepper salad, page 93

moroccan carrot salad with cumin, page 117

orange, onion, and olive salad, page 151

israeli chopped salad with avocado, page 163

gazpacho bread salad, page 188

lentil salad, page 199

bean puree, page 201

catalan salt cod and pepper salad, page 213

tuna, roasted pepper, and avocado salad, page 225

roast pork, page 253

beet salads

carrot salads

creamy dressings that double as dips

WITH THEIR RICH TEXTURE and voluptuous mouth feel, these creamy dressings not only complement salads with contrasting crunchy textures and a bit of body but also serve as dips for both raw and cooked vegetables. They do not penetrate the food but rest upon it, and they make wonderful finishing sauces as well.

Creamy dressings add richness to foods that are already rich in texture. It's the icing-on-the-cake concept, or "more is more." Roasted eggplant, mashed chickpeas or lentils, cooked fish, and poultry and meat salads do well with creamy dressings. They can be too weighty for tiny, delicate leafy greens, but crisp romaine, the chicories, and purslane, as well as cucumbers, celery, fennel, carrots, beets, eggplant, asparagus, and toasted nuts, are natural foils.

A creamy salad dressing can be based on tahini, yogurt, or mayonnaise, or it may be a vinaigrette or citrus dressing enriched with cream or cheese. Like most vinaigrettes, yogurt- and cream-based dressings are assembled in a bowl with a whisk. Tahini- and mayonnaise-based dressings, however, should be assembled in a blender or food processor or with an electric wand or immersion blender, which emulsifies them, holding the ingredients in suspension so they won't separate.

Cheese- and cream-based dressings strike a better balance when lemon juice or *verjus*, rather than vinegar, is the acid component. To arrive at the proper level of acidity, dip a lettuce leaf in the dressing; if it is not tart enough, add a bit of mild Champagne or Cava vinegar. Red wine vinegar often brings out bitterness in cheese. And please keep in mind that cheese is salty, so care should be taken in seasoning the greens.

CREAMY DRESSINGS

tahini dressing (303)

tarator dressing (305)

yogurt dressing (306)

CREAM-BASED DRESSINGS

basic lemon cream dressing and variation (308)

tarragon mustard cream dressing (310)

NUT-BASED CREAM DRESSINGS

hazelnut cream dressing (311)

walnut cream dressing (312)

CHEESE-BASED CREAM DRESSINGS

gorgonzola or roquefort cream dressing (313)

MAYONNAISE-BASED DRESSINGS

basic mayonnaise dressing and variations (315)

tahini dressing

TAHINI IS A PANTRY STAPLE in Israel, the Arab nations, Turkey, and the Middle East. A rather thick paste made from grinding sesame meal and oil, it comes to the market in cans, jars, and plastic containers. For years tahini was found only in stores specializing in foods from the Middle East or health-food stores, but today it is on many supermarket shelves. Not all tahini is of equal quality, so I advise sampling a few different brands to find one that is rich in flavor and has no bitterness. (Some of the "natural food" brands are not mellow enough for my palate, and a few have a nasty aftertaste.) My favorite, Al Wadi, comes from Lebanon.

After packing and shipping, the sesame paste settles to the bottom of the container in a dense lump and the oil floats on top. You will have to stir the tahini rather vigorously before use. A whirl in the blender or food processor will do it, or use a strong wrist and a fork. After you take what you need, put the rest back in the original container. Every time you need to use tahini, you will have to repeat the stirring process, as it will resettle.

Tahini becomes a salad dressing when you blend it with lemon juice and thin the puree with varying amounts of water. It can be thick or quite thin. Garlic is usually added, as are spices such as cumin and cayenne or another ground hot pepper. Creamy tahini dressing may be served as an appetizer dip for pita bread, spears of cucumber, carrots, radishes, and green onions. Thinned with water, it can be drizzled over a simple salad of sliced tomatoes or beets and greens. Tahini dressing can also be used to dress a salad of romaine lettuce, sliced cucumbers, and radishes. It is superb spooned over sautéed or grilled eggplant or zucchini. Stir it into mashed roasted eggplant and you create baba ghanouj. Stir it into mashed chickpeas and you create hummus.

Tahini dressing is also a superb finishing sauce. As you will see from the recipes in this book, it can be spooned into pita bread along with a bit of chopped cucumber and tomatoes to moisten falafel (page 203), mussels (page 229), or kefta (page 256). It may also be spooned over cooked fish and seafood as a finishing sauce. To lighten this rich, creamy dressing, some cooks beat in 1/2 cup plain yogurt.

1 cup sesame tahini, preferably Al Wadi brand
1/2 cup fresh lemon juice
2 cloves garlic, finely minced
1 cup cold water, plus more if needed
Sea salt and freshly ground black pepper
1/2 teaspoon toasted cumin seed, ground (optional)
Pinch of cayenne (optional)
Chopped fresh flat-leaf parsley, for garnish (optional)

makes
2 1/2 cups

(continued on next page)

Combine the tahini, lemon juice, and garlic in a food processor or blender and puree. Add water as needed to thin to a spreadable consistency for a dip and even thinner for salad dressing. Season with salt and pepper to taste, and with cumin and cayenne if you like.

To serve as a dip, spoon into a shallow bowl and sprinkle with chopped parsley. (Some cooks stir the parsley into the dressing.)

VARIATION:
Add 1/2 cup chopped fresh cilantro and 1/2 teaspoon cayenne to the tahini mixture when pureeing.

THIS DRESSING GOES WITH THE FOLLOWING RECIPES:

crunchy garden salad, page 47

greek parsley salad, page 63

cooked wild greens, page 67

slow-roasted eggplant, page 81

turkish eggplant puree with walnuts, page 83

roasted eggplant, page 86

zucchini and eggplant, page 100

roasted winter squash with bitter greens, page 105

carrots and celery root, page 118

beets, goat cheese, and arugula, page 123

beets and greens, page 124

lebanese bulgur wheat salad, page 168

chickpeas, page 202

chickpea croquettes, page 203

fish with tahini sauce, page 236

middle eastern hamburger, page 256

crunchy leafy salads (romaine, purslane)

cucumber and tomato salads

a dip for pita and for crisp vegetables

a dip for fried seafood and vegetables

beet salads

carrot salads

tarator dressing

NUT-THICKENED SAUCES ARE SIGNATURES of the Arabic kitchen and are found in the cuisines of Greece, Turkey, Lebanon, and Spain, whose cuisine was heavily influenced by the Moorish Arabs for seven hundred years. A creamy tahini dressing enriched with toasted nuts, usually walnuts or hazelnuts, is called tarator or teradot. Some cooks prefer to use almonds, which are more delicate. Tarator can be made hours ahead of time but will need to be thinned with additional water, because it thickens as it stands. Be aware that over time, walnuts may stain this dressing an odd shade of purple.

Any combination of romaine, watercress, spinach, parsley, and mint will take to this dressing. Cucumbers are also a natural partner. Tarator can be used to dress a salad of cooked chicken, cucumbers, and greens. It is also used as a sauce for cooked shellfish, fish, and vegetables. In Turkey, deep-fried mussels served with a tarator dipping sauce are a popular street food.

1 cup walnuts or hazelnuts, toasted
1 cup tahini dressing (page 303)
Water
Up to 1/2 cup mild or fruity olive oil
Minced garlic (optional)
Sea salt and freshly ground black pepper
1/2 cup yogurt (optional)

makes
2 cups

Put the nuts in a food processor and pulse to make a crumbly paste. Beat in the tahini dressing. Add water and olive oil until the dressing has a smooth, heavy, creamy consistency. Add more garlic if you like and season to taste with salt and pepper. You may lighten this dressing with the yogurt if you wish.

THIS DRESSING GOES WITH THE FOLLOWING RECIPES:

turkish eggplant puree with walnuts, page 83

carrots and celery root, page 118

beets, goat cheese, and arugula, page 123

beets and greens, page 124

lebanese bulgur wheat salad, page 168

shrimp salad, page 223

fried mussels, page 229

turkish chicken salad, page 243

beet salads

yogurt dressing

NOTHING COULD BE SIMPLER TO ASSEMBLE than this cool and creamy yogurt dressing. Cooks in Greece, Turkey, Iran, and the Arab nations find many uses for this versatile dressing. It is served on beet salads, carrot salads, and cucumber salads as well as those with cooked eggplant and zucchini. In Greece and Turkey, it is used to dress a salad of purslane. In Iran, it is mixed with cooked spinach, beets, mushrooms, eggplant, carrots, and cucumbers. The most common additions to the basic yogurt dressing are chopped fresh mint or dill and minced garlic.

To make this creamy dressing, you need thick yogurt. The imported Fage brand of Greek yogurt does not require any draining, but most commercial yogurts need to be drained of excess water. To get 2 cups of thick yogurt, spoon 4 cups of yogurt into a strainer lined with cheesecloth, set it over a bowl, and let the water drain away for a few hours in the refrigerator.

makes about 2 1/2 cups

2 cups thick yogurt
1/3 cup extra-virgin olive oil
1/4 cup fresh lemon juice
Sea salt
2 to 3 teaspoons minced garlic (optional)
2 tablespoons chopped fresh mint or dill (optional)

In a bowl, whisk the yogurt with the olive oil and lemon juice. Season to taste with salt. Fold in the garlic or herbs if desired.

THIS DRESSING GOES WITH THE FOLLOWING RECIPES:

crunchy garden salad, page 47

collard green salad, page 65

cabbage slaw à la politika, page 66

slow-roasted eggplant, page 81

turkish eggplant puree with walnuts, page 83

zucchini with mint and vinegar, page 99

zucchini and eggplant, page 100

carrots and celery root, page 118

beets, goat cheese, and arugula, page 123

beets and greens, page 124

cucumber salad, page 145

persian mushroom salad, page 146

persian spinach salad, page 147

persian eggplant salad, page 147

potato and egg salad, page 148

melon, cucumber, watercress, and goat cheese salad, page 150

lamb kebabs, page 255

beet salads

carrot salads

mixed with mashed grilled eggplant

used as a dip on the meze table

cream-based dressings

MOST CREAM-BASED DRESSINGS ARE FRENCH in inspiration and use lemon juice as the acid component. Occasionally a few drops of *verjus* or one of the "drinking" vinegars (which are less than 6 percent acid) such as a fragrant, sweet balsamic vinegar, or Minus 8 ice wine vinegar, Spanish muscatel vinegar, or a very mild Champagne or tarragon vinegar, may be added for accent. Stay away from a sharp red wine vinegar, as it will conflict with the cream. The cream may be heavy whipping cream or the thicker crème fraîche. The latter is a bit tart in its own right, so you may need less lemon juice to balance the dressing.

Cream-based dressings are good on leafy salads, especially those with bitter greens, spinach, Belgian endive, and romaine, as well as salads with walnuts and hazelnuts or those featuring cucumbers, fennel, beets, green beans, mushrooms, leeks, or asparagus.

basic lemon cream dressing

**makes
1 cup**

**1/2 cup mild olive oil
3 to 4 tablespoons fresh lemon juice
1/4 cup heavy cream or crème fraîche
Sea salt and freshly ground black pepper**

Whisk the olive oil and lemon juice together in a small bowl, then whisk in the cream. Season to taste with salt and pepper.

NOTE: *Want to make a simple cucumber or Belgian endive salad spectacular? Stir a bit of caviar or salmon roe into lemon cream dressing and you have a very festive salad.*

VARIATION:
lemon mustard cream dressing

**makes
1 cup**

**2 tablespoons strong Dijon mustard
3 to 4 tablespoons fresh lemon juice
1/2 cup olive oil
1/4 cup heavy cream or crème fraîche
Sea salt and freshly ground black pepper**

Whisk the mustard and lemon juice together in a small bowl. Gradually add the olive oil and cream. Add salt and pepper to taste.

NOTE: *For a classic French cucumber salad, slice cucumbers and sprinkle with salt. Let sit for 15 to 20 minutes, then rinse and pat dry. Dress with lemon mustard cream and sprinkle with lots of chopped chervil.*

THESE DRESSINGS GO WITH THE FOLLOWING RECIPES:

romaine, gorgonzola, and walnut salad, page 45

crunchy garden salad, page 47

spinach salad with mushrooms and walnuts, page 52

belgian endive, fennel, mushroom, and walnut salad, page 53

arugula, mushroom, gruyère, and prosciutto salad, page 54

cabbage slaw à la politika, page 66

beet, celery, potato, and mâche salad, page 125

grilled leeks, page 128

steamed asparagus, page 131

green and white asparagus, page 133

melon, cucumber, watercress, and goat cheese salad, page 150

smoked trout salad, page 215

shrimp salad, page 223

seafood, potatoes, and green beans, page 230

leafy salads, especially those with bitter greens, spinach, endive

beet salads

salads with nuts (walnuts, hazelnuts, pine nuts)

mushrooms, cucumbers

cooked salmon, chicken salads

BASIC LEMON CREAM DRESSING ALSO GOES WITH:

figs, almonds, greens, and cabrales cheese, page 155

figs, greens, and prosciutto, page 157

pear, fennel, endive

tarragon mustard cream dressing

THIS MAKES AN IDEAL DRESSING FOR cucumbers, cooked aspar-agus, carrots, leeks, and potatoes, cooked salmon salads, and a salad of shrimp and artichokes or shrimp and asparagus.

**makes
about 1 cup**

**2 tablespoons Dijon mustard
1/4 cup fresh lemon juice or 2 tablespoons lemon juice and
    1 to 2 tablespoons tarragon vinegar
1/2 cup fruity or pure olive oil
1/4 cup heavy cream, plus more to taste
1 to 2 tablespoons chopped fresh tarragon
Sea salt and freshly ground black pepper**

Whisk together the mustard and lemon juice or lemon juice and tarragon vinegar. Whisk in the olive oil and then the cream. Add the chopped tarragon and season to taste with salt and pepper.

THIS DRESSING GOES WITH THE FOLLOWING RECIPES:

nut-based cream dressings

NUT OILS ARE INTENSE AND FRAGRANT because the nuts are toasted before they are pressed, which maximizes their flavor. Because these oils are assertive, they need to be used with finesse. In classic vinaigrettes they often are mixed with olive oil to cut their intensity, but in cream-based dressings they do not need another oil to become mellow. The cream brings out the sweetness of hazelnuts and tempers the bitterness of the more intense walnut oil. There are now almond and pistachio oils on the market, but walnut and hazelnut are the nut oils most commonly used in European salads.

Store nut oils in the refrigerator, because they have a tendency to go rancid quickly. As added insurance, taste them before using; rancid oil is a very unpleasant trick to play on your palate and your guests.

Nut cream dressings are excellent on salads with green beans, beets, grilled or steamed leeks, celery or fennel, mushrooms, cucumbers, endive, ripe pears or figs, crisp apples, and cooked poultry. Hazelnut cream is especially good on asparagus. To enforce the nut flavor, garnish the salad with nuts that echo the oil in your dressing.

hazelnut cream dressing

Juice of 1 lemon (about 1/4 cup)
2 shallots, finely minced
1/3 to 1/2 cup toasted hazelnut oil
1/2 cup heavy cream
Sea salt and freshly ground black pepper

makes about
1 1/4 cups

In a small bowl, whisk together the lemon juice, shallots, 1/3 cup hazelnut oil, and cream. Season to taste with additional oil if needed and with salt and pepper.

THIS DRESSING GOES WITH THE FOLLOWING RECIPES:

spinach salad with mushrooms and walnuts, page 52
belgian endive, fennel, mushroom, and walnut salad, page 53
green beans and fennel, page 126
grilled leeks and asparagus, page 129
green and white asparagus, page 133
figs, greens, and prosciutto, page 157

walnut cream dressing

YOU CAN FOLLOW THE INSTRUCTIONS for hazelnut cream dressing (page 311), substituting walnut oil for the hazelnut oil, or try this variation, which uses mild, sweet balsamic vinegar in place of lemon juice.

makes
about
1 1/3 cups

1/2 cup toasted walnut oil
1/4 cup mild olive oil
1/2 cup heavy cream
2 tablespoons balsamic vinegar
Sea salt and freshly ground black pepper

In a small bowl, whisk together the oils, cream, and vinegar. Season to taste with salt and pepper.

THIS DRESSING GOES WITH THE FOLLOWING RECIPES:

green salad with cucumbers and walnuts, page 42

spinach salad with mushrooms and walnuts, page 52

belgian endive, fennel, mushroom, and walnut salad, page 53

beet, celery, potato, and mâche salad, page 125

green beans and fennel, page 126

grilled leeks, page 128

crab salad with walnuts, page 224

turkish chicken salad, page 243

cheese-based cream dressings

THERE IS A WORLD OF DIFFERENCE BETWEEN a salad with cheese and a salad with a cheese-based cream dressing. Some salads are topped with shavings of Parmesan or pecorino; the cheese is the garnish, not a component in the dressing. The greens may be dressed with vinaigrette, but the cheese is usually strewn on top and not dressed. Mild, bland cheeses like fresh mozzarella and burrata do not react badly with salad dressings because they are lightly dressed with oil, and vinegar, if there is any, is barely detectable.

When I talk of a cheese-based cream dressing, I mean a dressing in which cheese is pureed or folded in. With cheese-based dressings, lemon juice usually is the acid of choice. Vinegar can make cheese taste bitter unless the cheese is mild and sweet. Just as red wine is not the perfect drink to pair with every cheese and white wine is often a better match because of its acidity, so lemon juice is a better choice for a salad in which cheese plays an important part.

gorgonzola or roquefort cream dressing

GORGONZOLA AND ROQUEFORT ARE the best-known of the blue cheeses, but you can use any other creamy blue in their stead. This intense and creamy dressing makes an ideal contrast to crisp textures. Fennel, celery, carrots, crisp-tender endive, mushrooms, beets, potatoes, crisp apples or sweet ripe pears and figs, and crunchy toasted nuts are ideal foils for its richness. You can also spoon this dressing on grilled steak or use it as a dipping sauce for fried potatoes. Remember to go easy on salt, as the cheese brings a good deal of salt to the dressing.

1/2 cup mild olive oil
1/4 cup finely crumbled Gorgonzola dolce or Roquefort cheese
1/4 cup heavy cream
2 tablespoons fresh lemon juice, or to taste
Pinch of freshly ground black pepper
Sea salt (optional)

makes 1 cup

Place all the ingredients except the salt in a food processor or blender and pulse quickly just until combined. Do not overprocess. Taste and add salt if needed. If the dressing is too thick, thin it with water.

(continued on next page)

THIS DRESSING GOES WITH THE FOLLOWING RECIPES:

romaine, gorgonzola, and walnut salad, page 45

spinach salad with mushrooms and walnuts, page 52

belgian endive, fennel, mushroom, and walnut salad, page 53

belgian endive, pear, fennel, and walnuts, page 58

beets, goat cheese, and arugula, page 123

beet, celery, potato, and mâche salad, page 125

green beans and fennel, page 126

grilled leeks and asparagus, page 129

figs, greens, and prosciutto, page 157

beet salads

leafy salads, especially those with bitter greens, spinach, endive

salads with nuts (walnuts, hazelnuts, pine nuts)

green beans

mushrooms, cucumbers

cooked salmon, chicken salads

gorgonzola cream good on grilled steak

mayonnaise-based dressings

TO MAKE CERTAIN MEDITERRANEAN SALAD DRESSINGS, cooks drop an egg yolk into a bowl and then whisk in olive oil to partially emulsify. It is then thinned with lemon juice and more oil. This technique is quite close to the way one makes mayonnaise or the much-loved Caesar salad dressing. (In fact, many chain restaurants start Caesar dressing by whisking a few tablespoons of commercial mayonnaise with oil and lemon and adding garlic and anchovy.) Homemade mayonnaise is better than bottled, as you can control the texture, density, and tartness. It is also free of sugar and additives. But if you are worried about using raw eggs, start with a few tablespoons of bottled mayonnaise and thin it with lemon juice, oil, and water if needed.

For the dressings that follow, start as if you are making mayonnaise but do not fully emulsify the mixture to mayonnaise thickness. Whisk in the oil and lemon juice and then thin with water to the consistency you want to dress the salad.

A strongly flavored extra-virgin olive oil will dominate all the other ingredients. For mayonnaise, you want a mild and neutral oil. If all you have is strong oil, cut it with a mild salad oil like canola.

basic mayonnaise dressing

1 egg yolk
1 teaspoon Dijon mustard
3 tablespoons fresh lemon juice, plus more if needed
1/2 to 3/4 cup pure olive oil or part canola oil and part extra-virgin olive oil
Cold water
Sea salt and freshly ground black pepper

**makes 1 to
1 1/2 cups**

It is tempting to assemble this dressing in a blender or food processor, but it may emulsify too quickly and become thicker than if you prepare it by hand. If you want to use the blender or food processor, just don't let the mixture get too thick.

To make in a blender or food processor: put the egg yolk, mustard, and 2 tablespoons lemon juice in the container and blend. Gradually add 1/2 cup oil in a slow stream. (I use a plastic squeeze bottle, as I can control the flow of the oil better than by pouring it from the bottle.) Transfer the mayonnaise base to a bowl and stir in the remaining 1/4 cup oil, the remaining 1 tablespoon lemon juice, and enough cold water to create the desired consistency. Season to taste with salt and pepper.

(continued on next page)

To make by hand: put the egg yolk, mustard, and 2 tablespoons lemon juice in a mixing bowl and whisk in the oil very slowly, until an emulsion is formed. Add up to 2 more tablespoons lemon juice and thin with water as needed. Season to taste with salt and pepper.

VARIATIONS:

For lemon mayonnaise:
Thin basic mayonnaise with lemon juice and cold water.

For mustard mayonnaise: Increase the mustard to 2 tablespoons.

For tarragon mayonnaise: Add 1 to 2 tablespoons chopped fresh tarragon and 1 tablespoon tarragon vinegar in place of some of the lemon juice.

For saffron mayonnaise: Add 1 tablespoon saffron infusion: a pinch of saffron filaments heated in 2 tablespoons white wine or water and steeped for 10 minutes.

For aioli: Add up to 1 tablespoon finely pureed garlic.

For anchovy mayonnaise: Add 1/4 cup pureed anchovies.

For tuna mayonnaise: Fold in 1/2 cup pureed oil-packed canned tuna and 1 to 2 tablespoons anchovies; add a bit of vinegar to taste if needed. (Pulse the tuna and anchovies in a food processor along with the lemon juice and vinegar.)

For remoulade: Add 1/4 cup finely minced white onion, 2 tablespoons minced chives or green onions, 2 tablespoons chopped fresh flat-leaf parsley, 2 tablespoons minced cornichons, and 2 tablespoons capers, rinsed and coarsely chopped. Thin with some of the vinegar from the cornichons.

The emulsified mayonnaises, unthinned, are fine as sandwich spreads.

NOTE: *If you have emulsified the dressing too much and the mixture is too thick and creamy, add 1/4 cup cold water to each 1/2 cup thick mayonnaise.*

THESE DRESSINGS GO WITH THE FOLLOWING RECIPES:

composed salads with hard cooked egg, green beans, potatoes, tomatoes, and olives
egg salad, deviled eggs
potato salads
chicken salads
crabmeat, tuna, and salmon salads
sandwich spreads
romaine salads
caesar salads—anchovy garlic mayonnaise

tapenade

moroccan
charmoula

pesto
vinaigrette

yogurt dressing
with chopped mint

harissa
dressing

romesco sauce

sauces with multiple personalities: pesto, tapenade, romesco, charmoula, and harissa

IN THIS CHAPTER WE EXPLORE the versatility of five classic Mediterranean sauces: Italian pesto, French tapenade, Spanish romesco, Moroccan charmoula, and Tunisian harissa. While traditionally used as finishing sauces for fish, poultry, and meats or as condiments, these classic sauces may be turned into lively vinaigrettes and dressings by whisking in enough olive oil and vinegar or lemon juice to make them more fluid and easy to spoon onto salads and cooked foods. The sauces may also be folded into prepared mayonnaise to become flavorful sandwich spreads.

Pesto, tapenade, and romesco are most efficiently assembled in a food processor, but charmoula and harissa and the sauce-based dressings can be assembled in a bowl with a whisk. Start by making the sauce and then whisk in additional oil and vinegar or lemon juice until you attain the desired consistency. You may also emulsify the dressing by whirring it in a blender or beating it with an electric wand or immersion blender. Emulsification is not necessary but will hold the dressing in suspension a while longer than is the case with one that is simply whisked together.

After thinning the sauces, you will see that they do not resemble traditional vinaigrettes or citrus dressings, as they are not as loose and transparent. They are more viscous in texture owing to the additional base ingredients such as nuts and olives, and are infused with color from the spices and herbs. Tapenade and romesco dressings are the densest in texture, so they are used on composed salads and cooked foods; in other words, they are finishing sauces spooned on top of the ingredients. If sauce-based dressings are sufficiently thinned, you can toss them with the salad ingredients.

Sauce-based dressings are not usually put to work as marinades. Charmoula is the exception; it can be used as a marinade for fish, seafood, poultry, and lamb, as well as a spoon-on finishing sauce. The powerful harissa can be used sparingly as a spice rub on meat.

By themselves, without thinning, tapenade, romesco, and harissa have a very long shelf life in the refrigerator. Pesto will keep for a month in the refrigerator and even longer in the freezer. Please be aware that once you add the acid component to turn pesto into vinaigrette, it will lose its bright green color rather rapidly, after an hour or two. In fact, any sauce made with fresh herbs, such as parsley, cilantro, basil, and mint, and mixed with acid, such as lemon juice and vinegar, will fade in color. Charmoula and pesto vinaigrettes are best made an hour or so before use. Any leftover dressing will taste fine, but the lively color will be lost.

pesto and pesto vinaigrette

THE CLASSIC BASIL PESTO from the Italian region of Liguria is most widely used as a sauce for fresh pasta. It can be transformed into fragrant vinaigrette just by thinning it with a little extra-virgin olive oil and mild vinegar. Traditionally this emulsified sauce is assembled with a mortar and pestle (hence its name, from *pestare*, "to pound or crush"), a technique that requires considerable practice and elbow grease. I am a realist and know that most of us will use a food processor or blender. We are not from Genoa and pesto is not part of our tradition, so there's no need to apologize for our expediency.

No matter what tools we use to create the emulsion, the same culinary advice applies. Select Genovese basil, not the more exotic Thai, purple, or lemon basil, with the smallest, most tender leaves you can find. Do not use large, tough leaves that have been baked in the sun. Tender little leaves break down more easily and are sweeter. Add garlic and pine nuts and crush them all together, then beat in the oil gradually to emulsify the sauce. Once the pesto is prepared, transfer it to a jar or container and film the top with a thin layer of olive oil. This will help preserve its green color. Every time you scoop some out, refilm the top with oil.

I prefer to use Ligurian or Provençal olive oil. These oils are light and fruity because the olives are harvested when quite ripe. Strong, peppery Tuscan oils, prepared with underripe green olives, will overpower the basil. If that is all you have, cut it with a pure olive oil or mild vegetable oil. I don't add cheese to pesto or to pesto dressing, but may offer it as an option for sprinkling later on.

makes about 2 1/2 cups

2 cups tightly packed fresh basil leaves
2 teaspoons finely chopped garlic (about 4 cloves)
2 tablespoons pine nuts or walnuts, toasted
1 teaspoon sea salt
1/2 teaspoon freshly ground black pepper
Up to 1 cup mild and fruity olive oil, or half extra-virgin oil and half pure oil, or all pure oil

Combine all the ingredients except the olive oil in the container of a food processor or blender. Pulse a few times to chop the ingredients into small fragments. Add about 1/2 cup oil and pulse or puree quickly. Gradually add more oil, as much as you need to make a thick puree. Do not overblend or overprocess. You should be able to see tiny pieces of basil leaf rather than a homogenous green paste.

Transfer the pesto to a jar and film the top with a little olive oil to keep its bright green color. The pesto will keep for 1 month in the refrigerator and 3 to 4 months in the freezer.

VARIATIONS:

For a Sicilian variation called *pesto alla trapanese*, add 1 cup diced tomatoes to the basic mixture and use almonds instead of walnuts or pine nuts. Given the acid of the tomatoes, you may not need very much vinegar if you should decide to turn this into a salad dressing.

Pesto vinaigrette: Thin 1/2 cup pesto with 1/2 cup olive oil and just 1 to 2 tablespoons mild wine vinegar. You do not want this to be too tart, as excessive acidity will obscure the flavor of the basil. The vinaigrette will hold well and stay green for up to 2 hours, either in the refrigerator or in a cool pantry. If you don't care about the faded color, it will keep for a few days.

Pesto vinaigrette is good on tomatoes, mozzarella cheese, roasted peppers, cooked chicken, cooked seafood, rice, pasta and bread salads, bean salads, roasted or boiled potatoes, green beans, carrots, and beets.

Pesto mayonnaise: Add 1/2 cup pesto to 1/2 cup mayonnaise.

THESE DRESSINGS GO WITH THE FOLLOWING RECIPES:

slow-roasted eggplant, page 81

cheese-stuffed eggplant rolls, page 89

roasted peppers filled with herbed goat cheese, page 98

pasta salad, page 181

tuscan bread salad, page 182

gazpacho bread salad, page 188

cannellini beans, page 193

seafood, potatoes, and green beans, page 230

sliced tomatoes or tomato and mozzarella salads

roasted peppers; roasted peppers and mozzarella

rice salads

farro salads

on cooked fish, poultry

pesto mayonnaise for sandwiches with tomatoes, seafood, poultry

tapenade and tapenade vinaigrette

TAPENADE IS A PROVENÇAL olive spread traditionally served as a condiment for cooked and raw vegetables and hard-boiled eggs or slathered on toasted or grilled bread as an appetizer. It can also be spread in a thin layer on a pizza crust before you add tomatoes or cheese. Thinned with olive oil and vinegar or lemon juice, it becomes an intensely flavorful dressing. It is rather dark in appearance, but it tastes wonderfully rich and olive-y. It is up to you how you choose to use it. Do you want to spoon it only on dark salad items like broccoli or beets, where its deep color won't show? Or are you going to take advantage of the dramatic blackness and proudly spread it in a graphic line on the salad ingredients? As a partial glamour remedy, you have the option to pretty it up with a garnish of chopped parsley or minced hard-boiled eggs.

Of course you can use one of the numerous tapenades sold in the gourmet section of the market, but it's easy to make your own, and you can customize it. You might add some grated orange or lemon zest or a drop or two of Cognac.

For the real taste of Provence, I use black Niçoise olives, even though Kalamata olives are easier to pit and are even sold pitted. (Yes, there are green picholine or Niçoise olives and you can try them as a variation. But traditional tapenade is black, as is its Italian counterpart, olivada.) An olive pitter is not very practical for small Niçoise olives, which is why many cooks choose the larger Kalamatas for this condiment. I prefer the milder, less acidic taste of Niçoise olives, so I think they are worth the effort. To remove the pits easily, gently hit the olives with a meat pounder; it will loosen the flesh from the pits, and then it's easy to pick them out with your fingers.

As for the capers, you can use salt-packed capers from Pantelleria in Italy or brine-soaked capers. I prefer the salt-packed capers, as they have none of the residual sourness that a strong brine imparts. In either case, rinse the capers well and pat them dry.

**makes
1 1/4 cups**

1 cup pitted black olives, preferably Niçoise
2 tablespoons salt-packed capers, rinsed and chopped
2 teaspoons chopped anchovies
1 tablespoon minced garlic
1 tablespoon freshly grated lemon or orange zest (optional)
4 to 6 tablespoons fruity extra-virgin olive oil, preferably Provençal
1/2 teaspoon freshly ground black pepper
1 tablespoon Cognac or brandy (optional)

Combine the olives, capers, anchovies, garlic, and zest, if using, in the container of a food processor. Pulse a few times to combine. Gradually add the olive oil; you can make this a very smooth puree or keep some texture. Add pepper to taste and the Cognac, if using. Store the tapenade, covered, in the refrigerator. Bring to room temperature before using.

Tapenade vinaigrette: Thin 1/2 cup tapenade with 1/4 cup olive oil and 2 tablespoons mild white wine or Champagne vinegar.

Tapenade citrus dressing: If you have added lemon or orange zest and want to play up the citrus, thin the tapenade with 2 to 3 tablespoons fresh lemon juice.

Both of the above variations are good slathered on grilled vegetables, cooked tuna, and hard-boiled eggs, tossed in rice salads, and drizzled on roasted peppers and mozzarella salads, broccoli and cauliflower, orange and celery or fennel salads, and oranges and beets.

Tapenade mayonnaise: Fold 1/2 cup tapenade into 1/2 cup mayonnaise. Excellent on sliced chicken and leg of lamb sandwiches, and great for egg salad.

THESE DRESSINGS GO WITH THE FOLLOWING RECIPES:

spinach and chicory salad with cauliflower and artichokes, page 50

cheese-stuffed eggplant rolls, page 89

roasted peppers and onions, page 96

roasted peppers filled with herbed goat cheese, page 98

beets, oranges, and greens, page 121

tunisian cauliflower, artichoke, and potato salad, page 136

broccoli and potato salad, page 140

salade niçoise, page 227

leg of lamb, page 249

tomato salads, tomato and mozzarella, or goat cheese salads

roasted peppers and mozzarella

finishing sauce for cooked fish

combined with mayonnaise for sandwich spread

sliced chicken

romesco sauce

EVER SINCE TASTING ROMESCO SAUCE in Barcelona, I always have
a jar of this Catalan "ketchup" in my refrigerator. I slather romesco on grilled
lamb chops or use it as a dip for cooked asparagus, shrimp, fried calamari,
and fried potatoes. I dollop it liberally on hard-boiled eggs. Thinned with oil
and vinegar, it's a great dressing on tuna salad with grilled vegetables or tuna
tossed with greens.

**makes about
2 cups**

2 medium ancho chilies or 1 rounded teaspoon ancho chili powder
1 cup blanched almonds or skinned hazelnuts, or a combination, toasted
4 large cloves garlic, minced
1 large red bell pepper, roasted, peeled, seeded, and chopped
1 cup peeled, seeded, and diced tomatoes, fresh or canned, or
   2 tablespoons tomato paste
1 tablespoon pimentón dulce or sweet paprika
1/2 teaspoon hot pimentón or cayenne, plus more to taste
3 tablespoons red wine vinegar or sherry vinegar
1 teaspoon sea salt
3/4 cup extra-virgin olive oil, preferably Spanish

If using whole anchos, remove the stems and seeds, and then soak the
chilies in hot water to cover for about 1 hour. Drain, and cut up into small
pieces. Transfer the chili pieces, or the ancho chili powder, if using, to
a food processor along with the nuts, garlic, roasted pepper, tomatoes,
sweet and hot pimentón, vinegar, and salt. Pulse a few times to make
a chunky paste. Add the oil a tablespoon at a time until the mixture
emulsifies. Taste. You are looking for a balance of sweetness, nuttiness,
and acidity. Add salt if necessary to bring up these flavors.

Let the sauce rest for about 15 minutes for the flavors to come together,
taste again, decide whether you want it spicier, saltier, or more vinegary,
and adjust the seasonings accordingly. The sauce keeps, tightly covered,
in the refrigerator for up to 6 months. If the oil rises to the top, you may
want to reemulsify it in the food processor, or you can mix it back to a
smooth consistency with a small whisk.

VARIATIONS:

Romesco vinaigrette: Thin 1 cup romesco with 1/2 cup olive oil and add a few tablespoons of red wine vinegar or sherry vinegar.

Romesco Mayonnaise: In a small bowl, whisk together 1/2 cup romesco and about 1/4 cup mayonnaise. Adjust the seasoning, as you may want more salt or a bit more acidity. The mayonnaise keeps for about 3 weeks in the refrigerator.

This is a flavorful spread for sandwiches: try it on grilled chicken breast, cold roast pork, and grilled sliced eggplant with a few greens on a ciabatta roll. Or toss cooked chicken or shrimp and a bit of chopped celery with romesco mayonnaise for a salad. Add the mayonnaise to fish soup, as you might add a dollop of rouille or aioli, or serve it as a dip for fried potatoes, grilled or steamed asparagus, green beans, cooked beets, artichokes, or hard-boiled eggs.

THESE DRESSINGS GO WITH THE FOLLOWING RECIPES:

beet salads

composed salad of grilled tuna, asparagus, potatoes

avocado salad

sandwich mayonnaise—for cooked chicken, pork, lamb, grilled sliced eggplant

condiment for grilled pork, lamb chops, and cooked seafood

a dip for fried potatoes, fried seafood

toss cooked chicken or shrimp and a bit of chopped celery with romesco mayonnaise for a salad

add the mayonnaise to a fish soup as you might add a dollop of rouille or aioli

grilled or steamed asparagus, green beans, cooked beets, artichokes, or hard-boiled eggs

moroccan charmoula

CHARMOULA (SOMETIMES SPELLED *CHERMOULA*) is a signature sauce in the Moroccan kitchen. Aromatic spices such as cumin, sweet paprika, and black or hot pepper are combined with chopped parsley, cilantro, and garlic in a base of olive oil, with either lemon juice or vinegar as the acid component. There are many different versions of this traditional sauce. Some have sweet spices such as cinnamon and ginger, and some include saffron. Others have grated onion or slivers of preserved lemon. Charmoula is most often used as a marinade for fish, poultry, and lamb.

Charmoula is incredibly versatile. Just like the Moroccans, we can use it as a marinade for fish, poultry, and lamb. It can be a finishing sauce and can be spooned over grilled fish or shellfish or stirred into fish soup for an herbal jolt. As a dressing, it is excellent on grilled vegetables, bean salads, potato salads, grain salads, and couscous salads. For the acid factor, I usually opt for lemon juice, but if the lemons are mild and you want greater acidity to set off the spices, add some red wine vinegar.

makes about 2 cups

About 1/2 cup fresh lemon juice, or 1/4 cup lemon juice and 1/4 cup red wine vinegar
6 cloves garlic, very finely minced
2 teaspoons sweet paprika or pimentón dulce
2 teaspoons ground cumin, toasted
1/2 teaspoon cayenne
1/4 cup chopped fresh flat-leaf parsley
1/4 cup chopped fresh cilantro
1 cup extra-virgin olive oil, plus more if needed
Sea salt and freshly ground black pepper
Chopped preserved lemon (optional)

Mix the lemon juice, garlic, paprika, cumin, and cayenne in a mixing bowl until smooth. Whisk in the parsley, cilantro, and olive oil. Taste and add more oil if necessary and salt and pepper to taste. Sprinkle in a little preserved lemon if you like.

VARIATIONS:

Charmoula citrus dressing: Make the charmoula, then add more lemon juice to thin it to the consistency of a dressing.

Charmoula vinaigrette: Make the charmoula, then add wine vinegar as needed to make a sharper-tasting dressing.

Charmoula mayonnaise: Mix 1 cup charmoula with 1/2 cup mayonnaise, or a bit more to taste. This is a great spread for a sandwich of grilled salmon and sliced fennel in pita bread, with a few sprigs of watercress.

THESE DRESSINGS GO WITH THE FOLLOWING RECIPES:

moroccan chopped salad, page 74

slow-roasted eggplant, page 81

chopped eggplant with preserved lemon, page 85

cheese-stuffed eggplant rolls, page 89

spanish salad of grilled eggplant, onions, and peppers, page 90

moroccan pepper and tomato salad, page 92

roasted peppers and onions, page 96

roasted pepper and celery salad, page 97

roasted peppers filled with herbed goat cheese, page 98

artichoke and fennel salad, page 107

moroccan carrot salad with cumin, page 117

beets, oranges, and greens, page 121

cauliflower zahlouk, page 135

tunisian cauliflower, artichoke, and potato salad, page 136

couscous salad with grilled shrimp, page 175

cannellini beans, page 193

tunisian-inspired chickpea salad with peppers and capers, page 195

bean puree, page 201

tuna, roasted pepper, and avocado salad, page 225

leg of lamb, page 249

lamb kebabs, page 255

moroccan lamb sausage, page 257

carrot salads

beet salads

grilled vegetable salads, peppers, tomatoes, eggplant, zucchini

composed salad of tuna or chicken, potatoes, peppers, and eggplant

marinade for lamb, fish, seafood, chicken

finishing sauce for lamb, fish, seafood, chicken

stirred into fish soups

added to mayonnaise for sandwich spread—grilled salmon, sliced fennel, watercress

grilled tuna or chicken sandwich, with eggplant and peppers

harissa

HARISSA IS A NORTH AFRICAN HOT SAUCE used in both Morocco and Tunisia. Moroccan harissa is mainly a mixture of chopped chili peppers, garlic, cumin, and olive oil. Although you can buy this harissa paste in a tube, it will never be as good as when you make it yourself. The Tunisian version is a bit more distinctive, as it is infused with *tabil*, a signature spice mixture in North Africa that includes caraway, coriander, garlic, and lots more hot pepper. It is a rather incendiary condiment and needs to be thinned with plenty of olive oil and lemon juice, along with hot water, so it does not blow your head off. This version of Tunisian harissa certainly will invigorate bean salads, peppers, eggplant, potatoes, beets, seafood, and hard-boiled eggs.

makes about 1 cup

4 small dried ancho chilies or 1 to 2 tablespoons ancho chili powder
5 cloves garlic, minced
2 tablespoons tomato paste or 1/4 cup pureed oil-packed sun-dried
   tomatoes
3 to 4 tablespoons extra-virgin olive oil, plus more if needed
1 teaspoon sea salt
2 teaspoons ground coriander, toasted
1 teaspoon ground caraway, toasted
1 teaspoon ground cumin, toasted (optional)
1/2 teaspoon cayenne, plus more to taste
Fresh lemon juice

If you are using dried anchos, remove the stems and seeds and discard. Then cover the anchos with boiling water and let stand until softened, about 10 minutes. Drain well and grind in a mini food processor.

When you have ancho powder, whether homemade or store-bought, grind it with the garlic, tomato paste, olive oil, salt, and spices. Add a drop or two of lemon juice.

Harissa can be stored in the refrigerator for up to a month.

Harissa dressing: Thin 1/4 cup harissa with a bit of warm water and then whisk in 1 cup olive oil and 1/3 cup fresh lemon juice. Add more oil if the dressing is too intense for your palate.

Harissa mayonnaise: Fold 2 to 3 tablespoons harissa into 3/4 cup mayonnaise and add fresh lemon juice to taste. Use on a sandwich of grilled merguez, grilled onions, and grilled peppers on a roll.

THESE DRESSINGS GO WITH THE FOLLOWING RECIPES:

moroccan chopped salad, page 74

spanish salad of grilled eggplant, onions, and peppers, page 90

tunisian roasted pepper salad, page 95

tunisian squash puree, page 106

artichoke and fennel salad, page 107

tunisian carrot salad, page 116

moroccan carrot salad with cumin, page 117

cauliflower zahlouk, page 135

tunisian cauliflower, artichoke, and potato salad, page 136

tunisian-inspired chickpea salad with peppers and capers, page 195

lamb kebabs, page 255

moroccan lamb sausage, page 257

spooned into fish soups

thinned and drizzled over cooked meats, fish, poultry

rub on meat for kebabs

Note: Page numbers in **boldface** refer to recipes; page numbers in *italics* refer to photographs.

about the author

JOYCE GOLDSTEIN IS A CONSULTANT to the restaurant and food industries. For twelve years she was the chef-owner of the ground-breaking Mediterranean restaurant Square One in San Francisco. She is the author of many cookbooks and has written for *Fine Cooking*, *Gourmet*, *Wine & Spirits*, *Food & Wine*, *Vegetarian Times*, and the *San Francisco Chronicle*. She lives in San Francisco.